Cruel,
Poor
and
Brutal
Nations

THE
UNIVERSITY
PRESS
OF
HAWAII

Honolulu
1975

THE
UNIVERSITY
PRESS
OF
HAWAII

Honolulu
1972

John Cawte

CRUEL, POOR AND BRUTAL NATIONS

the assessment
of mental health
in an Australian
Aboriginal community
by short-stay
psychiatric
field team methods

|Contents|

[Contents]

|Illustrations|

|Tables|

|Foreword|

The study of the relationship between mental disorder and the cultural traditions or beliefs of a people is of recent origin. At the 1961 World Congress of Psychiatry we had difficulty in assembling sufficient speakers for one peripheral session on the subject; at the 1966 congress there was one plenary session and a number of additional papers; in 1971 we planned for three formal sessions and many additional papers. However, this growth has been largely in the directions of simple observation and theory, with practical applications being rare. When a practitioner or an organizer in the mental health field encounters a specific problem that might have its roots in the culture of the patient or society in question he is more likely today than formerly to uncover some information about mental disorder in people of that culture, but he is still quite unlikely to find the answers he seeks. Moreover, it is still rare for someone specializing in this aspect of psychiatry to be invited to advise on such problems, and probably rarer still for him to risk giving advice. The practitioner usually sees his work as complicated enough without inviting further complications, and the researcher is too aware of the mass of unknowns that crowd like ghosts just beyond the small circle of his knowledge.

It is in this context that the work of John Cawte and his collaborators in Australia possesses a truly pioneering character. Here we have a group that is invited year after year to give practical advice and does dare to do so, operating very economically but at the same time seeking answers to questions of general as well as of local import. Obviously then, this is something which other countries should be paying attention to, asking themselves whether the model would apply under their conditions also. One knows that a program can be highly successful in one country and either fail or be found inappropriate in another, so Dr. Cawte's success does not automatically mean that others would be successful if they copied his methods in a different setting. Perhaps a foreword such as this, therefore, is an appropriate place in which to ask what preconditions are necessary for the model to succeed.

The first prerequisite concerns the man. Once such a program has developed its own tradition the personality of its director becomes less important, but until such time it is necessary that he possess certain definite characteristics. The first of these is that he should be practical, that he should have worked successfully under the conditions that those whom he seeks to help are working and that he should be able to make decisions which satisfy the immediate demand, however uncertain he may be about their propriety and theoretical soundness. Unfortunately, many of those whom I see showing the most interest in transcultural psychiatry lack such experience and ability, and few have them to the extent that John Cawte has. Secondly, he must have the breadth and flexibility of approach to see beyond the immediate urgencies and to accept as possibly valid cultural traditions very different from his own. Unfortunately, those psychiatrists that show the greatest practical sense often lack this width and flexibility. Thirdly, as with all successful pioneers he must be persistent and persuasive. Administrators and practitioners do not welcome proposals which imply that they should eventually look at their own work in a new light —which is what social psychiatry usually demands—and it needs tact or charisma to persuade one's university colleagues to join in such unpaid or underpaid ventures (for even when the fieldwork is officially paid for, the months of preparation are unlikely to be) after the first flush of originality has faded. All these abilities were present in the man who directed the study discussed in this volume.

The second prerequisite concerns the studied communities. In a relatively short field trip (though not necessarily as short as Dr. Cawte is using) the research team has to carry out a psychiatric census, grasp the essentials of the community's social life, study individual patients, pursue related matters such as the prevalence of significant infestations or the adjustment of children to schooling, and provide both general and specific recommendations. Obviously, this can be done only if the population is small, highly visible, communicative, and relatively cohesive. Size and visibility interact, for one can make direct observations on a much larger population if it lives in the open, as is true not only in Australian settlements but in some Asian and African cities, than if it lives largely behind doors, as is true both of northern communities with their fierce winters and some desert communities with their fierce sun. However, even with high visibility and with extra time there is a limit to the size of population to which this approach can be applied, the limit being determined mainly by how much information can be carried in one's head. If one cannot remember the details one has learned regarding a person one sees or a name that one hears, then there is not the same value in trying to do direct observation. I think probably that two thousand is about the maximum population one should attempt to cover by the approach which this volume describes, although if there is genuinely little psychopathology that ceiling could be raised.

These factors of size and visibility affect the amount of work that has to be put into selecting suitable research locations more than they affect the actual application of the program to a given cultural minority, but community cohesion and readiness to communicate may affect its application. To take an obvious example, this is not an approach one would normally wish to apply to the average sector of a large modern city where neighbors usually know very little of each other but have social networks extending far beyond their district. Similarly, it is not an approach that can be easily applied if the population is uncommunicative, either from distrust of the outsider or from distrust of each other or simply because their culture frowns on what is regarded as gossiping or inquisitiveness. Yet here also the restrictions are probably less than one might expect. Cultural minorities usually form enclaves even within cities, and if the population is suspicious this can often be overcome by a more gradual entrée (making single visits over a period of months or years before bringing in one's team) or by winning the confidence of a powerful leader. Such solutions are not always possible and even when possible may have their disadvantages. But it remains broadly true that although the approach cannot be applied to all communities, there are likely to be some communities in any culture where it can apply. If one has the right type of leader, the major question is probably not whether appropriate types of communities can be found but rather whether studying such communities will provide the type of guidance that is needed.

The problem here is twofold. In the first place Australia is a rich country while its Aboriginal population is small, scattered, and for the present relatively submissive, so that both the type of guidance sought and the type of help available should theoretically be very different from those found in most other countries. In the second place the size of the population actually covered by such a program, even if running full time throughout the year, would seem to be very small in relation to the forces deployed. For these reasons it could be argued that the Australian experience *cannot* offer a useful lesson for the many countries where an improved understanding of the relationship between culture and mental health is desired but where the populations involved are very large and the resources few.

On this I would disagree. Rural psychiatric patients in most developing countries (and even urban patients from cultural minorities in some developed countries) are either neglected or sent away to a central mental hospital, since the hard-worked district doctors and dispensers do not know how to handle them and have been trained to disregard or even despise the help they might receive from the (sometimes) more psychologically sophisticated folk healers. If that pattern is to be changed and if we cannot rapidly produce and pay for an army of mental health workers, then the district practitioners must be won over to a more modern view, and this can only be done by giving them practical help. Academic researchers and government administrators can produce theories and plans, but if the practitioner is not given very concrete and effective guidance he is not likely to pay much attention to them. Moreover, if the researcher is not forced to think in practical terms he is very tempted to pursue questions that promise a quick answer but that bear little relevance to local needs. A model that combines service with research and that extends out into the population in response to local demand is thus much more suitable for most countries than the other patterns that transcultural psychiatry is at present following, particularly if the research can be part applied and part basic.

Naturally the model will have to be modified somewhat if it is to be adopted as a permanent governmental program in countries with relatively large cultural minorities. A central team would obviously work too slowly and part of its function would therefore have to be the training of local personnel to imitate them on a more modest scale. Also, if social psychiatry were to develop in this direction then one might expect other health and welfare services to do likewise, something which would call for coordination and collaboration during which the mental health specialist might not always find himself head of his own team. Such matters are of secondary concern, however. What I feel to be important about the present book is that it not only gives us an interesting picture of a specific situation but also shows a way of applying transcultural psychiatry that deserves to be taken up and developed further by many other countries.

H. B. M. MURPHY, M.D., PH.D.
Head, Section of Transcultural
Psychiatric Studies
McGill University

|Acknowledgments|

Contributions by members of the field team in the preparation of this book are acknowledged with gratitude.

While all members played designated parts in the research plan, the work of Dr. Barry Nurcombe deserves special mention. He wrote chapters 8 and 9 on childhood socialization and psychiatric disturbance. His contribution in planning and discussing the work materially assisted the author in writing the other chapters.

The surveys reported in chapters 6 and 7 were carried out through the joint efforts of Drs. Cawte, Kiloh, McElwain, and Bianchi. Dr. McElwain guided the construction of questionnaires and scales, and Dr. Bianchi was chiefly responsible for the form in which the data so gathered are presented. Dr. Singh contributed the genetic data in chapter 2. Mr. Belcher provided the Lardil myths from his collection, and a wealth of background information. Mr. Baglin furnished the photographs of facial types and housing.

John Cawte and Barry Nurcombe would like to dedicate their work to the Commonwealth Fund of New York, in recognition of the fact that without their Harkness Fellowships they might have remained too confined in the grooves of prior experience to have undertaken this work. Sometimes used in connection with the Fund's work is the phrase "to do something for the welfare of mankind." In modest extension of this aim, royalties in excess of the cost of producing this book will be set aside for the assistance of scientific and artistic activity for and by the people of the Wellesley Islands.

The assistance given the author by the Social Science Research Institute (NIMH Grant MH 09243) and the East-West Center at the University of Hawaii in the preparation of this book is appreciatively acknowledged.

Chapters 6 and 9 originally appeared in slightly different form in *The Australian & New Zealand Journal of Psychiatry*. Chapter 7 was originally published in slightly different form in *Social Science & Medicine*. Their permission to reprint is gratefully acknowledged.

This study of the Aboriginal community on Mornington Island was a project of the University of New South Wales, Australia.

one

Introduction: The Psychiatric Field Unit Survey

TRANSCULTURAL PSYCHIATRY

Wittkower and Rin (1965) define transcultural psychiatry as an extension of psychiatry in which the purview of the observer goes beyond his cultural unit to another. "Transcultural" emphasizes the special feature—that in making a cultural and conceptual jump of this order the psychiatrist utilizes knowledge from disciplines broadly related to his own. He builds upon a foundation of the ethnographic study of the people, including child development and linguistics. He familiarizes himself with the traditional medical system of the culture, especially its view of causation. He scrutinizes the sociology of alien contact of relevance to health, such as rapid acculturation and social fragmentation. He devotes attention to such concepts as "cultural exclusion," emphasized by Brody (1966) as being of psychiatric importance. He uses the resources of epidemiology, which involves the thorny problem of the definition of psychiatric disorders. He studies his population at first hand in the field in preference to relying unduly upon the observations of others or upon hospital admission data. He tries to evaluate the influence of ecological factors in adaptation, and of economy, industry, demography, and territoriality. For the Australian Aborigine as for people in transition elsewhere, such factors play a part in psychiatric adaptation that has been underestimated.

Transcultural psychiatry shares with applied anthropology a common interest in practical aspects of welfare, based on an understanding of the society and of the stresses, resources, and symptoms of the people. The extent of the common interest is apparent if one accepts the scope of psychiatry as concerned with private discomfort and social inefficiency in addition to overt mental disorder. The World Health Organization's (WHO) definition of health as "a state of physical, mental, and social well-being, and not merely the absence of disease or infirmity" similarly emphasizes the dependence of health upon social factors such as education, employment, housing, and recreation.

There are distinctions between transcultural psychiatry and applied anthropology that give rise to confusion whenever the two disciplines

1

have insufficient opportunity to work together. For this reason we should like at the outset to outline the methods, goals, ethics, and general theoretical position of those who participated in the present research. In general, the special contributions of the transcultural psychiatrist relate to the fact that his background in clinical theory and practice gives him an appreciation of the individual and a skill in interviewing, coupled with an expectancy of providing relief or prevention wherever possible.

In an academic sense, psychiatry and Australian Aborigines have already come together: the ethnology of these people has been utilized as a text for inductive reasoning by psychiatric writers from Freud (1912) to Roheim (1945). A generation of observers of Aborigines from Malinowski (1913) to Warner (1937) and Montagu (1937) established the practice of employing or testing the then current psychiatric concepts in their anthropological writings. Our expeditions have been concerned, on the other hand, with Aboriginal psychiatry in its own right. A brief description of our modus operandi illustrates this. In the field we usually seek an approach through tribal practitioners. We attempt to understand the medical system by working out the details of traditional illness, including diagnosis and management. Our approach corresponds in some ways with the anthropologist's proverbial ploy of working out kinship ties: it serves to break the social ice, quite apart from the possible value of the data brought to light. Our "medical convention" attracts the cooperation of indigenous doctors; the mutual familiarity with illness and its management, coupled with the privilege of sharing secrets not normally available to the rank and file, creates some feeling of rapport between the representatives of the two medical systems.

Once satisfactory levels of collaboration are established, the next objective is a census of psychiatric disorders. The census is designed to reveal not only the syndromes associated with traditional magical-animistic beliefs indicated by the tribal practitioners. It also uncovers the familiar psychiatric conditions such as personality disorders, neuroses, and psychophysiologic complaints. The next objective is to learn enough of the sociocultural circumstances of the people to make the psychiatric data meaningful. These circumstances range through economics, ecology, child-rearing practices, health and heredity, the social credit network, and indeed the whole network of roles, transactions, and aspirations enmeshing the people. Since the orientation of our expeditions is medical, a final objective is to determine the extent to which community members, indigenous and European, have it in their power to act to the psychiatric advantage of the community. Those factors which promote the realization of individual capacities within the community have therefore to be identified.

2

Epidemiology should make a fundamental contribution to trans-cultural psychiatry. Data from clinical observations, hospital admissions, field surveys, censuses, court records, and sociometric scales are often available for the population under scrutiny. The hope cherished for this activity is that of finding a population with either a high or a low incidence of a particular disorder, and then correlating this with specific features of the physical or social environment. In this way something is discovered about the aetiology of the disorder.

Transcultural psychiatry in theory provides a rich opportunity for epidemiology. If this opportunity is not being realized at the present time it is because of inherent difficulties. In the first place, comparability of statistics is impossible to achieve between populations using different criteria for mental disorder. Some populations have large hospitals maintaining extensive admissions data and using sophisticated statistical techniques for the medical records; others have small field services. Others—such as the areas with which we are concerned —have no psychiatric services at all; in such populations psychosis and neurosis are invariably recorded as having a low incidence. Another difficulty concerns classification. It is not easy to assign conditions observed transculturally to Western "Bleulerian" taxonomy. Because of this difficulty some transcultural psychiatrists utilize a local "anthropological" classification (Margetts, 1959) or try to evolve a cross-cultural psychopathological system such as that proposed by Kaelbling (1961) from the work of Honigmann (1954). Such taxonomies may be expedient for the fieldworker, but comparability is sacrificed. Another difficulty is that transcultural psychiatrists, with some notable exceptions such as Leighton, Lambo et al. (1963), have to carry out their work without adequate assistance in the areas of anthropology, linguistics, sociology, and psychology. Their work suffers from the inevitable crudeness of the frontier or marginal situation.

In its broad sense, mental hygiene includes both formal and informal activities designed to promote social efficiency and to provide relief from psychological discomfort. Informal activities are wide-ranging, concerned as they are with hazards of human ecology. Factors such as overpopulation, underemployment, deficiencies in education, industry, housing, recreation, and the care of the aged, the sick, and the underprivileged are all relevant. Formal activities are concerned with the development of mental health services. Each country has its own specific problems of economic resources, availability of trained personnel, and capacity of the population to appreciate health principles. These factors operate to different degrees in different countries and circumscribe the development of health services. Transcultural psychiatric studies therefore include the consideration of the design feasible for such services. In some places little more can be provided than "first aid"—an offering not to be despised in the present era of potent psychopharmacology. Despite national variations in what is possible, some objectives are universal. They have been appropriately summarized in the WHO report on the African Seminar on Mental Health held at Brazzaville. This report, inter alia, advocates a team approach. "To serve these regions, psychiatric field units might well provide a satisfactory answer. If psychiatric field units were organized, they might remain in a given area for several weeks and offer the usual somatic treatments. They could, at the same time, collect information about the prevalence of mental disorders in the region and thereby provide the information necessary for the planning of an effective mental health service." (1959, p. 2.)

THE PSYCHIATRIC FIELD UNIT SURVEY

The notion of the rapid field survey of mental health in a non-Western population was not born in an armchair. We do not claim it as an original idea. As indicated, it was suggested by the WHO report on the African Seminar on Mental Health (1959). In our case it was the denouement of psychiatric participation in several field expeditions that had primarily anthropological, medical, and dental objectives. These expeditions were generally of one month's duration taken during university vacation time—necessarily brief in order not to disrupt the participants' teaching and clinical duties. Since the expeditions were to faraway places, a week was consumed in travel—by airline, chartered small aircraft, truck, or ship—leaving only three weeks for fieldwork.

By anthropological standards three weeks seems a ridiculous period to attempt to gather useful data. Three weeks can pass by in organizing a camp—hewing wood, drawing water, and defending against the smaller species of camp-sharers such as ants, flies, mosquitoes, and snakes. There are time-consuming domestic roles in camps: on an anthropometric expedition led by A. A. Abbie, the psychiatrist member was elected, with what appeared a sense of playful fitness on the part of the leader, officer in command of latrine. Such roles are onerous. Apart from the chores necessary for survival, preliminary tasks such as finding informants and developing rapport take time. Despite this, such is the nature of biological studies, at least, that by using well-oiled systematic approaches and by working hard, data are actually obtained in the time left for the main purpose. Often, more is gleaned than there is time to write up at home. Is it in the nature of psychiatry to gain anything of value in less than a month in the field? At first sight this seems doubtful, especially to anthropologists. But medicine has a natural pace that should not be discounted. Years of slavery in

4

outpatient clinics accustom the psychiatrist-physician to days filled with brief, and mostly new, encounters. He is used to systematic information-gathering from people who may be less than communicative, even bewildered, frightened, or antagonistic. Though field interviewing can hardly be compared with clinical interviewing in one's own culture, this training does not go amiss. The clinician has another advantage over other kinds of fieldworkers. He has a generally understood and socially sanctioned access to the sick and disturbed members of the community, and to their friends and relations. He is in a position to exploit his therapeutic role—even if it is only the simple provision of an effective medication for bedwetting. Though his work may be regarded as contributing to anthropological description, he is present as an agent as well as an observer, prepared to make on-the-spot applications of his knowledge. As a further advantage, he can utilize his "medical association" to cross the cultural gap to relate with the traditional practitioners, to see something of the indigenous medical system in operation, perhaps to gain the support and goodwill of influential elders.

This recital of some features of the medical fieldworker's position is not of itself intended to justify the rapid field survey. The plain truth is that developing countries are not able to retain psychiatrists in the field. Those psychiatrists who visit the field inevitably do so for a brief time. It is merely suggested that this time can be fruitful. A sample of mental disorders can be seen, and a sample of social conditions taken. Descriptive information of this kind, gained in this way, forms the material for *Medicine is the Law* (John Cawte, The University Press of Hawaii, forthcoming), describing from a medical viewpoint the activities of traditional practitioners.

Description is unsatisfying where comparative, correlational, and experimental measurements could be obtained. Clinical and epidemiological findings are of little value if there is not adequate social and cultural information to match. In order to achieve this more systematic information, a concentrated attack by a team of investigators is needed. Because a prolonged team study, in the manner of Leighton and Lambo's classical "Psychiatric Disorder Among the Yoruba," is rarely feasible, a rapid team study is the logical procedure—a "poor man's Yoruba" is better than none.

In planning the distribution of these field labors amongst participants of our team, four areas were viewed as cardinal points to be surveyed: Ecology-Biology; Anthropology-Sociology; Psychiatry-Epidemiology; Psychological and Personality Testing. These areas are broad and overlapping, and the subcategories of information relevant to mental health could be expanded indefinitely. The time factor limited us to choosing, rather arbitrarily, the following model that we proposed to

Ecology—Biology

History	Levels of health
Topography	Endemic disease
Climate	Medical zoology
Vegetation	Nutrition and subnutrition
Marine biology	Children's disorders
Demography	Prematurity and dysmaturity
Culture contact	Anthropometry
Economics	Genetics (blood groups)
Industry	Genetics (fingerprints)
Poverty	Individual variation

Anthropology—Sociology

Traditional social organization	Westernization
Ethos, "the ideal man"	Christianity
The family	Education
Sex	Socioeconomic stratification
Marriage and domesticity	Work
Traditional child-rearing	Contemporary child-rearing
Ritual, religion, magic	Recreation, leisure
Art, song, dance	Housing, zonation
Indigenous medicine	Group conflict
Law and order	Miscegenation

Psychiatry—Epidemiology

Patterns of illness (traditional)	Patterns of illness (Western)
Morbidity census (indigenous judgments)	Morbidity census (Western judgments)
Validity of census	Degree of correspondence between indigenous and Western judgments
Sorcery	Neurosis
Possession	Personality disorder
Culture-bound syndromes	Psychosis
Children's disorders:	Organic disorders
anxiety-inhibition	Developmental disorder
tension-discharge	Mental subnormality

Psychological and Personality Testing

Measures of Symptomatology	Measures of Cultural Identity
Cornell Medical Index (C.M.I.) (adapted to the society)	Acquisition of Western culture scale
	Emulation of Western culture scale
Patterns of response to C.M.I.	Retention of traditional activities scale
Effects of sex, age, subgroup	Retention of traditional beliefs scale
The "key" health questions	Correlation with symptomatology
The sickest subgroup	Cognitive (intelligence) Testing:
The healthiest subgroup	The Queensland Test

6

pursue in the field. Our book will reveal in which areas our task was accomplished and in which it fell short.

Every researcher appreciates that it may take as long to prepare for a study as to carry it out; in the case of an innovation such as the Field Psychiatric Unit it takes longer. We had to find funds, choose a locale, recruit a team, arrange for leave, make the physical preparations, and establish working conditions.

Funds for transport and subsistence were granted us by the Australian Institute of Aboriginal Studies, Canberra. By its original charter the institute supports studies of traditional Aboriginal culture rather than studies concerning culture-contact and social welfare. Since it was our real and avowed intention to study traditional medicine it did not perturb us that we planned to study other aspects of medicine as well. The areas overlap and mutually illuminate, and we felt confident that the council of the institute would view our endeavors in this way.

Choosing a locale to suit the survey was an interesting process rather than a difficult one. Since our previous studies had led us mostly to the arid zone of Australia we hoped to turn our attention to the wet tropical regions. We narrowed the choice to populations that had not been closely studied by a resident anthropologist. We chose a mission rather than a government settlement for reasons of expediency: administrative arrangements were simpler, and personnel such as the mission nurses or teachers were likely to have a longer tenure and to be better informed on matters of concern to us. The first mission that we approached happened to have a staff member whose correspondence revealed an antagonism to psychiatry and a feeling of threat as to what the study involved. While conceding that such misconceptions should not be evaded, we had little enough time for our program so we accepted the proffered alternative of going to another mission. As it proved, the choice of Mornington Island (Presbyterian) Mission in the Gulf of Carpentaria, Queensland, could not have been more fortunate in many ways.

The research team when finally established was not balanced in the way initially envisaged. It did not include an experienced cultural anthropologist, because none could be found at that time to accompany it. The team was heavily loaded with psychiatrists, but they had a wide range of skills. Besides the leader, there was a child psychiatrist, an adult psychiatrist with an interest in formal testing, a psychologist whose special field was cognitive testing in settings of reduced communication, and a human geneticist. Most had some knowledge of the indigenous people, but in only two members was this experience extensive.

The team was recruited largely from a group of colleagues at the

University of New South Wales, on the basis of personality judgments as well as skills. The intensive approach—described as the "blitz" technique by one team member—necessitates teamwork in which each member focuses upon his appointed section of the investigation. This compartmentalization requires that members interact regularly, referring their progress to other team members for a running commentary. It is preferable not to have to cope with rigid personalities on such an expedition, which is usually an anxious experience despite its rewards of sociability. Days of frustration often succeed each other, with data collection faltering and uneven. Will the level of acceptance by the community hinder the work? Will the census and sociometric technique prove adequate and workable? Will something of value be accomplished for the indigenous people in the time available? Correlations remain in question until the computer has done its work, long after the expedition is over; in some areas one is working in the dark. It is an anxious and challenging time.

The expedition was scheduled during a university vacation to simplify leave-taking. Some members obtained special leave, others took recreation leave. The board of Prince Henry Hospital in Sydney where several of us worked was generous over the matter of leave; we took this as a sign of growing interest on the part of well-equipped city hospitals in the medical problems of remote regions.

Physical preparations were straightforward. Several months in advance we shipped to the island some crates of groceries, tobacco, and small gifts. We planned, in the evenings, to have guests from the Aboriginal community share the food and talk at our table, and we wanted as hosts to be able to offer something different from the regular bill of fare on the island.

We finally added two more members to the team. Michael Friedman, a Stanford University Medical School student, upon learning of our activities, used his elective to visit our school. We were happy to incorporate such a capable and hardworking young man. He remained on Mornington Island for two weeks after the main expedition and filled in several gaps found in the data. The other member whom we were grateful to include in the team was the mission superintendent, the Reverend D. L. Belcher, who acted as host to the expedition and who entered actively into its program. He had an experienced awareness of individual and social problems of the Islanders. Correspondence with him after the field trip served as a check for many of our observations. Above all, it is through him and his staff that implementation of medical or public health policies stemming from our findings will come.

two | The People in Ecological and Biological Outline

The islands in the Gulf of Carpentaria, vast backwater of the Arafura Sea between New Guinea and Australia, were long overlooked by the bearers of European culture. Nearly three centuries passed between their discovery by Dutch traders sailing from Batavia and their settlement by Europeans. Tasman, dispatched by Van Diemen, governor-general of the Dutch Indies, to find a passage between New Guinea and the South Land into the South Seas, sighted them during his voyage into the Gulf of Carpentaria in 1644. Tasman not only failed to find a passage; he fabricated a coastline. The charts recording his voyage, including one in the British Museum, show solid land connecting New Guinea to the South Land, with a note to the effect that these lands "form all one continent together. . . . This large land of New Guinea was first discovered to join ye South Land by ye Yot Lemmen" —one of Tasman's vessels. Commented the historian Jose "the probability was that Tasman was horribly afraid of landing anywhere he might meet warlike savages—the mere trace of some scared him from Tasmania. He ignored Van Diemen's instruction to seek a passage between New Guinea and the South Land and saved himself trouble by drawing lines on the map." (1928, p. 139.) Tasman called the land he sighted in the southern reaches of the Gulf Cape Van Diemen— in fact it is the eastern extremity of Mornington Island—and, uninterested in taking a closer look, he depicted it on his chart as part of the mainland.

In 1802 Lt. Matthew Flinders of the Royal Navy entered the Gulf of Carpentaria from the east and recognized that what Tasman had seen was a group of small land masses (see map 1). Flinders quoted Jan Carstens, the earlier Dutch explorer, who described the low coastal islands as "altogether thinly peopled by divers cruel, poor and brutal nations" (1623). Flinders named them after his British patrons (Flinders, 1814, p. 159). The group became "Wellesley's Islands" in honor of the Duke of Wellington; the largest was named "Mornington's Island" after the governor-general of India, and the second largest "Bentinck's

9

Map 1. The Wellesley Islands

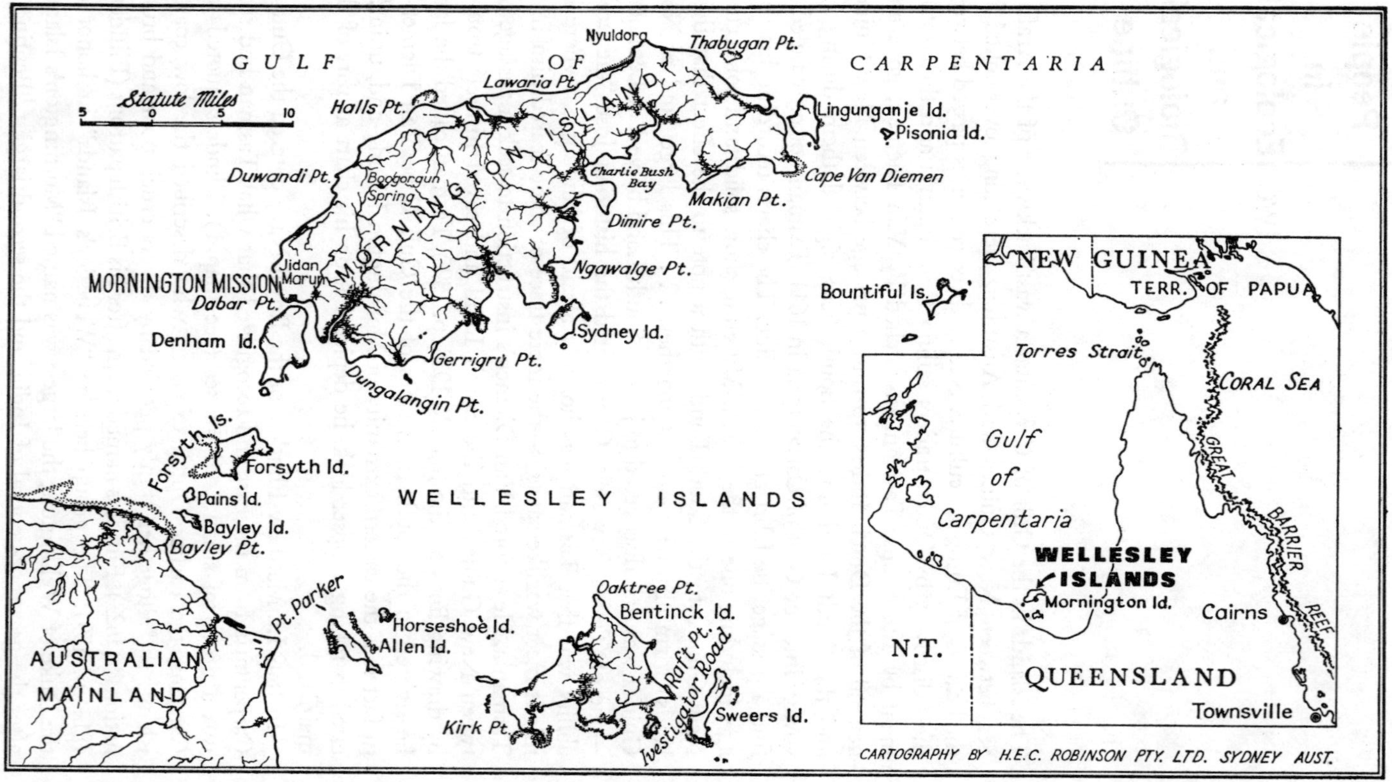

CARTOGRAPHY BY H.E.C. ROBINSON PTY. LTD. SYDNEY AUST.

Island" after the governor of Madras. Flinders' meticulous survey of these waters was prematurely terminated by the discovery that the planks of H.M.S. *Investigator* were in a rotting condition, and by his own and his crew's scurvy; he turned back from the Gulf of Carpentaria to Sydney via Timor. It was not until the day of his death in 1814 that Flinders' *Voyage to Terra Australis* was published and readers learned of the existence of the Wellesley Islands. Flinders had been detained for seven years on his voyage home by the French governor of Mauritius, who evidently considered that the discoveries of the British explorer might prosper France's hopes of trade and empire after the Napoleonic Wars.

Trade and empire came slowly from Europe to the coastal islands of the Gulf of Carpentaria. The Aboriginal inhabitants were people of few wants in domestic or other industries and the islands had nothing to offer in external trade. Even the Macassar praus on their annual voyages to Arnhem Land to procure trepang (*bêche-de-mer*) for the gourmets of China had left them alone. To Western eyes, no native culture was less attractive or more negligible than that of the Australian Aborigines. So far as Europe was concerned the islands remained no more than outlines on a map, bearing Dutch and British coastal place names, for a further hundred years.

The European names were gratuitous. Mornington Island, the home of the Lardil, and Bentinck Island, the home of the Kaiadilt, already had place names of an appropriate kind that identified the human tenants with the sea they fished and the earth they trod. Tasman's Cape Van Diemen is Bargia to the indigenes, the country of the people having affinity with *banbadyi,* the pigeon.

What became of the Lardil and the Kaiadilt, the "divers cruel, poor and brutal nations"? At the time when they were feared by Tasman and approached by Flinders their lives and fulfillment were regulated by totemic concepts such as the sea serpent and the tide. The trade by Lardil Aborigines that did exist was cultural rather than commercial, part of the Australian network of exchange of artifacts of spiritual significance. Recently the Kaiadilt have abandoned their island home to live alongside the Lardil on Mornington Island. Enough of the pristine world of the Kaiadilt and Lardil remains to reveal traditional modes and customs. The behavioral repertoire of the Mornington Islanders includes unique culture-bound disorders such as the totemic possession syndrome, *malgri,* a condition that must be incorporated in the psychiatric record of man.[1]

The first Australian of European descent to turn his attention to the Wellesley Islands was a Mr. Jackson, a geological surveyor for the

1. Described as a culture-specific psychiatric disorder in *Medicine is the Law* (forthcoming).

Queensland government, who visited in 1902. His visit was followed by more general journalistic descriptions (Hedley, 1903). Dr. W. E. Roth, chief protector of Aboriginals in Queensland, made limited ethnographic studies in 1906, but many of his records have presumably been lost. After this, annual reports (1908 et seq.) were made by the chief protector of Aboriginals in the Queensland Parliamentary Papers, and since 1914 by the Australian Presbyterian Board of Missions. Studies of the region include those of Tindale (1962a and b) who concentrated on demography; Simmons et al. (1964) on blood group genetics; Winterbotham (1959) on medical practices; and Hale (1964) on linguistics. Shortly after our team visited, in the latter part of 1966, the region came under study by an anthropologist, Mr. David McKnight, from the department of anthropology of the University of Queensland and the Australian Institute of Aboriginal Studies.

THE ISLAND ENVIRONMENT

The largest of the Wellesley group, Mornington Island, lies some 80 miles north of Burketown in the southern waters of the Gulf of Carpentaria in latitude 16°30′ south and longitude 139°30′ east. Mornington is some 40 miles long with an average width of 8 to 10 miles and an area of 372 square miles. A chain of small islands leads to the nearest part of the Australian mainland 17 miles away at Bayley Point and Point Parker. The next largest island, Bentinck, is in the South Wellesley group and is separated by a wider expanse of open sea from the mainland. This separation is of some significance for the history and, as will be seen, the adaptation of the Kaiadilt people.

The climate of the islands is monsoonal with an annual rainfall of forty-five to fifty inches falling mostly between December and March with at most only light showers for the remainder of the year. Summer is the season of the wet northwest monsoon; from March to November the wind reverses its direction and the dry southeast trades blow persistently and bleakly. So prevailing is this wind that the Lardil people living on the south side of the island traditionally referred to themselves as "Windward" and those on the north side as "Leeward," a division that became the basis of factions. Low hills rising to about three hundred feet above sea level give little opportunity for the catchment of water. During the wet season, mud makes the hinterland difficult of access but the streams flow briefly, dwindling to chains of ponds along their flat beds for most months of the year.

A moderately dense savannah woodland covers Mornington Island; trees of the *Eucalyptus, Acacia, Melaleuca,* and *Grevillea* genera predominate in varieties locally called bloodwood, messmate, white gum, white box, and wattle. In the rocky areas are tufts of *Spinifex* or porcupine grass that make walking difficult. Elsewhere there is much

12

fodder grass on the plains and in the bush. In areas of damper soil the ti-tree (*Melaleuca*) thrives, affording the natives bark utilizable for wrappings and one of the few timbers to resist the ravages of the endemic termites. On the coastline, clumps of mangroves extend beyond the water's edge and alternate with low headlands of wave-cut rock platforms. On the northwest coast are sandy beaches vivid green with tall casuarinas. The numerous reefs are backed by sand dunes growing pandanus and macrozamia palms. A few clumps of recently introduced coconut palms are conspicuous but difficulty has been experienced in enlarging the plantations (children have foraged some of the seed coconuts for food, others have succumbed to lack of care and to termites).

A phenomenon of the southern reaches of the Gulf of Carpentaria is the occurrence of one tide only each day. The tidal range is four to six feet for most of the year but in the monsoon season it is greatly increased by the prevailing north wind. The tide is a vital factor in the human ecology of the Gulf of Carpentaria. Today, shipping of even shallow draught must await high tide to approach the island; formerly, fishing was so dependent upon it that elaborate propitiatory rites were evolved by the Aborigines. In 1948 an exceptionally high spring tide occurred in the Gulf and Torres Strait, inundating land which had never been covered in living memory. It was a misfortune for Mornington Island but for the inhabitants of Bentinck Island an event of historic importance, leading to emigration from their homeland. This at least is the interpretation by Tindale (1962*a*); the Kaiadilt themselves give fighting and killing as the main factor forcing their exodus.

The biotic zone between high and low tide yielded much of the traditional diet of the Islanders; crabs, oysters, and other shellfish were foraged by women and children. The women maintained rock-walled fish traps on the reefs. The men's part was to spear and net the larger fish along the edge of reefs and sandbars, often by moonlight. Flinders noted native use of light rafts of dried mangrove stems joined by their broad ends to make fishing platforms that could also be used for voyaging to outlying islands in search of turtle eggs. Tindale described the rafts as measuring approximately fifteen feet by five, and commented that they were still in use by the dugong (sea cow, an aquatic herbivorous mammal with a bilobate tail) hunters in 1962. The sea is generally so shallow that one may be out of sight of land in three fathoms of water. Rafting can be dangerous because gusts of wind stir up rough water and blow the rafts off course. The mission superintendent, Mr. Belcher, doubts that the dugong were ever hunted from rafts. In the days before the comparatively recent advent of canoe and harpoon, these large creatures were trapped with nets in the mouths of estuaries.

The people in ecological and biological outline   13

Although fishing provided most of the traditional diet of the Islanders, foraging was also important especially in winter when the littoral became chilly. Lizard, frog, duck, turkey, flying fox, and honey from the wild bee were sources of the terrestrial diet. Nothing now pleases the older men better than to demonstrate the traditional ingenuity in capturing these prizes. Wallaby became rare on the island as a result of hunting aided by scrub-firing. Vegetable foods in season were wild cucumber, bush banana, water-lily root, acacia, gum, pandanus nuts, wild turnip, and grapes. Much of this edible flora has disappeared since the introduction of cattle. Seasonal harvests of yam and nail-fruit (an onion-like bulb growing in swamps) permitted gatherings for feasting and ceremonies.

The first alien contact in this home of the Lardil was tragic. In 1914 a Presbyterian mission was established on partly consolidated sandhills providing the most sheltered anchorage along the Appel Channel, a boomerang-shaped stretch of water separating Mornington from Denham Island. From the outset mission relationships with the Islanders were not easy and the function of the first missionary, the Reverend Robert Hall, appears to have been appreciated merely as that of a man who handed out provisions. Mr. Hall made regular tours of friendship and evangelism through the island. In 1917 an Aborigine called Peter, who had spent some time on the mainland, quarreled with him. One night while Mr. Hall was camped in the Sandalwood River region, Peter and his companions clubbed him to death as he slept. A group of Aborigines then attacked the mission house using Hall's gun to shoot the sleeping assistant missionary, Mr. Owen. Though wounded, Mr. Owen struggled with the assailants and regained the gun. With its aid Mrs. Hall and Mrs. Owen were able to defend the mission house for ten days until help arrived. (*Brisbane Daily Mail,* Nov. 5, 6, 29; Dec. 7, 1917). The missionary couple who followed, the Reverend and Mrs. R. W. Wilson, worked from 1918 to 1940 shaping much of the present administrative, educational, and religious life of the mission.

THE ISLAND PEOPLE

The entire population of the island is congregated nowadays in the village which nestles between the jetty on Appel Channel and the airstrip on higher ground half a mile inland. The ground plan (see fig. 1) gives an impression of the general organization. The population is not homogeneous. Three distinct groups of people inhabit the island: Mornington Island indigenes (Lardil); Bentinck Island indigenes (Kaiadilt) who immigrated in 1948, and their progeny; and mainland Aborigines (representing various tribes). The total population, recorded in 1965 as 556, consisted of 337 Lardil, 98 Kaiadilt and their

14

progeny, and 121 mainland Aborigines.[2] Of the 98 Kaiadilt, 47 were born on Bentinck Island, 40 were born after their Kaiadilt parents arrived on Mornington Island in 1948, and 11 are the progeny of Kaiadilt mothers with fathers from other areas, including one European.

This threefold division of the population is of fundamental importance to the social organization of the community, and to our survey separating the dependent variable (psychiatric disorder) from the independent (social factors of various kinds). The salient points of the survey are finally summarized in chapter 10 under the heading "The Sickest Society: the Search for Determinants." In the present chapter some of the major distinctions between Lardil, Kaiadilt, and mainland Aborigines will be outlined, including an account of distinguishing genetic features. There will be frequent allusions to the three population subgroups in the course of our comparative studies of social contingencies and mental disorder.

The largest subgroup, the indigenous Lardil of Mornington Island, live monogamously as conjugal families in the Western manner. Their level of acculturation as indicated by command of spoken and written English is comparatively high. This is particularly so among the middle-aged people, testifying to the effectiveness of the Reverend R. W. Wilson's school and the now defunct dormitory system, in which the younger people were retained at night for training and supervision. English is the lingua franca of the island; the Lardil language is used by the older indigenes but not by their children. Lardil have mostly adopted English names, some having surnames which are anglicized versions of original totemic names; for example, the name of the influential Roughsey family derives from "rough sea," the English translation of their totemic name.

Because of the totemic and territorial identifications, the population subgroups on Mornington Island remain relatively distinct. The mainland Aborigines hail not only from the neighboring tribal areas (Janggal, Jokula, and Karawa) of the Gulf country but from Cape York Peninsula; one comes from as far away as the Aranda country of central Australia. Their peripheral but scattered distribution in the village reflects their diverse origins. They have settled on Mornington Island from circumstances ranging from removal of waifs to the mission, to marriage, and in some cases to migration associated with personal difficulties. The mainlanders who came in early childhood

2. Population figures of Mornington Island are taken from *The Annual Report of the Australian Presbyterian Board of Missions, 1965*. Fifty-five part-Aborigines, having Chinese and European progenitors, are present in this total, but are socially identified with one or other of the three main groups. For present purposes they are not considered as a separate group.

now identify themselves as Islanders and even partake through adoption in the totemic and estate affiliations of this group, so that in certain contexts, this subgroup is not clearly distinct from the main Lardil group.

The third population subgroup, the Kaiadilt, evacuated in 1948 from Bentinck Island, is of special interest as the last group of coastal Aborigines to make contact with Western civilization. Bentinck Island people are visible by physiognomy, by their poorer command of English, and by signs of lower Western identification in their appearance. They live in a peripheral and chiefly endogenous community in shelters and humpies on the sandridge between Mornington village and the sea (see fig. 1).

The recent history of the Kaiadilt has been documented by Tindale (1962a). Although Bentinck Island is closer to the mainland it is out of sight of both the mainland and Mornington Island, leading to difficulty in navigation by raft and to a degree of isolation manifest not only in culture and language differences but in biological peculiarities as shown by blood-group and fingerprint genetics. The Kaiadilt community in its ecological relationship with its island was subject to the phenomenon of fluctuating abundance. In 1947 the missionary from Mornington Island, the Reverend J. B. McCarthy, visited Bentinck Island and found the natives in considerable distress. He concluded that they were rapidly dying out and ascribed their decline to tribal warfare and malnutrition among the young. Killing between the hordes was common because of subsistence problems. When a final catastrophe came in the form of the freak tide which contaminated coastal water holes, survival became so precarious that the decision was taken to evacuate them to the Mornington mission. The necessary contact for this step had been painstakingly built up for some years by Gully Peters, a Lardil man of energy and altruism who had come to know the Kaiadilt while on trepang-gathering trips to their shores. Gully and his wife Cora, now elderly, remain as protectors and interpreters for the older members of the Kaiadilt community. Kaiadilt children attend the mission school and are the only bilingual children on the island.

BUILDING AN ECONOMY

The transition from bionomics to economics has been exceptionally difficult and disruptive for Australian Aborigines. One of the more obvious obstacles confronting all subgroups of Mornington Islanders in their aspirations toward modernity is the lack of economically viable industry. The traditional fishing and foraging is superseded but not replaced by any activity resembling it in its capacity to motivate, inspire, and organize human existence. While the lack of industry is a

The Kaiadilt enclave borders the sea's edge and is mostly composed
of simple shelters or "humpies," and single-room corrugated iron
huts. In the foreground, at a small distance from the main body of
his people, is the rough shade of a disturbed (psychotic) man.
Lardil housing is on the landward side, and mission buildings can
be seen on the rise in the distance.

Lardil housing consists of more permanently constructed huts, often containing more than one room, and some with flooring. They are placed in regularly spaced rows and occupy intermediate ground between the Kaiadilt enclave at the edge of the sea, and the mission where the Europeans live.

A socially isolated and blind Kaiadilt man (Case Q., chapter 10) spends much of his time by this rough bush shade. Since becoming blind he has been absorbed in autism and is sometimes troubled by threatening auditory hallucinations.

A well-integrated Lardil man, normally employed in responsible jobs in the village (as well as being captain of the mission launch), spends some of his leisure time in traditional dancing. Here, his preparations include testing a spear, and body decorations of pipe clay, ochre, and leaves.

The Kaiadilt, who are genetically distinct from the Lardil, have a characteristic facial appearance, often with higher cheek bones and narrower noses.

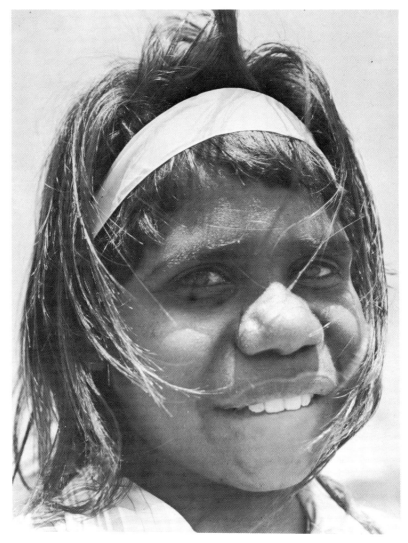

A vivacious Lardil girl shows the straight hair, chocolate-colored skin, and facial features common in her group.

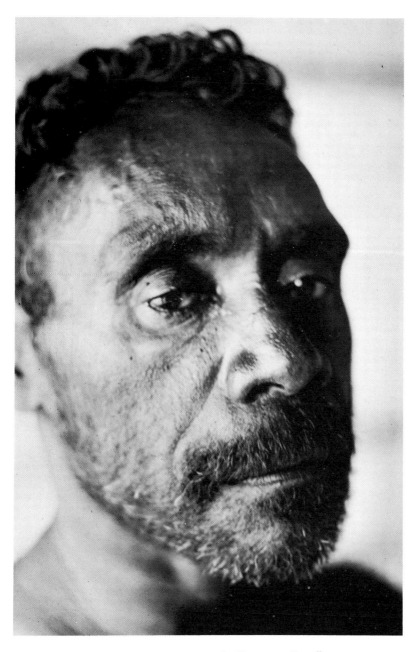

The wistful expression of the first Kaiadilt generation (born on Bentinck Island). The facial morphology is also fairly characteristic of this group.

In addition to a distinctive physiognomy, the second generation of Kaiadilt (born on Mornington Island) tend to have distinctive temperamental features (see chapter 9). Comparatively fair hair is not unusual in young Aborigines.

problem shared by many outposts inhabited by Aborigines, islands pose the further problem of the transport of primary produce across the sea to the nearest market. It seems certain that Mornington Island, though reasonably endowed with natural resources, cannot achieve economic security until "Australia's Open North" (Holmes, 1964) is sufficiently populated to offer greater local markets. In the meantime the inhabitants face the psychiatric and personality sequelae of the "poverty culture" described by Lewis (1959). Public officials in Queensland have even asked if it is desirable to maintain at public expense on a remote island a native population that cannot support itself. The economy of this question was studied after the tidal wave in 1948 created temporary water difficulties on Mornington Island. A proposal was made to evacuate the population to Weipa, on Cape York. It collapsed in the face of local resistance. It may also be that since this occurred shortly after World War II strategic considerations concerning the value of maintaining an offshore island population had some bearing on the issue.

The mission on Mornington worked toward defining and developing the island's potential. An early industry was trepang or *bêche-de-mer* fishing, with preservation by smoke of a variety of holothurian known locally as chalk-fish for Thursday Island agents. "Trepanging" had been the basis of the first trade known in Australia, when the Macassar praus came down to Arnhem Land from the Celebes with the monsoons, to return with the trade winds carrying the esteemed food for the Chinese market. Flinders in 1802 had been astonished to meet a fleet of sixty Macassar praus manned by a thousand men on the western shore of the Gulf. A fall in market price in 1929 destroyed the trepang industry and recent attempts to revive it have failed. The older Islanders were dugong trappers, using bark rope nets in the estuaries. The Gulf is one of the few places in the world where this species remains plentiful. Its meat is esteemed by Aborigines and Europeans alike. It is protected here by law against commercial exploitation; only Aborigines are permitted to kill it, and then only for their own food. Traditional fishing interests are declining in the younger generation, though fishing with hand lines provides a supplement for the diet. Dugong is now harpooned by the Aborigines from open boats. Barramundi and other fish favored in Australian markets are prolific, but commercial exploitation of fishing opportunities requires an investment of capital for boats, refrigeration, and air freight not warranted by the returns.

A cattle industry is being developed on the island but the country is too heavily wooded to be ideal for the purpose. On the few clearings and pastures the rate of sapling and undergrowth regeneration is high. Perhaps 2,000 Hereford and mixed-breed cattle run on the island. Some are wild from infrequent handling, especially those in the north. They are subject to heavy tick infestation in drought and to buffalo fly in the wet season. As an experiment in transportation, in 1964 300 cattle were taken off by hired barge to Cairns, a large town on the eastern coast of Queensland. Unfortunately, the barge ran aground on a sandbar just off the island so that a trip planned to take four days took three weeks, and the beasts that survived it were in poor condition on arrival. Notwithstanding the doubtful profit, cattle provide an industry by which the men of the island find activity and training and whereby meat is provided for the Islanders. The attempt to run dairy cattle was given up; little fresh milk was produced and at a cost greatly exceeding that of powdered milk, which is more convenient in the tropics. Agriculture and kitchen gardening are tentative, hampered by the shortage of water between June and December and by the Islanders' lack of inclination toward such pursuits.

The mission has encouraged local craftsmen to produce Aboriginal artifacts for sale on the mainland—boomerangs, clubs, spears, spearthrowers, and musical instruments such as dronepipes and clapping sticks. Some of these articles are not derived from Lardil material culture. This is not necessarily a mission imposition on the people; the Islanders have themselves copied dances and songs of Arnhem Land and Cape York, interweaving them with their own. Corroboree parties from the island have recently given concerts under the missionary's direction at Cairns and Mt. Isa, the nearest large towns, achieving artistic if not commercial success and contributing to the general level of self-regard. If the dancing should flag in the village corroborees, some wag out of school is apt to cry: "Step it up, boys, or you'll never get to New York."

An inference frequently made by visitors is that the Islanders will not move further toward Western modes of adaptation and out of their present dependence until the economy is more heavily capitalized. The present budget is sufficient for subsistence only. A characteristic mission budget is that for 1965, which allowed $16,800 for rations, $1,200 for clothing, $9,000 for wages, $2,400 for maintenance, and $7,200 for sundry expenditures, including a large single item, medical expenses. In a population of 550, this comes to about $60 per head per year, excluding money that emigrant workers can send home. Of the rations and clothing grant, the bulk is not available for the general exchequer but comes in the form of the pensions and child endowment provided for all people in Australia. The government of Queensland provides 90 percent of the remaining budget, the Australian Presbyterian Board of Missions the balance.

Poverty cannot be defined in terms of income alone, but by the unavailability of the necessities and benefits of life. Nevertheless, some poverty on the island is indicated by the wages. The total weekly budget of $180 for Aborigines employed by the mission permits payment of wages of the following order: store clerks $14 per week; head stockman $12; policeman and head gardener each $8; married working man $6; single working man $5; cook $5; domestics $4 to $2; boy recently left school $2; part-time laundress $1.50. Since these wages represent a third of the amount that can be earned for comparable work on the mainland and since food, clothing, and other essentials are not cheap, a common practice is for young men and women to work for some years "outside," until the wife and sometimes the husband return when their children are old enough to attend the mission school. Seldom do married couples with children go out. In 1965, 67 men and boys and 43 women and girls were employed "outside," representing a large drain of those of good working capacity and initiative. By a special arrangement many of these workers have two-thirds of their wage packets paid to the government district officers who bank it on their behalf. The wife at home on the mission is able to draw on this account by authority of her husband. In an average year a capable stockman on a cattle station can allot $400 in this way. This constitutes the major part of the island's income, somewhat in the way that modern Greece and Southern Italy bolster their economy through emigrant labor. On Mornington Island in 1965 store receipts totalled $66,000; of this, "outside earnings" contributed $28,500; mission wages $18,500; pensions and child endowment (government subsidy for children) $19,000. Very few workers emigrate finally, unless in the course of transfer to other missions and settlements of the Gulf and Cape York regions. To do so they must overcome ties to their homeland and families. A fear of the mainland is deeply rooted, often expressed in the form of concern for its superior sorcery or *puripuri*. As will be seen, successful adaptation to the outside world does not come easily to the Islander.

HAZARDS TO LIFE

The sea from which the Islanders traditionally subsisted holds hidden hazards. Loss of life from drowning in raft mishaps and from shark or stingray attack was not rare. The stingray, the stonefish, and even the prettily marked cone shell in these waters all possess venoms that cause intense pain and may lead to death from cardiac arrest. The most toxic venom is that of the sea wasp, *Chironex fleckeri*. The adult form of this jellyfish concentrates in shallow water and spreads out as far as twenty feet a web of almost invisible tentacles to catch prawns and small fish. It does not attack but if its appendages brush naked skin they shoot out thousands of microscopic threads which inject a venom capable of causing death in two or three minutes. The victim screams and becomes irrational with pain. A Mornington child died around the time of our visit from this cause. People avoid entering the water in summer (December to March) as far as possible; no part of these waters is considered safe for swimming in summer. The Islanders' dependance upon the sea as a food source is declining and with it the incidence of deaths and injuries caused by the sea.

The home of the Lardil has hazards to health. The level of physical well-being on Mornington Island, while inferior to that in Australian towns and cities, is superior to that found in Aboriginal settlements in less favored parts. Initial impressions of the village are of reasonable cleanliness and order despite the poverty. Adults and children have comparatively clean eyes and noses for an Aboriginal community. An uncharacteristic feature and one that contributes to hygiene is the absence of dogs. Dogs are presumed to have come to Australia with the first Aboriginal Australians ten to twenty thousand years ago. Every Aboriginal camp is alive with them; they help in the hunting by day and warm the children by night. Elimination from the island of this traditional companion of Aborigines was accomplished around 1946 by order of the then superintendent, though not without resistance. Accounts of the incident in the village contain rationalization as well as reason. For example it is said that the dogs were destroyed so that their barking would not attract the enemy Japanese to the village. Gully Peters, an elder of acknowledged charm and integrity who was influential in the immigration of Kaiadilt to Mornington, declined to permit the shooting of an old white terrier that had been presented to him by a previous missionary. A police constable from the mainland was introduced into the impasse and a melee took place in which Gully, passively resisting, was handcuffed, locked up, and removed to Palm Island for a year. His friend, Paddy Marmies, who tried to protect Gully, was beaten. Serious tension seems to have been engendered between mission and village, but dogs were banished and a stride toward Western standards of hygiene taken. Dogs may be absent, but large numbers of cats infest the village, basking in the trees and grass, scavenging the scraps, and preying on the birds.

Mornington Island lies just below the line that marks the southern limit of the malaria-bearing *Anopheles* mosquito. Of endemic diseases only hookworm and subnutrition are of much consequence. Hookwork infestation (revealed by microscopic examination of fecal smears for ova) affects 16 percent of the population (*Mission Annual Report,* 1966). The incidence is decreasing gradually, though few of the population wear shoes. A campaign is under way to dose the people twice yearly with Bephenium and Alcopar. Village sanitation is provided by a system, under supervision of the policeman, for disposal of waste into the Appel Channel from a special jetty. Sealed pans on some of the communal toilet cabinets are installed and maintained at what appears a trifling expense, but which is in fact a strain on the mission exchequer, when the budget as outlined is considered.

Subnutrition in children is countered by a compulsory daily ration of cheese, yeast extract, and fruit juice, and each child's progress is checked by monthly weighing. The Kaiadilt children, whose supply of food from their own parents has proved uncertain, were until recently fed in a special kitchen in the village together with the old folk. Infants are breast-fed for long periods—often to the fifth or sixth year. After the first year or two the breast is more a pacifier than a supply of milk. One reason the people give for prolonged breast feeding is convenience, another is contraception. None of the women have any practical knowledge of contraception and serious difficulties are being encountered because of the rapidly rising birth rate and the improved survival rate of infants.

Chronic bronchitis is prevalent and is probably associated with the heavy exposure to dampness, cold, and smoke from fires in the winter. Tobacco smoking is heavy. The Kaiadilt people use a bamboo pipe with a curled tin tobacco burner that appears copied from the Malay design. They did not smoke before 1948. Others smoke European-style pipes or roll their own cigarettes. Nobody has chewed plug tobacco on this island for twenty years; it is regarded as a distasteful mainland habit. Many of the older people suffer from visual defects, the sequelae of trachoma. "Tropical ear," a non-specific otitis media and externa, is responsible for deafness in children which may in some instances be linked with impaired psychological development. The periodic exanthemata are becoming less devastating but are still important in this immunologically isolated region; for example, a measles epidemic recently caused the death of four children, whereas the previous epidemic in 1953 caused ten deaths.

The risk of leprosy, though not so high as in some other communities in the Australian tropics, is always present; in fact a physician in the visiting team detected an early case.

GENETIC DIFFERENCES

The cultural and psychiatric differences readily discernible between the three population subgroups should not lead the observer to overlook biological differences that exist. In fact there are fundamental differences in the genetic constitutions of the Lardil and the Kaiadilt, of a degree amazing in peoples inhabiting neighboring islands. How they relate to psychiatric disorder is open to question, though the possibility must be borne in mind. Differences in genetic constitution are exemplified by the blood group work of Simmons and his coworkers (1962) and by the fingerprint studies by Singh on our expedition.

They are summarized here as evidence that differences exist, without any implication as yet that they have or do not have particular significance for mental health.

In the A-B-O blood group series, Aborigines are mainly A and O like Europeans; B is more characteristic of Asia. The Aborigines around the northern shores of Australia possess group B, which has been thought to be imported from Indonesia and New Guinea. In 1962 Simmons, Tindale, and Birdsell published a report of investigations carried out on Mornington Island, including the blood group gene frequencies for 42 Kaiadilt and 67 Lardil people. Further investigations were reported in 1964 by Simmons, Graydon, and Tindale. In 1960, when the material for the first series was collected, the tribal populations numbered 78 Kaiadilt, 350 Lardil, and 20 mainland (Janggal); nearly all the adults contributed blood samples. No differences in blood group distribution between Lardil and Janggal could be found and the two were combined for the purpose of the report. The results were compared with those for other Australian Aboriginal tribes.

The most remarkable feature was a complete absence of the A gene from the Kaiadilt, a complete absence of the B gene from the Lardil and Janggal (0 gene frequencies 0.756 and 0.922 respectively). There was an almost equal distribution of M and N in both populations, with a complete absence of S. The B gene has been found lacking in the majority of Aborigines in Western Australia, South Australia, and New South Wales, except in the north. The high frequency of the B gene in Cape York Peninsula has been attributed to Indonesian and Melanesian admixture over many centuries. No mainland tribe has shown a complete absence of the A gene, though the frequency in Cape York was low. The highest was in New South Wales (0.646) and the lowest in Queensland (0.217). All mainland tribes have shown a preponderance of the N gene, with the highest frequency (0.857) in South Australia and the lowest in the small series in New South Wales (0.688). All Australian Aboriginal tribes appear to be completely lacking in S, a situation not found anywhere else in the world. In the Rh system the South Australian tribes and the Kaiadilt gave the lowest frequencies of R_1 (CDe) with 0.530 and 0.521 respectively. The Lardil frequency of 0.652 was similar to those from Western Australia, Northern Territory, and South Queensland. High frequencies of R_1 were found in Cape York, especially at Mitchell River (0.790). The Kaiadilt had a low frequency of R_2 (cDE) in common with the Cape York tribes and at variance with other mainland tribes, while the Lardil resembled Western Australia, still well below the frequency for South Australia. The Kaiadilt were also unique in their remarkably high frequency of R_0 (cDe) at 0.426, the next in order being the Northern Territory with 0.232.

In 1960 Cummins and Setzler published an analysis of the finger- and palm prints they had collected from mainland Aborigines during the 1948 Arnhem Land expedition. The subjects were 41 males and 51 females from Yirrkala in northeastern Arnhem Land and 43 males and 38 females from Groote Eylandt. They gave details of finger and palm patterns but did not analyze finger ridge counts. Macintosh (1952) analyzed fingerprints only from 82 males at Old Beswick and Mainoru in Arnhem Land and from 53 males in the files of the Western Australian police department in Perth. Pattern frequencies but not ridge counts were reported. Rao (1964a, b) reported the finger pattern frequencies and total finger ridge counts of 44 males and 40 females from the Kuini, Kulari, and Walambi people at Kalumburu on the coast northwest of Wyndham in Western Australia. Mader et al. (1965) collected fingerprints from four tribes in central Australia (Aranda: 86 males, 102 females; Pintubi: 64 males, 57 females; Pitjantjatjara: 139 males, 148 females; Walbiri: 73 males, 109 females). They reported pattern indices calculated from the total triradius count of each population. They found some significant differences in inter-tribal pattern indices. Mean total ridge counts in the same tribes were reported by Robson and Parsons (1967). Rao (1965) examined finger- and palm prints of 61 boys and 44 girls of the Walbiri tribe at Yuendumu Settlement, northwest of Alice Springs in the Northern Territory, and reported the pattern frequencies.

While the present team was on Mornington Island in June 1966, finger- and palm prints were obtained from 19 males and 19 females of the Kaiadilt and 55 males and 65 females of the Lardil. A detailed report is given by Singh (1968). In brief, the frequencies of whorls and loops and the pattern intensity indices are lower for the Kaiadilt than for the Lardil in both sexes. The pattern intensity difference between the females of the two tribes is statistically significant; for the males it approaches the level of significance. In both tribes the females have a mean total ridge count higher but not significantly higher than the males. Mean ridge counts for individual fingers show some tribal differences. The Lardil counts are significantly higher than the Kaiadilt counts for male right index and right middle fingers (RII and RIII) and for female right middle finger (RIII). It should be noted, however, that the Kaiadilt sample is small. Table 1 shows a comparison of finger patterns in the Kaiadilt and the Lardil with those of other tribes so far reported. There are few tribal differences in the frequencies of palm patterns. The exception is the second inter-digital area, where there are significantly more patterns on the left hand of the Lardil males and on both hands of the Lardil females. The available data show no significant differences in palm prints between the tribal groups; these prints have not been included in table 1 and will not be discussed further.

Table 1. Comparison of Finger Patterns in Some Tribes of Australian Aborigines

LOCATION	TRIBE	MALES						FEMALES					
			PERCENTAGE OF ALL PATTERNS			MEAN PATN. INDEX	MEAN TOTAL RIDGE COUNT		PERCENTAGE OF ALL PATTERNS			MEAN PATN. INDEX	MEAN TOTAL RIDGE COUNT
		NO.	WHORLS	LOOPS	ARCHES			NO.	WHORLS	LOOPS	ARCHES		
Western Australia: Kuini, Kulari, Walambi[a]		44	64.32	35.08	0.45	16.23	160.40	40	64.75	33.00	3.00	16.25	148.00
Western Australia[b] (Mixed groups from police file, Perth)		53	52.4	46.4	1.1	15.12							
Central Australia[c]	Aranda	86				15.93	154.90[g]	102				15.06	144.60[g]
	Pintubi	64				16.78	166.20[g]	57				16.46	160.80[g]
	Pitjantjatjara	139				16.33	160.80[g]	148				15.50	157.10[g]
	Walbiri	73				15.64	158.90[g]	109				14.06	137.50[g]
Central Australia[d]	Yuendumu	61	50.66	48.03	1.31	14.94		44	43.41	55.00	1.59	14.18	
Arnhem Land (NT): Old Beswick[b]		82	60.9	38.0	0.9	15.98							
Arnhem Land (NT): Yirrkala[e]		41	79.0	20.5	0.5	17.85		51	78.2	21.6	0.2	17.80	
	Groote Eylandt	43	76.3	23.8	0	17.64		38	66.3	31.9	1.8	16.45	
Mornington Island: Lardil[f]		55	54.7	44.7	0.7	15.44	169.33	65	63.5	35.8	0.6	16.29	172.17
Gulf of Carpentaria[f]	Kaiadilt (formerly of Bentinck Island)	19	45.8	54.2	0	14.5	158.11	19	47.4	52.6	0	14.74	163.42

SOURCE: Rao (1964a,b); b. Macintosh (1952); c. Mader et al. (1965); d. Rao (1965); e. Cummins and Setzler (1960); f. Singh (1968); g. Robson and Parsons (1967).

The analysis of finger- and palm prints confirms the striking genetic difference between the Lardil and Kaiadilt previously noted in studies of blood group gene frequencies. These variations are probably explained by such natural forces as genetic drift and mutation operating over a long period in isolated groups of people. It is possible that these little nations originated from single family units. The geographical and geological conditions of the Wellesley Islands area, particularly as they affect Bentinck Island, could contribute to the isolation of a rafting people although the mainland is only a few miles distant. Simmons et al. (1962, 1964) have discussed this aspect. It is suggested that the Kaiadilt have been in occupation for a shorter period than other Aborigines in Australia. Since they do not possess the A gene their ancestors probably did not accompany the original wave of migration in the post-Pleistocene. Estimates of their occupancy range from three to six thousand years. As Abbie (1969) observes, they are peculiar in not having the A blood group, in not having the dog, and in not having the aspects of material culture that most Aborigines possess. The picture is that of a family unit marooned on an island that became a natural prison—with their initial arrival possibly occurring after Indonesian contact.

Despite their genetic differences, indicated by fingerprint and blood group patterns, the Lardil and Kaiadilt peoples share cultural features suggesting some contact. Some common nouns are similar; land rights or estates on Mornington Island are *dulmara,* on Bentinck Island *dulnoro.* The Mornington Island possession syndrome *malgri* has its counterpart *malgudj* on Bentinck Island. About half of the fish names are similar. The contact suggested by these similarities is lost in prehistory. The passage from Mornington Island to the mainland by stages via Denham and Forsyth islands ensured that the people of Mornington, Denham, and Forsyth islands regarded themselves as related; Bentinck Island, twenty miles away across windswept sea, was bypassed, a backwater within a backwater. Informants from the two peoples maintained to us that these peoples had no traditional awareness of each other prior to the mission's arrival.

Gully Peters likes to relate how it was that while engaged in the Mornington *bêche-de-mer* fishing in the 1930s he paid regular visits in the mission launch to Bentinck Island. Camped there collecting and processing his trepang, he gradually developed contact with the Kaiadilt with whom his conversational exchange steadily improved. Gully's enterprise opened the way to Western society for people whom some judges have called the earth's most primitive men, but who are perhaps better described as the earth's most excluded and isolated. Their approachability seems to have improved in recent years, as will be seen in the epilogue to this book.

The people in ecological and biological outline   25

three

The People in Social and Cultural Outline

The immediate impressions gained by a Western visitor to the Mornington village are of poverty and lack of privacy. The impact of this is softer than in many other Aboriginal settlements situated in remote, and in some cases not so remote, parts of Australia. To the visitor unfamiliar with Aborigines it is still overpowering. It is first apparent in the housing. The houses of the Lardil people are no more than huts, erected with galvanized iron, usually with one room for the whole family; the cooking, laundry, and toilet are done outside. Latrines are adjacent, for family and communal use. A very few houses have fenced enclosures and gardens. Hardly any have electricity. The Kaiadilt mostly live in shelters on the ground made of sheets of iron and bark supported on a framework of boughs; a few have erected galvanized iron houses like those of the Lardil.

It is doubtful whether the impression of poverty and lack of privacy conveyed by the housing can be attributed to the visitor's Western ethnocentricity. Village life is not traditional to the Islanders; it is an artifact of European settlement. In the pristine society the people lived in small bands fishing and foraging within the confines of littorals and estates which divided the island into territories. These divisions are now abandoned and most of the island is deserted because everybody has congregated at the new village. Traditionally there may have been poverty in the sense of few possessions and periodic survival difficulties; the poverty of the village is of a different kind. It is more a culture of poverty associated with exclusion from Western economic life, imposing its characteristic design on living, famliy life, and child-rearing.

SPACING BEHAVIOR IN THE VILLAGE

The mission itself is half a mile distant from the village on higher ground overlooking the Appel Channel. In this preserve are the church, offices, school, hospital, workshops, jetty, and some houses for European staff. Other staff houses are built on a less convenient but more elevated site adjoining the airstrip. The separation of the mission from the village at first glance appears repugnant to the Christian ideal and to the administrative intention of assimilation. But it is understandable. Adjacent to the mission office, the grave of murdered missionary Robert Hall—"martyred" is the term on the gravestone—is a reminder of the risks of too early an intimacy. Discomforts and sacrifices in the lives of missionaries and lay workers are substantial, and life in the village might make them unendurable. Europeans find the humidity of the wet season so oppressive that they have to use housing of a type that villagers cannot afford. Housing, electricity, refrigeration, and sanitation set them apart. Westerners of whatever status or occupation would find it very difficult to bring enough of their culture for their own well-being into the village, and once there they would feel threatened by involvement in quarrels and sexual invitations. Probably the most difficult feature of living in the village would be the pressure toward a more intimate incorporation into kinship obligations. By living at a little distance the mission staff feels it has a better chance of retaining objectiveness, which is desirable from the people's point of view. "Culture shock" in the sense used by Oberg (1960) would be a reality for most Westerners having to adapt to the village. It is an open question as to what extent the Aborigines resent the contrast. Seemingly, most accept it as the natural order, at least for the present.

The caste system of mission and village signifies an authoritarian social order with a European summit and a hierarchy of dominances and submissions unknown in traditional life. Unlike some mainland communities, little overt hostility is expressed between Aboriginal and European. Tension and frustration is disclosed passively by refusal to work or to cooperate in community projects. Some of it is dissipated by humor. Villagers have a favorite "play" dance called "No Store." A previous superintendent had closed the store as a coercive measure at a time of strife in the village. Pompey Wilson, the policeman, was charged at the time with turning people away from the store door. In the dance depicting the incident, women advance across the arena in a body towards Uncle Pompey who suddenly turns and says in grave tones "No store, no store." The women disperse in a mechanical shuffling step while everybody chuckles.

In the village the Aborigines' houses are elevated on several parallel ridges or sandhills as a protection against the occasional high tide. The arrangement of residential clusters in the village is revealing (see fig. 1). The low shelters of the Kaiadilt enclave line a sandridge near the water's edge at the Appel Channel. Two inner sandridges are occupied by traditional Windward and Leeward divisions of the Lardil people. Mainland people tend to distribute themselves a little farther inland, but though occupying peripheral positions in the village they show no tendency to form a cohesive cluster. A glance at the arrangement of

Figure 1. Mornington Village

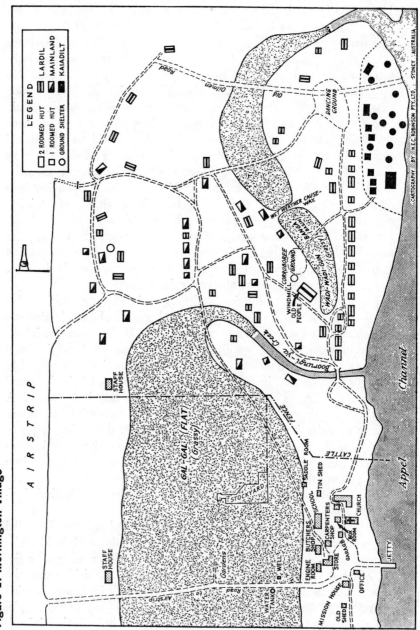

residential clusters shows how it affects some of the conflicts by preserving ethnic divisions. In a typical instance we observed Peggy Lorraine, an excitable Lardil woman who lives just outside the Kaiadilt enclave, claiming that Sally Bentinck's (Kaiadilt) little boy trod on her watermelon patch. This was probable because Peggy had not defined the patch with sticks or any sort of fence. Peggy chased him off and insulted the Kaiadilt group in general by calling him a dirty Bentinck boy who should use more soap. The offended community began to complain at Peggy across the boundary; Peggy, who does not understand the Kaiadilt tongue, took umbrage at Sally and ran at her with a stick. There was a fight in which Roonga Bentinck's scalp was split and had to be stitched up in the hospital. The council (see table 2) held an emergency meeting with all injured parties, and uttered grave injunctions in the hopes of forestalling further fighting, but next day the fighting resumed. Some Bentinck girls were at the well when Norma, Peggy Lorraine's daughter, came to draw water armed with a butcher's knife, which she said was to protect herself in case the Bentinck girls mobbed her. At this tempers were lost and more epithets were exchanged including the ultimate "Big Prick" (male insult) and "Red Cunt" (female insult). There was some stone-throwing and hand-fighting in which Netta, Sally's daughter, defended her mother and had her new dress torn. At a second council meeting called to control the situation, a leading councillor, Prince Escott, suggested that everybody stop talking about "wild Bentincks" and call them "New Mornington Islanders." He was thinking of the rapid assimilation of European immigrants into Australian society, where newcomers are termed "New Australians."

The closeness of the village allows no private life. There is no possibility of anonymous social experiment except by going to the mainland, and even there word gets back to the village. Gossip is pervasive. When a person wanders away from the village there is a hue and cry until he returns. Eccentric behavior tends to be inconvenient and to create anxiety. The pressure to conform is reinforced by the church elders' approval of changes for the better, as more frequent attendance at church would receive favorable comment from them. The closeness of village life creates problems of apartness and loneliness; thus young people of opposite sex have little opportunity to stop and talk. They are in the public gaze and tension from gossip does not permit unstrained relationships.

Some stratification has arisen in the village through the establishment of social class conferred by the degree of Western self-identification shown by education, dress, and earning capacity. Some of these distinctions are in the nature of caste; most Lardil, for example, regard themselves as socially superior to mainlanders and in a different category altogether from the Kaiadilt, to whom they tend to be patronizing. There is some value for the Kaiadilt in this patronage; sick Kaiadilt are scarcely fed if the chore is left to their kinsmen, while Lardil are attentive with food and visiting. The latter attitude may be an artifact of re-enculturation by the mission but it also reflects the abundant subsistence on Mornington Island. By contrast with Bentinck Island, it is implied, on Mornington Island even sick people get something to eat.

The administrative organization diagram (see table 2) gives the names of place-holding Aborigines at the time of our visit. Councillors, appointed by secret ballot amongst villagers, have vaguely defined duties which are still evolving. They are entitled to take disciplinary actions including fine and imprisonment, but do not exercise these; penalties for the occasional crime usually consist of extra work such as chopping wood. Rarely, a man may be sent away to camp by himself for a week. Councillors complain that their authority is disregarded by the villagers. The importance of the council lies in its potential for the future administration of the island, but achieving this is likely to be a lengthy process in an institutionalized and dependent community. Law and order is upheld officially through the superintendent and his councillors. Remnants of traditional control remain, operating in an increasingly haphazard way. They include the traditional medical system with its associated possession and sorcery syndromes, and to a small extent that is hard to guess, traditional values concerning "proper" behavior. The latter, exercised through the ties of kinship, is probably the only strong traditional control today. Traditionally, the system of initiation and advancement provided the possibility of coercing non-conforming younger men through the threat of excluding them from admission. To this extent traditional government could be called gerontocratic, but there appears to have been no powerful council of elders, certainly no authoritarian overlords. The new council runs into difficulties because it is an alien concept with no clear counterpart in traditional life. Disputes in the pre-mission era were settled on an ad hoc basis through argument, manipulation, factional pressure, and physical clash—as they tend to be today.

THE DISPLACEMENT OF TRADITION

Closer acquaintance with the village reveals cultural diversity within. The people vary in the degree to which they retain traditional interests or have acquired Western ones, or aspire to them. One of the aims of our research was to investigate the relationship between these aspects of an individual's cultural identity and his psychiatric adaptation. We constructed scales to measure these factors, obtaining results that will be detailed in chapter 7; in the meantime impressions of a relationship

Table 2. Administrative Organization of Mornington Island, 1967

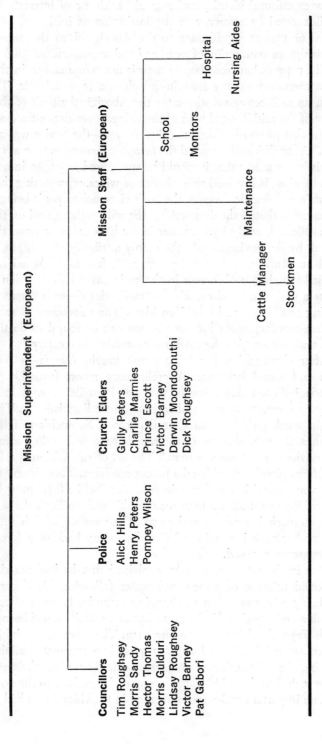

Mission Superintendent (European)

Councillors
Tim Roughsey
Morris Sandy
Hector Thomas
Morris Gulduri
Lindsay Roughsey
Victor Barney
Pat Gabori

Police
Alick Hills
Henry Peters
Pompey Wilson

Church Elders
Gully Peters
Charlie Marmies
Prince Escott
Victor Barney
Darwin Moondoonuthi
Dick Roughsey

Mission Staff (European)

Cattle Manager
Stockmen

Maintenance

School
Monitors

Hospital
Nursing Aides

between cultural identity and mental health are of interest. They will be illustrated by reference to the institution of initiation, normally a ritual of utmost significance to the Aboriginal as the outward dramatic sign of assumption of manhood and responsibility.

The progression from boy to man is not now marked in the village by a ceremony or any meaningful change in social role. There has been no satisfactory substitute for the Aboriginal rituals of this epoch. Most of the middle-aged men of the village were circumcised as novices in the first phase of initiation, called *lurugu*—the novice was a *"lurugu* boy."* As traditionally enacted the *lurugu* ceremony was so at odds with Christian practices that it would be suppressed as pagan in any Christian mission. It involved an exchange of wives, representing the mating of male and female dingoes, the boy's circumcised penis being thought to resemble that of the dingo. After the wife-exchange coitus, the semen was collected, washed with water into a bark container, and the liquid drunk by the novice to gain the manly attributes of strength, courage, skill at hunting, and sexual prowess. A few middle-aged men who missed the chance of *lurugu* in the early days of the mission now express a desire to be circumcised—"made clean"—in a ceremony combining traditional and Christian ideas. The missionary is receptive to such a rapprochement but no surgeon can be found to do the operation with the aseptic safeguards now considered necessary.

After circumcision the initiate was taught *Damin*—a remarkable sign and sound language. A preliminary report from Dr. K. Hale (1965) indicates that some of the "nasal snuffle" sounds in this language are extremely rare and of importance linguistically. The novice might speak only in *Damin* until released. Subincision of the penile urethra, the second phase of the *rite de passage,* is called *warama* and the novice was a *"warama* man."* The act of subincision is called *linga* and *linga* blood is considered a potent medicine. There is an association between subincision and certain fish. The "white fish" must be slit in the midline ventrally; a man may tell his wife to *linga* the white fish. The stomach is retained and eaten. The stomach of fish such as the cod and salmon is evaginated like the rolling back of a foreskin and the contents removed.

One important *warama* man explained that he had not drunk the collected mixture of semen and water following his circumcision— probably as a concession to changing attitudes brought about by the mission and associated influences—but as a substitute had been anointed with *linga* blood from a *warama* man. The most recent initiation on Mornington Island was *lurugu* only, and an attenuated affair at that, lacking the wife-exchange and semen-drinking. Nevertheless it meant a great deal to the middle-aged group and especially to the novice himself, an important and responsible man in the village who had regretted

32

his failure to be circumcised previously. The noteworthy transitional feature is the drying up of the flow of understanding and information. Younger men and women know little of the traditional mysteries and are little influenced by them. These customs are now important for mental health in the village only by default, by their inability to motivate and organize the individual into a secure place in society.

It is also noticeable in the village that the sons of the men who are traditionally oriented are poorly adjusted to the present situation. Sons of the Lardil men most attached to tradition are failures in work; none are stockmen and generally they do not assist in the ordinary chores of village life at home or in hunting. These young men who do not seek mission employment are teasingly called "pensioners." So far as habits of industry are concerned they compare unfavorably with two peer groups: the ex-mainlanders, who have been more involved in cattle work, and the new generation of Kaiadilt men, who are selected to work with the stock in preference to the Lardil men. Habits of Western industry represent only one form of adjustment of interest to our survey; no conclusions are ventured on other forms at this point.

To what extent have traditional customs and observances been replaced by those of Christianity? Opportunities for the church to influence village life on Mornington Island are plentiful. Brief services are held daily before work starts—a hymn, a prayer, Bible reading, and a comment. A Sunday morning service of worship is held, usually in the church but occasionally in the village, with the elders taking part. Frequently, Gully Peters interprets the sermon in the Lardil or Kaiadilt languages. A midweek meeting is held in the village, alternately in the Lardil or the Kaiadilt sections. Every two weeks a Bible study group meets in the church, the chief attenders being European staff members and a few village women. There is a Sunday school taught by staff members assisted by several Aboriginal women. The choir practices on Sunday nights. A young people's fellowship meets on Thursday night.

These religious observances have a mixed reception. The midweek meeting held in the village is poorly attended. The eight elders do not take an active part in church life with the exception of three, Gully Peters, Dick Roughsey, and Victor Barney, who possess relatively high acculturation. The position of church elder, like that of councillor, is more one of status than function. Choir practice is mainly of interest to some of the women. The young people's fellowship comes in for village criticism. Apart from its official object of religious study it allows young people of both sexes to meet socially, which they cannot easily do in the village. Village folk are sensitive about this and blame the "fellowship" for promiscuity and embarrassments to the kinship system

The people in social and cultural outline 33

—the half-mile walk between village and mission being an opportunity for dalliance. Regular attenders at Sunday services are mainly those who are paid mission wages. In earlier years there was a firm connection between mission employment and obligation to attend church. Attendance is better at the bi-monthly communion service, which suggests that the sacrament has some appeal. Religious fervor is not noticeable among the Lardil or the Kaiadilt; Presbyterians, if any have become such, are fairly conservative. Parents bring infants for baptism and adolescents become members of a communicant class in preparation for being received as members of the church, all after the somewhat desultory pattern of church life elsewhere in Australia.

Uneasy about the difficulty of making the Christian faith meaningful to Australian Aborigines, the present missionary over many years has tried to find a relationship between biblical thought and local tradition. This effort achieved a response from the Islanders, so that much of his preaching became a search for common theological ground. The Old Testament is rich in tribal laws and myths that lend themselves to local comparison. We heard some of these comparisons in his sermons in the corrugated iron church. Jacob's journey to the country of his mother's brother, Laban, in order to marry his mother's brother's daughter (Genesis 28:2) illustrated the practical problem of working out satisfactory marriages within a kinship system. In Canaan, Isaac abhorred the idea of Jacob marrying a local woman. Mother's brother's daughter may not have been a good marriage in kinship terms and involved a long journey for Jacob. In his sermon, the missionary stresses that Isaac did the best he could under the circumstances and that this is what Aborigines have to do under their kinship system today. Another sermon took for its text the treatment of Joseph by his brothers (Genesis 42). Such conduct among the sons of one father was a sin against kinship values. The retribution in Egypt—when the brothers came begging to Joseph and realized that their misfortune was divine "payback"—is the retribution acknowledged by Aborigines.

It appeared to us that in these sermons the missionary was seeking not to synthesize two systems of abstract religious thought but to illustrate the concrete themes of social life—marriage, kinship, land tenure. He felt that biblical references to interference with the ancient landmarks (Deuteronomy 19:14; Proverbs 22:28; Job 24:2) could well reinforce the Aborigines' feelings concerning their own land, at a time when tenure rights are violated while they remain politically unorganized and silent. To take another example, the reaction of the apostle Peter and his friends to the apparent defeat of Jesus at the crucifixion is found in Peter's "I am going fishing" (John 21:3). This is readily understood by the Islanders, as is the picture of the homely preparation of fish on a beach fire by Jesus (John 21:9-10). The correlations became interesting to us especially when the illustrations were made in the reverse direction. One discourse starts with a description of a visit to some island caves in the country of Gully Peters' father. It is from these that the "cave people" or Widamanda come—a popular myth celebrated in corroboree song and dance. The sermon then leads on to David's sparing Saul's life when he found him asleep in a cave in the hills. (I Samuel 26:1–12). After all, we felt, the Aboriginal story may have antedated the Old Testament!

The mental health implications of a quest for theological credibility are open to question. But insofar as it does not represent the too rigid imposition of an alien religious system, it may elicit some cooperative response from Aborigines who are commonly confused by Western traditions and values. The team on Mornington Island was impressed by the intent, although not familiar with the extent to which it may or may not be part of missionary practice elsewhere.

THE ORGANIZATION OF TIME AND LEISURE

Time on the island is structured in ways that to the Western outlook seem unsatisfactory, ways possibly unsatisfactory for the Islanders' adaptation to the new milieu. Aborigines in the alien contact situation acquire a good capacity for sitting and apparently doing nothing. Long before this pastime is terminated a Westerner would have become restless for further stimulation. It would seem that to engage in feverish activity, except perhaps in sport or at times in hunting, is not part of the Aboriginal makeup. It is hard to judge what provides the sensory input during these periods of inactivity. Conversation and story-telling make up a part; gambling with cards takes place at the instigation of some ex-mainland Aborigines, for whom it has become the main time-filling activity. There is no evidence on the island of compulsive gambling in the sense of a need to continue until all money is gone. In the case of a man who recently lost his mission wages through gambling, his wife made such trouble that some village control was brought to bear; it remains a rare occurrence. At the Christmas season gambling intensifies as more money and people are present. But to the European, the modes of arousal and stimulus seem disarticulated from the business of livelihood.

Village football is played with local rules, men and women together on sides unlimited in number. Some broken legs have resulted. Listening to the radio and record player is popular, and many people write to the nearest radio station at Mt. Isa three hundred miles away, requesting special numbers and greetings to folk in other places. Adolescents have adopted the guitar and dancing from the mass media. Some imitate through contact the singing of the Torres Strait islanders, a style more Melanesian than Aboriginal. Marbles is played seriously

The people in social and cultural outline   **35**

by the young and old of both sexes, especially around Christmas time. Marbles has features in common with traditional manipulative ground games and is played with a skill that would amaze the Western schoolboy. Coinciding with the school vacation all mission workers have a paid holiday and usually establish camps, at the Dugong River for Windward people, or Birri in the north for the Leeward. Hardly anybody expresses the wish to travel to the city, Brisbane, for a holiday. Occasionally somebody will visit a relative on Palm Island near the Barrier Reef on the other side of Cape York Peninsula, though the cost is considerable. More frequently people visit relatives at Doomadgee, the neighboring mainland mission a mere two hundred miles away, or Burketown, sixteen miles inland from the southern shore of the Gulf.

Seemingly, the most meaningful leisure activity is the corroboree in which dancing, music, oral literature, body and artifact decoration are combined. The artifacts are well-made "props" and have a natural balance and beauty which transcend any Western art influence. The singing, accompanied by tapping boomerangs and more recently by the introduction of the didjeridoo (dronepipe) from Arnhem Land, has rhythm and vitality. Corroboree themes derive from the locality and the natural phenomena of animals, weather, sea, and stars. Myths relating to these subjects are enacted after sundown in the dance clearing in the village and almost everybody comes to watch the more important dances. There appear to be few instances of a dance related to fighting or to tension of a hurtful kind between people. Three examples of oral literature converted into dance were provided us by Dick Roughsey.

Dick's stories, some of which we heard on the dancing ground, some while camping on the beach, forced us to ask whether myths do more than illustrate and personify religious and artistic themes and fantasies. Do they conceivably enshrine actual historical events? Dick's story of the coming of the Lardil from the south, from the center of Australia, might have seemed to us unlikely, but for the fact that their blood group resemblances to central tribes agree with it! (See chapter 2.) We decided we would do well to look closely at the myths, not only for their undoubted interest for psychoanalysis. The latter interest, naturally, is almost irresistible for Western psychiatrists.

The Coming of the Balamanda People
Told by Dick Roughsey

Our story tell us the first people who came to Goonana or Mornington Island were Marnbil, Gingin, and Duwaliwal. The word Balamanda means west so that most of our customs and laws come from the tribes around the center of Australia. Their work was to dig wells for the people who came after them, to make fish traps, taste all land and sea foods, and to show how to cook them. Duwaliwal was uncle of Gingin, Marnbil's wife. Marnbil and Gingin his wife went round the south side of the island while Duwaliwal went around the north side to work. When they reached the top end of the island they made their camps. One day both men went out to do their last work on the two remaining islands, Bountiful and Turtle Island. Gingin stayed home gathering pandanus palm nuts. Duwaliwal came home early from his work, heard Gingin cracking nuts, came over and said to her, "Niece, I feel that I must have wife. Will you be my wife for a moment?" "No, you are my uncle, I won't do that, it is not right." But he kept on asking her. At last she gave in to him. At the moment Marnbil came home and saw all that had happened. But he never said a word. Next day, Marnbil asked Duwaliwal to dig the last water hole. Marnbil found water and asked Duwaliwal to taste the water. This was the moment Marnbil wanted. He leaned back, picked up a spear and speared him in the buttocks.

The Story of Thuwathu

Told by Dick Roughsey

Away in the Dreamtime there lived an old Rainbow Serpent named Thuwathu. He lived at a place we call today Lalgagindiboo which today is under water, between Timber Point and the opposite side of the mouth of the Dugong River. This is called Mooloorra in our language today. Here he lived until one day his sister Bulthugoo and her baby Yindidboo or Willy-wag-tail came and stood outside his humpy or shelter as we should call it today. She stood outside and looked up into the sky and saw the rain clouds gathering. She knew her brother was inside and she called out, "Brother, will you put my little daughter, your niece, inside your humpy?" But old Thuwathu was sound asleep. She could hear him snoring and she called out louder than the first time, "Brother put my baby inside, it might rain soon!" But he could not hear her, he was very tired and was sound asleep. The rain started to fall and she decided to make a little fire, and in that way might keep her baby warm. She covered her baby with a piece of bark and went and gathered more wood until she had a big fire, and sat down by the fire.

She got up after a while and yelled out at the top of her voice "Brother, you're awake? Put my baby in that corner over there, I can see a place for my baby there!" Then old Thuwathu woke up and moved over to where she saw that place and he said, "No, that place is for my two knees!" After saying this, he put his two knees there and went back to sleep. Suddenly the sister called out again and with tears in her eyes said, "Brother, put my baby in that corner over there—my baby is shivering with cold now!" But he was a selfish brother. He opened his eyes and said, "Oh no—that room's for my two elbows!" He rolled over and put his two elbows at the spot where his sister pointed. That left other parts of his humpy bare, as he moved over. So this kept on, every place that was bare his sister saw and asked him to put her daughter in, he would say, "No." It was for his two ears, or two feet, or his big tail.

So at last she looked at her baby and she was shivering with cold, and she knew it must die soon. She left her baby to die, and went and made a big fire and cried and cried. She picked up the fire and threw it on the back of his humpy and got some bark and tied it together. When she thought it was long enough she put one end in the fire and lit it and ran around the humpy until she burnt it and the fire got bigger and bigger. When she did this she stood a distance away and looked, and she heard him crying and talking and cursing her. All she wanted was to pay him back for what he done to her.

Old Thuwathu came out, groaning and saying bad words to his sister Bulthugoo and rolled in pain and afterwards decided to leave, and he began to crawl away, groaning as he went on his way. Soon after he left, the fires began to spread and burn all the country between Timber Point and the mouth of the Dugong River, and the place was covered with salt water. That is why all that part is called Lalgagindiboo today, after the baby of Bulthugoo, Willy-wag-tail. On and on he went, and as he went he left his tracks, and in some places he would rest for a while and in those places there are some very deep water holes today.

He went on inland and our story says he almost reached the other side of Mornington Island. There he met another mob of his countrymen the Rainbows, and they asked him what happened and he told them his story. After listening to his story they got sharp stones and began bashing themselves and made a big mourning. He stayed with them for a while, and one day he left and went away. He was going to come back to die in his own country, but it wasn't so, he died half-way, under a big pandanus tree, and where he died there is a spring we call Boogargun. It is on a ridge, away from other waterholes. The nearest would be about three miles and so here on this high ridge is where Old Thuwathu the Rainbow died. Out by the mouth of the Dugong River is a big inlet or bay where he made it, and the river itself runs about seven miles inland.

Where the people or his mob mourned for him, there are piles of little pieces of stones—some have been collected and mixed in cement for housing. Today when my people see the rainbow they say, "There look —there is the spirit of Thuwathu" and now if anyone takes land food such as sugarbag, yams or roots or goanna down to the sea the spirit of the rainbow serpent will enter their stomach and make them sick.*

The Stars and Their Stories
Told by Dick Roughsey

The woman star, Booldingoo [Venus?], is the first star to go down in the evening in the west. Her husband Bidgingoo, the hunter [Orion?], always sends her back to the camp first, so that she can get wood and make a big fire to cook the food on his arrival. Bidgingoo, the great hunter, always tells the old people when to get up in the morning and when to go to bed at night. He also told us when it is time to go down

---

* This refers to the *malgri* sickness, a culture-specific disorder of which a detailed account and examples are included in *Medicine is the Law* (forthcoming).

to the reefs at night to hunt fish with the small scoop net—about midnight depending on the tide.

The Gooridnid Sisters [Pleiades?] are stars for good luck in hunting and food gathering. To make sure that there will be good hunting my people have a song and dance for the Gooridnid Sisters. Men and women gather round at night when we first see these Sisters. A fire stick of pandanus is thrown towards the stars and we sing this song:

> "Give us plenty of fat snake, goanna, swamp turtle,
> fish, dugong, crab, prawn, roots."

The corroboree art form at Mornington Island is in the throes of change. From the degree of interest we observed in the village we might have expected that the young men would become proficient dancers and songmen, but this is not happening. Effectiveness in the corroboree comes from participation in the traditional life. The younger men seem to think the future lies in identifying with Western ways, so that the guitar is more important than the tapping of boomerangs—an electric guitar if possible. But the cowboy songs and the strumming seem nervous and ambivalent. Some of those who persist with the corroboree art form are discovering commercial possibilities. The group from the island that visited the mainland towns of Mt. Isa and Cairns as a concert party had its presentations applauded enthusiastically. This has stimulated interest in the dance and in the other creative activities associated with it. Tape recordings made of the songs and music have been edited to make a phonographic disc available commercially, with a cover design drawn by one of the Islanders. The resurgence of the dance heightens the ambivalence of the young men. They come to watch the village corroborees but take little part. At a showing of photographic slides of the dancing it was noticeable that they felt free as a group to make derisive remarks. "Film star!" they cried at the picture of one highly decorated dancer. "Stick 'em up" they cried at a picture of dancers raising hands in the Thuwathu story. At the corroboree they had never been so disrespectful. "Jealous! Jealous!" accused an angry older man. This was not the permissible joking expressions in the context of a teasing kinship relationship. The incident expressed the derision of the young men for tradition from which they are excluded by lack of skill and knowledge, and the older man's defense of an identity of which he is proud.

The brother artists, Lindsay and Dick Roughsey, are in a situation which can be sketched here as a portrait of the Aboriginal artist as a transitional figure. *Ars gratia artis* is no more conspicuous in the artistic life of the Islander than in that of Westerners; Dick as the most successful bark painter is no exception. He calculates what lies ahead of each painting effort; sales bring money, which buys a house or an outboard motor for his fishing dinghy. The same consideration applies to the manufacture of artifacts that are now supplied to meet the demand. The Western techniques used for making the artifacts are far removed from the traditional, but the finished product brings a better price; steel tools and sandpaper produce a more efficient boomerang than does a shell knife. A leader of the art industry, Dick is probably one of the most socially competent of the men and has had extensive contact with Western ways. At corroborees he is frequently master of ceremonies and is capable, comical, ironical—in a way skillful and appropriate. He has adapted the Arnhem Land style of bark painting to his use, and his natural talent ensured the success of his exhibitions held in Brisbane and Canberra. He plans to leave the island and move his family to Cairns to establish himself as a painter, a somewhat unusual ambition in that he is hoping to enter a different class from that into which most Aborigines are assimilated. It is a form of individuation of which the island has no experience.

Dick's ambition poses his mission advisers with a dilemma. They feel that he is one of the few who takes Christianity seriously. They know him as kind, affectionate to his children, loyal to his wife and, perhaps like an artist, easily imposed upon, erratic. His charm of manner is widely recognized. Once a bystander found him drawing eight legs on a bee and when this was pointed out Dick smiled and said, "All artists are a little bit liars, eh?" A party of visitors organized a spear-throwing contest in which Dick, Lindsay, and some others took part. Dick took a spear and thrower and exaggerating the Aboriginal hunting walk pretended to be stalking the visitors. His clowning made fun of the Europeans putting him to the test in the Aboriginal role. When they offered money for the longest throw, Dick in return offered one of the visitors a tin of tobacco if he could hit a target. When the throws were a long way off target and one of the bystanders was nearly hit, Dick commented that white people are probably better when they aim at live targets.

One European who held Dick and his personality in affection and who was concerned about the outcome of his ambition to go to Cairns described Dick's exhibition of bark paintings held in Brisbane the previous year. He said that Dick had blended well with Brisbane society; he met his viewers with wit and charm. Yet Dick's inexperience with money matters and in looking after himself in town was revealed by the trip. He could not calculate where his money went and was amazed when his pocket was empty. During his exhibition he was constantly worried about how he was doing; he depended on aspirin and could not sleep for worry about his show. He ate little and when the show was over collapsed with exhaustion. His friend worried whether he would withstand the availability of alcohol and whether he would gain the necessary experience of Western society without undue trauma. Home on the island, Dick is the epitome of social ease and relaxation.

This adviser has Dick's welfare clearly at heart and is discouraging him from moving to Cairns. He feels that Dick has underestimated the difficulties of breaking into Western society and of inducing it to give him enough money. He feels he could not cope with its value system despite his valiant efforts, nor with the exclusion from the many aspects of the Western world that would be his lot. Moreover, away from the island he might lose much of the inspiration for his traditional art; his repute as an artist arises out of his background at Mornington Island. In his opinion it was the capable Dick who deserved Western help more than some of his disturbed confreres. Dick's art chiefly depicts the oral literature of the island; his inspiration is Lardil mythology.[1]

Dick's elder brother Lindsay paints on bark using graphic designs and rarely depicting human figures, but with a deeper spiritual significance than Dick's. In his secondary style Lindsay paints figures and landscapes in a "primitive" but non-traditional manner. Unlike Dick, Lindsay does not aspire to live in Cairns or anywhere else. His business is to learn all he can of the tribal life of his people and he has gained status with them through his knowledge. Functionally, if not physically, he is a *warama* man, contrasted with Sam Bush who is a *Damin*-speaking *warama* yet who has always been dependent and uninterested in traditional life. A *warama* man has no foreskin and his urinary stream sprays wide from the subincision. Lindsay has expressed the desire to be circumcised—"to be made clean" as he expresses it.

Lindsay is in the ambiguous position of appreciating the mission on the one hand and being the participant in traditional resurgence on the other. Three years ago he felt obliged to support a kinsman who led a faction that advocated leaving the mission and going back to the bush. Although the rebellion arose out of an incident now forgotten it brought to light the ever-present sense of loss concerning the way of life that regulated the island. In consequence of these activities Lindsay is ambivalently regarded at the mission. Some people there view him as "a tricky man"; others respect him because he directs his people and does not always conform with mission requirements. The psychiatric

1. Dick comments: "Since you wrote this, I had a successful show in Canberra, and I only painted in oil, the everyday life of my own people on Mornington Island. Marnbil and Gidigil paintings are like paintings of Christ carrying the Cross, and different artists have done them differently through the ages, still do. Grog—well, I have been in Cairns nine or ten weeks and I am learning how to use alcohol as a pleasure, without drinking too much. Instruction in drinking is badly needed. Now I am making between fifty and sixty dollars a week for my paintings. I have a great friend who teaches me how to live in the white community, how to use it, when, and I am happy." (The friend is Captain Percy Tresize, an airline pilot.)

Subsequently, Dick and Captain Tresize collaborated in writing Dick's autobiography, *Moon and Rainbow* (Wellington, N.Z.: A. H. and A. W. Reed, 1971).

The people in social and cultural outline   **41**

team formed an impression of Lindsay as a man of high social awareness, potentially in conflict with Western values but well adjusted personally. He adapts to the social situation insofar as his integrity as an Aborigine permits. Recently some businessmen friends of the Lardil returned to the island bringing gear with which they hoped to train the men to net and salt the more highly fancied fish as a commercial venture for the gourmet market. The project did not succeed. One of the friends despaired of enlisting Lindsay's support; he was interested in fishing only to the extent of its usefulness as food, here and now. Somehow it was Lindsay who emerged dominant; he made kinsmen of the business friends, engaging them in mutual appreciation of both lifestyles, the more poignant in that it camouflaged the Aborigine's disinclination to come to grips with commerce.

The case of the Australian Aborigine is of supreme interest to behavioral science because he is commonly regarded as Early or Stone Age Man who is suddenly confronted by modern Western society and asked to adapt and assimilate. From the social-psychiatric point of view that we represent it seemed that one of the fundamental changes involved in this confrontation is the abandonment of nomadic or semi-nomadic foraging life in small bands in favor of life in a settled village community. We made a hypothesis about preparedness to live in a village. It seemed to us that the social organization, social institutions, and social character that had evolved to suit nomadic life were unlikely equally to suit village life. Our hypothesis was that because social organization, social institutions, and social character would not be erased or replaced rapidly, their persistence was likely to introduce elements adverse to village life. This was a hypothesis that would suggest itself not especially to psychiatrists but to anybody taking a sympathetic interest in what goes on in a village.

In this chapter we plan not so much to test the hypothesis as to elaborate upon it through the observations of individuals interacting with those around them in the business of living in the village.[1] It seemed that certain regular transactions—conflicts, impasses, collisions, submissions, evasions, frustrations were among the various terms we employed for them—were making it hard for Islanders to become socially integrated in the village. In our view some of these transactions had pathogenic elements. We selected for our scrutiny three: the periodic violence that shook the village, the peculiar difficulties in achieving domesticity, and the stresses involved in finding satisfactory work through emigration. Each of these three, periodic violence, do-

---

1. The "social adaptational" and "interactionist" emphases in this book do not imply our lack of concern for the classical "adjustment" motifs of psychiatry such as instinctual drives, intrapsychic conflicts, and ego defenses. In situations of reduced communication it is inevitable that conflict is focused transactionally rather than intrapsychically.

mesticity, and emigration, was highly relevant to the Islanders' opportunities for adaptation to village life.

PERIODIC RIOTS

The even tenor of life in the village is interrupted by explosions of rioting. These riots are periodic violent group conflicts, of psychiatric importance in that they disrupt harmony and constructive purpose in the community. We also considered that by their cumulative effect on the individual according to the principle described as schismogenesis by Bateson (1936) they resulted in the differentiation of certain character traits. These character traits put Aborigines at a disadvantage in their transitional world. One of these traits that has become part of the island ethos we entitled "evasion of confrontation."

We observed two riots of a self-generating or reverberating type, one during the team's visit and one during the brief follow-on visit by one of the participants. They are common over the Christmas holidays when the village is crowded with people returned home from mainland cattle station jobs. The wet monsoonal season adds to the charge in the emotional atmosphere by making it difficult to work and to move about outside. It is open to question whether the reverberating type of conflict is a characteristic of traditional Aboriginal society or is an artifact of a camp-life developed at the fringes of Western settlement. Whatever the historical origins, it seems that inflammatory feelings heightened by close living are ignited in these periodic fights.

In the characteristic sequence, the precipitant is an incident concerning a child. A mother punishes her little daughter for something; the father takes the child's side. In the ensuing argument the father hits the mother with his hand; she retaliates with a stick. Soon the in-laws and other relatives join in. Alternatively, the precipitating event is a children's squabble. One child beats another in a fight and the parent of the defeated child goes to the house of the other child to complain to the parents. Harsh words are exchanged and somebody is clubbed. More distant relatives rally around and the argument spreads. Coalitions crystallize in the village, perhaps along the lines of ancient divisions, for example, between Windward and Leeward people. Eventually fifty or a hundred people are milling about. Men and women not fighting are watching the fighting, or are busy appeasing, arguing, carrying off combatants, bringing to the hospital scalps split and fingers broken by boomerang clouts. In most fights the mission superintendent is expected to remain impartial but in bigger ones he sometimes accepts a popular appeal to quell the riot. Then he too is to be found in the middle of the fracas, appealing, ordering, threatening, and cajoling. By getting in the way and by exploiting the fairly general concern for his safety he usually succeeds in exerting a dampening effect on the tumult.

The use of children's squabbles as an excuse for letting out tension is a pattern sufficiently common on Mornington Island to merit closer examination. The use of children by parents to communicate in a hostile or deceptive way with each other is frequently observed in Western families by psychiatrists—for example the "pawn child" described by Wilmer (1966). The island children sometimes see their parents—and possibly half the village—shedding blood over children's squabbles. One of the older men, Gully Peters, claimed that it was a new pattern on the island: "A long time ago when children would fight, their parents would say, 'That's only a children's fight.' They wouldn't take part. Now parents step right in and take sides." He explained that for many years children did not live in the village but in the dormitory and that the sudden parental responsibility thrust upon the community when the dormitory system was abolished might be a factor. Whatever the truth of Gully's claim, the pattern seems to have been in existence long enough to contribute to the differentiation of certain character traits and perhaps a certain island ethos.

The ethos of the island conspicuous in the periods between the reverberating conflicts is one of tolerance, concern, and evasion of confrontation. This ethos makes it hard for adults to pick fights for legitimate reasons. The lack of confrontation is reflected in the attitude toward children. Adults are extraordinarily tolerant of young children and disinclined to set limits. If it is pointed out that a child is doing something destructive in the mission yard—something the adults might not have even thought of otherwise—everyone descends forcibly on the child.

On a fishing trip members of the team noticed the general disinclination to speak firmly. Scarcely a hard word passed between any two people for several days. The strongest disapproval witnessed on this trip was a complaining type of admonition addressed to two boys by Doris, the wife of the village policeman, Henry Peters. In fishing along the river, Henry waded into waist-deep muddy water with the net. As he proceeded slowly up the river nobody went in after him although obviously somebody had to follow him up with the other end of the net. No orders came from Henry. The women started complaining in a jocular way to the boys standing on the bank that somebody had to get in. The moment was approaching when the end of the net was about to float free of the bank. Still no word came from Henry. A member of the expedition could tolerate the impasse no longer and plunged in. This won a small note of approval from the elderly Gully and his wife Cora but no mention was made of it by Henry either to the boys or to anybody else. On another occasion the launch was returning late at night and ran aground on a sandbar about a mile from the island. This was not unusual at low tide and reflected no discredit on Pompey, the captain of the launch. Getting the launch off the sandbar by the various possibilities—reversing the engine, pulling with oars from the two dinghies, or lightening the launch—required power of command from Pompey with the issuing of firm directions to the crew. Nothing of the sort was forthcoming with the result that everybody present suggested some different course of action.

It is tempting to trace the evasion of confrontation, or lack of attempts at dominance in the island ethos, to the fear of the conflict that could result and grow into a conflagration. The individual would not need to experience many such incidents to learn wariness and a disinclination to be provocative. The social character thus developed may have been illustrated by responses to our inquiries concerning the traditionally valued attributes of men and women. Responses about the ideal man included: "Strength not important for hunting and fishing, only skill . . . he gives things away, gives anybody anything at all, good hearted . . . he is a peacemaker, goes into the middle of arguments and separates fighting people . . . he will fight when somebody gets cheeky with him but he never starts fights . . . a cheeky man passes my place and helps himself to my food without asking . . . I carry water and a cheeky man asks me for a drink and then he tells me it doesn't taste good . . . a good dancer . . . looks are not important but good temper is very important . . . nowadays the young girls forget about good temper, they just go for looks." Traditionally valued attributes of women were cited: "She gets along with her co-wives, no arguing, cooperation . . . today, my word, you can't go near a woman without getting a stick thrown at you . . . a good woman is a good gatherer of crabs and roots . . . she makes a good fishing net . . . she is good looking."

An ethos characterized by reluctance to make a firm confrontation may have adaptive aspects in village life with the ever-present possibility of reverberating group conflict. But it puts the Aborigine at a serious disadvantage in his dealings with Westerners and the Western world which expects communication of a firmer and more direct kind. The anxiety-inhibition syndrome to be described in Kaiadilt children, and to some extent in the other Aboriginal children, represents a variant. It is an ethos incompatible with the attainment of competence in Western life. Nor does it help much in the village. If the "ideal" Aboriginal man who is generous and restrained does not confront another with his grievances until these become of a serious nature, he becomes the victim of the forgetful borrower, the dependent relation or guest, the stealthy manipulator, and the carping wife. Many Aboriginal adults seem to Western eyes indecisive and lacking in initiative. We saw this as related to the inhibition of confrontation and to the necessity to consult group opinion rather than get out of step inadvertently, in either case to avoid the risk of group conflict.

This apparent link between character and conflict represents a stereotype. Even though it possesses general validity, exceptions exist, such as the "cheeky men" described by the Aborigines. Over-conformity to the ethos or rebellion against it both contain the germ of a pathology that will be revealed in greater detail by the study of individual case histories, when we reach that section of our inquiries. But one thing stood out about the periodic riots: they did nothing to lessen the social distance between the "blackfellow" and the "whitefellow"—one of the basic sources of pathology in the culture contact.

DIFFICULTIES IN DOMESTICITY IN A CHANGING SOCIETY

Because the family is the chief context for acquiring and imparting mental health, changes in domesticity resulting from the cultural upheaval become of great importance. One of the more troublesome conflicts is that between the Western system of assortative mating and the Aboriginal system of tribal kinship rules. We collected instances of dissension arising from this conflict in mores, associated with various psychiatric disturbances.

It should not be inferred that finding a mate through tribal kinship rules proceeds smoothly and automatically. A small population attempting to operate under an eight-subsection kinship system copied from admired groups to the south is subject to a mathematical probability that mates will not be available when wanted. Even in a large tribe organized in eight marriage subsections limiting the degree of blood relationship possible between spouses, such as the Walbiri of Central Australia described by Meggitt (1962) and by Cawte and Kidson (1965), distribution of wives is uneven, and considerable departures from marriage rules have to be made through negotiation. Although Lardil are not especially rigid and do concede some second-best alternatives, one of the heaviest burdens that parents face is to arrange the "right-head" (correct kinship) marriage for their children. Western contact adds further complications to the making of village marriages: monogamy and miscegenation. Monogamy is enforced by the mission; a man no longer has rights to his wife's sisters either for marriage or for sexual union. Miscegenation—Chinese and European—has created a small stock of mixed-blood Aborigines that somehow has to be incorporated into the community. Each situation contains the seed of conflict, crisis, and altered adaptation for the individual.

Under tribal law a man has rights to his wife's unmarried sisters. A reliable and competent head stockman at the mission ran into difficulties in this context. Some years ago his wife declined sexual relations on the grounds that she feared pregnancy, whereupon he turned to his wife's unmarried sister as tribal law entitled. The sister became pregnant and amidst much gossip left the island. The same thing then happened with a second sister. Relieved of his duties as head stockman, he has since worked on the mainland. Interviewed at home on his holidays, he was anxious to return home to the island and to his job as stockman. Much of the trouble undoubtedly arose because the two unmarried sisters were nubile and eager but had no husbands eligible under the interpretation of kinship rules.

Miscegenation disconcerts the traditional kinship situation. In several recent instances part-Aboriginal females have been desired by full-blood males in preference to their chosen endogamous wives-elect. The opportunities afforded for dispute, crisis, and emotional disturbance by the presence of part-Aborigines in the marriage market may be illustrated by the courtship of the women of Olive's family.[2] Olive was born on the mainland of a European father and Aboriginal mother. In common with most of the part-Aboriginal women on the island she is a stable and adapted person. The mixed-blood people in general have a higher Western identification and help the work of the mission by meeting children's needs on a community basis through cooking, clothing, sewing, and teaching in school. Olive married a full-blood man and has three fine daughters, Trixie, Ivy, and Maud, who are technically quadroons. Each daughter was sought in marriage by young full-blood men in defiance of kinship rules but in compliance with the belief amongst the younger people that it is a step up the social ladder to marry a part-Aboriginal. John sought the first daughter, Trixie, but in the face of parental opposition on kinship grounds he capitulated and married his right-head wife-elect Sarah. Trixie went away to a country town where she became the de facto wife of a European man and bore him a child. Noel sought the second daughter, Ivy, but in the face of kinship opposition yielded and married his right-head mate Susan. Since then he has regularly visited the mission hospital for hypochondriacal complaints and symptoms of a hysterical type, including fainting. Bill, who sought the third daughter, Maud, overcame the opposition to the "wrong-head" marriage, succeeding where the others failed because Maud herself gave him more encouragement. The marriage has been satisfactory to both spouses. The only other part-Aboriginal young woman on the island, Ellen, is also at the center of domestic difficulties. She married David but was desired by Sam, to whom she bore a child. While David was employed away from the island she refused Sam's further attentions. At one point in the protracted argument Sam manipulated the situation by shooting himself

2. Names in these histories are fictitious.

through the hand with a rifle. It was abundantly clear that the presence of a few part-Aboriginal people, through no fault of theirs or of the villagers, left a trail of behavioral and emotional disturbances.

Several Kaiadilt girls away working on mainland cattle stations have conceived children by European men and all the children appear to have been well received by the Kaiadilt group home on the island. Many older people are in fact dependent on their daughters and would rather they had illegitimate babies than marry and leave home. One man sends money to support the mother and child and expresses affection for both. A factor in overcoming village and parental opposition to a "wrong-head" marriage is the birth of a child—a kind of shot-gun marriage with generation roles reversed. Leslie and Connie had a child when Connie was fifteen years old. Connie's parents were bitterly opposed to the marriage because her selected husband was Tom. Leslie's parents accepted responsibility for the child and cared for it. When Connie's father Steve died, her mother's opposition weakened; Leslie and Connie now keep company—for example they sat together on the launch during a trip made by the study team up the north coast of the island. At present they are employed at different cattle stations on the mainland but hope to marry. Three other couples whom we found to have married "wrong-head" in defiance of the rules —Wesley and Carol, Ian and Nell, Claude and Barbara—have achieved stable marriages. On the other hand some arranged "straight-head" marriages have failed; Henry will not live with his wife Winnie although he supports her and the child.

Another feature of domesticity affected by the new life in the village is the status of women and the balance of domestic power. In general, women's status has risen with the development of the Western pattern of conjugal family life. Access by men to women whom they previously called "wife"—such as wife's sister—is disapproved. The traditional code permitted and regulated sexual liaisons and although the advent of Western society overthrew this system, indiscriminate sexual union remains rare. Surprisingly little quarrelling arises in this village from marital infidelity; the cases that have occurred are so well remembered as to suggest that infidelity is the exception. We observed three "triangles" in which the relationship appeared to be tolerated without undue disharmony by the respective sides of the triangle.

We concluded that marital balance of power and the adoption of domestic roles in the village setting depends as much on personality as on tradition. There are only a few families in which the woman seems the dominant or decision-making partner: Norma is more dominant than Terence, Mary more dominant than Fred—both wives are part-Aborigines. There are several families in which both marital partners are passive and indifferent. In general husbands are dominant, possibly

Conflicts of village life   49

in part because on the whole island women have less opportunity to earn money. A quid pro quo sharing of labor is general between couples; under the hard economic conditions prevailing, little else is possible.

But our observations suggest that in the village the women work harder than the men. To begin with they have the supervision of the children, and most of the disciplining. Conditions on camping holidays perhaps more closely simulate traditional life and were therefore of special interest to us. On arrival the women immediately get a fire going and keep busy the whole time—fishing, cooking, collecting shells for necklaces to sell to the mission. The men relax and sleep between spells of fishing. On the other hand, the women do not spear fish in the deeper water as the younger men do, nor do they net fish in the river. But the balance of useful and purposeful activity lay with the women. This may contribute to the deteriorating situation, widely remarked in the mission, that young adult men are mere shadows of their fathers. With a couple of exceptions the sons of the leading Lardil men show much less initiative and industry than their fathers, and fail to apply themselves to the Western-type jobs that are offered.

The change in the marriage institution being undergone by modern Western society is commonly incriminated by psychiatrists as a source of personal difficulty and instability. Here is a society in which the marriage institution is changing more drastically, at a faster rate.

SUCCESS AND FAILURE IN EMIGRATION AND INDUSTRY

If lack of adequate industry can be accepted as "normal" on the island, emigration to mainland jobs becomes the special work problem. Since the economy depends heavily on exporting labor, the community has an eager interest in the success of those who take mainland jobs. Success in these jobs does not come easily to the Islanders. We found that a few of the more adaptable succeed beyond expectations: June became a nurse in Sydney, though at the cost of domestic instability; Trixie similarly trained in a country town before quitting her training to become the "wife" of a married European. Many of the girls who work as domestics meet with similarly mixed success. As mentioned, pregnancy is a common occurrence in those who venture out, especially with the Kaiadilt girls. Acute psychiatric disturbance is not rare. A Lardil girl who recently became severely disturbed after commencing work on a mainland station had to be sent home after a stay in a mental hospital; her transitory delusional state we found to be characteristic of such situations. (See chapter 5.) Homesickness and culture shock seem especially hard for the emigrant Islander to endure. The performance of some of the Islanders in mainland work situations is inferior to their performance on the island; this may be motivated by nostalgia and an active intent to be sent home. An aggrieved letter was recently received by the missionary from the wife of a mainland cattle station manager. It reveals much about this troublesome situation. As written, it reads:

Dear Sir,

I feel it is my duty to inform you of my reason for sending Edna Sampson back to the Island. The past 6 months I have had to stand over Edna to do her work and get it done, she would hide herself away and start reading and when corrected she would get moody and sulk all day.

On three occasions now when I have been away in town, and did not take Edna with me she has let our pet bird out of its cage, also killed my daughter's pet kangaroo, because she did not take Edna to town with her. We naturally thought the dogs killed it, until about three weeks ago, I had to go into town to see a Doctor and the men were on the road driving cattle so I left Edna home to look after the animals, she asked me to leave my pet fox terrier with her for company. This I did, as I usually take my little dog everywhere I go with me as she is just like a baby to me. When I returned the little dog did not meet me. Edna told me she followed the car and that she went looking for her but did not find her. I walked for miles the next day over the property looking for her thinking she was lost and perished. After I returned home I was very upset. Edna must have known I was determined to find the dog dead or alive so she handed me a letter and said it was going to upset me. The letter told me that Terry (the dog) was dead and that she had found her and put her in a bag and planted her in some bushes not far from the house. I had a look at the dog and examined it before I buried her. She had her head all crushed in, her legs broken and body mutilated. I knew then that Edna had killed my dog. My daughter cornered Edna and asked her how she killed Terry and why. She told us she did not know what made her do it, but could not help herself.

I had the dog eight years and it never once gave Edna any reason to hate it. I really think she did it for spite, as we could not take Edna to town, as I could not find her when ready to come home, she was after a white man baby. I think Edna is a very bad girl and should be punished. I was very good to Edna and treated her like my own daughter.

(Signed) Mrs.

Home on the island Edna is moody, though playful at times amongst other girls. She withdraws or becomes mute whenever European men are about. One of the team members spoke to her in the company of her father and she would not answer any questions. Throughout the conversation her father kept telling her not to be afraid, that the doctor was there to help her; Edna looked sullen rather than afraid. Two girls working as aides in the hospital knew Edna well and contributed the information that she had wanted to come home to Mornington Island

and had often asked the station manager's wife to send her back to see her family. The two girls said that Edna had killed the animals in order to be sent home. They thoght the whole thing was rather humorous.

The great copper mines at Mt. Isa offer opportunities for the employment of Mornington men but judging from previous experiences, unless the men are supervised it is not employment suited to them. This situation deserves study because the booming mining industry of outback and northern Australia could be the salvation of the bulging Aboriginal population—if the industrial psychiatric problems can be overcome in time. The first four Lardil men to be employed at the mines, Bob, Harry, William, and Keith, aged between twenty-five and thirty-two, were recently dismissed from their laboring jobs at Mt. Isa mines. They had been warned for "blowing shifts" (absenteeism) on the days after nights of drinking. When this persisted they were sent back together to the island. It was a great disappointment because they were believed at home to have been doing well; they had prestige as the first Lardil to have mining jobs and had held them for periods of three to ten months at excellent wages. The information received on the island was that the foreman had said that he was no longer interested in employing Aboriginal men who could not be relied upon to come to work. There had been no racial discrimination; they had been accepted by their workmates both as workmen and socially in the mines' hostel. Indeed the conviviality had been part of their problem.

A group interview of the four men back on the island revealed that all seemed genuinely disappointed at losing their jobs, but admitted "blowing shifts" because of hangovers. They had gotten into a pattern of regular heavy drinking—ten beers[3] each night in the hotel, and on Sunday nights a drive into the bush with members of the football club in cars stacked with beer. Beer cost eleven to sixteen dollars a week out of a wage packet of nineteen dollars remaining after the installment to be sent to their dependents by their own arrangement with the district officer had been deducted. There was not much left over for food or clothing. The men said there was nothing much to do in Mt. Isa with their leisure time; nearly everybody that they knew drank as much as they did. But the white men were used to it.

Although the four men had been dismissed collectively for persistent absenteeism in which all had participated, it appeared in the interviews that there were different degrees of negligence as well as other individual differences. Bob, the eldest, was the chief spokesman and his ease in conversation with Europeans bespoke his years of contact in football clubs and mainland jobs. He is athletic, genial, pleasure-seeking. William, although comparatively young, is the father of six children

---

3. Australian beer has a high alcohol content, usually of the order of 8 percent.

and a contemplative man regarded on the mission as an unusually good motor mechanic. Loss of the job at the mines has been a serious matter to him. Harry is a somewhat withdrawn person who scarcely spoke in the interview; he has a morose appearance. He usually lives apart from his wife who suffers from a personality disorder characterized by episodes of hostile excitement. Keith, though strongly built, has a history of job instability and lack of perseverance. Although the group at first denied that there was any difference in their individual amounts of absenteeism it soon transpired that Keith's was the highest.

From the men's account they had received fair consideration from their employers. But it appeared that they had been perhaps treated as a group at the mines. If a stereotype had arisen it would hardly be surprising. Public opinion of Aborigines consists largely of stereotypes; even much anthropological and sociological research has been concerned with social character and the delineation of shared traits. For example, the "ethos of generosity" by which Aborigines are obliged to share possessions and their aversion to authoritarian leadership in social organization are cited as group qualities that make it hard for them to adapt to Western industrial situations.

Although these generalizations are to some extent valid it is probably more helpful in individual cases to consider differences rather than shared characteristics. From the interview with the four unsuccessful emigrant workers and from a knowledge of their personal histories, it seemed that William and Bob possessed personal characteristics that might enable them to offset shared traits that lead to failure in industry. On the other hand Harry and Keith probably did not. Even so, it was obvious that if William and Bob were to succeed they would need supervision: somebody acting *in loco parentis* at Mt. Isa mines to help organize their leisure time and to prevent identification with the "poor white" and more alcoholic element of town society. It is the possibility of such supervision that the mission now has to explore if reinstatement is to be achieved.

A member of the psychiatric team on his way home pursued this matter by visiting Mt. Isa mines, where the four men are well remembered by the personnel officer and by their foreman on the "Roads and Rails" external division where they had worked as laborers. It transpired that each of the men had achieved the lowest rating on the intelligence and spatial aptitude tests administered by the company's psychologist. None of them was well developed physically, but despite this all had worked satisfactorily until "blowing shifts" became common. They did not seem to grasp the necessity of adhering to the work roster. In the personnel department there proved to be no bias against employing Lardil men as such, but a strong view that if they are to succeed several changes would be necessary. The welfare officer thought that to maximize ties to the job men should be taken on singly and not as a group; for the same reason it was thought advisable to distribute them to separate work sections and to separate barracks. He agreed that tribal men should not be left to sink or swim in industrial life; that they needed close supervision of their leisure time on an individual basis, and that if possible they should share accommodations with stable Europeans or Aborigines. This is asking a lot of the welfare officer. But it seemed necessary to him if this vanguard of full-blood Aborigines in modern industry is to have any success. If advance in this direction is to be possible, he held that a lot of attention to the individuals' needs had to be paid along social work lines. No company that is responsible to shareholders is going to hire labor that needs social support, when it can get labor that does not. But nothing is more crucial to the work future of the Aborigines.

five

Some
Make
Disturbances

As a method of medical research, epidemiology looks for populations having a high incidence of a disorder, or alternatively a low incidence, and seeks to relate this exceptional incidence to environmental factors. Transcultural and social psychiatry afford good opportunities for the epidemiological method, as in the Stirling County study in Nova Scotia under the directorship of Alexander H. Leighton of the Cornell program in social psychiatry (Leighton and Harding et al., 1963). In that study the field investigators recorded the occurrence of psychiatric disorders ranging from psychoses and mental subnormality to psychoneurotic and psychosomatic syndromes. As case-finding methods they used the interview and the questionnaire. Having established the prevalence of psychiatric symptoms, they analyzed the social background in terms of "social integration" and "social disintegration." "Social disintegration" was a pattern characterized by factors such as poverty, secularization (removal from a religious influence), rapid sociocultural change, inadequacies of leadership, recreation, communication, and control of crime and delinquency. The aim in Stirling County was to determine whether important correlations existed between psychiatric symptoms and residence in integrated and disintegrated communities. In the final analysis of the data, certain specific factors emerged that correlated with mental disorders: advancing age, being a woman, low occupational position, and living in a disintegrated environment. "Stirling County" was a classical, and elaborate, exercise in psychiatric epidemiology that has in some way influenced all subsequent workers in this field.

There is a widespread belief that the incidence of psychiatric disorder in preliterate and primitive societies is different from that in Western society. The important preliminary of any sound analysis is to determine whether the morbidity rates—for example suicide and depression—are valid. In preliterate societies methods of data-gathering are scarcely comparable with those in Western societies. On Mornington Island we obviously had to create our own indicator of mental disturbance, since no previous psychiatric data existed. Having gained our data we were not particularly interested in comparing them with morbidity data gained in another culture. We were primarily interested in providing a range or pattern of information, and in detecting differences in the pattern amongst the subgroups on the island. The three population subgroups would provide the opportunity for relating environmental conditions to observed patterns of psychiatric disorder. For example, if we chose to describe our environmental factors in terms of "social disintegration" as employed by the Stirling County workers, the Kaiadilt community would be deemed the most seriously affected, the Lardil community the least seriously affected, and the mainland community between these two extremes. It might be predicted on this basis that the Kaiadilt community would reveal a higher incidence of psychiatric disorder.

Our first step was an indirect census for psychiatric disturbances of the population above the age of fifteen years. The second step was the clinical examination of persons indicated by the census. Results of these investigations will be tabulated here with illustrative case histories and a running commentary, followed by a discussion. The epidemiological study of the adult inhabitants of Mornington Island was tackled separately but in a similar manner to that of the children (see chapter 9).

The data-gathering instrument or indicator that we prepared for the census was a simple one. Two sets of twenty questions were prepared, one set for use in the adult population (above fifteen years of age), the other for use with children. The twenty questions on the adult instrument were in phrases common to the lay description of disturbed behavior. (See table 3.) The categories were selected on the basis of previous field experience amongst Aborigines. From a list of disorders of conduct, we simply selected the twenty items that our experience suggested were the most prominent in an Aboriginal community. We do not pretend it is complete or exhaustive. The questions were administered to groups of informants chosen for their comprehensive knowledge of people. In order to avert a European or Aboriginal bias as to what constitutes an abnormality in behavior, two groups of informants were employed. The European group comprised the staff of the mission, including the missionary, his wife, the nursing sister, the cattle overseer, the carpenter, and the school teachers. The Aboriginal group comprised men and women from the village who possessed seniority and high status, including several councillors. The sexes were evenly distributed in the two groups of informants.

Each group of informants was instructed that individuals indicated by them would be examined by the visiting doctors, who would probably be able to help some of them by medical treatment. Experience at

Table 3. Mornington Island Morbidity Census of Inhabitants Fifteen Years and Over

SYMPTOMS	INDICATED BY ABORIGINAL INFORMANTS	INDICATED BY EUROPEAN INFORMANTS
1. DULL, backward, slow learner	12	5
2. CONFUSED, forgetful, gets lost	5	2
3. EPILEPTIC, takes fits, has black-outs	5	4
4. OVERACTIVE, restless, interfering, noisy at night	3	2
5. CRIPPLED, paralyzed, many burns, blind, deaf, deformed	6	5
6. BATTERED, many fight cuts, sorry cuts	"Old Bentinck people"	"Old Bentinck people"
7. QUARRELSOME, abusive, destructive	14	7
8. MARKED DOMESTIC UNHAPPINESS	4 couples	6 couples
9. JEALOUS, markedly so of husband or wife	7	2
10. CRIMINAL, frequent clashes with the law	"Most people a bit"	1
11. CRUEL, to men, women, or children	7	none
12. OVERDEPENDENT, poorly occupied, unable to keep a job	9	3
13. SEX PROBLEMS	Reluctant to say	1
14. DEPRESSED, miserable, frequent crying, suicidal	5	4
15. SUSPICIOUS, blaming, twisted outlook	"Nearly everybody"	3
16. FEARFUL, anxious, very worried	"common"	1
17. COMPLAINING, makes a fuss about many aches and pains	1	10
18. MAGIC, claims command and use of	4	5
19. MAGIC, claims caught by **puripuri** or bad magic	3	1
20. WITHDRAWN, solitary, quiet, dumb	3	2
TOTAL	88 [a]	64 [b]

a. 49 males; 39 females.
b. 37 males; 27 females.

previously visited Aboriginal outposts suggest that this was a fair promise. Good cooperation was obtained from each group of informants. Each group debated its responses with care and thoroughness. No doubt the offer of medical treatment helped, but the motivation to cooperate was characteristic of the general atmosphere of this particular community.

The number of adults indicated independently by the Aboriginal and European informants in response to the twenty behavioral items are shown in table 3. The Aborigines indicated eighty-eight individuals compared with sixty-four named by the Europeans, suggesting that the Aborigines employed a somewhat finer filter for behavior disorder. They also employ a qualitatively different filter, though there is a substantial degree of concordance between the two groups in many of the behavioral categories. Some of the major similarities and divergences are as follows.

In items 3 (epileptic), 5 (cripples), 14 (depressed), and 18 (claims magic), there is close agreement between the Aboriginal and European assessors.

In item 17 (complaining, makes a fuss about aches and pains), the Aborigines name only one person while the Europeans name ten. This difference in perception suggests that expressions of physical discomfort do not constitute "making a fuss" to the Aborigines as they do to the pain-suppressing—or better housed—Europeans.

In items 1 (dull), 7 (quarrelsome), 9 (marital jealousy), and 11 (cruel), the Aboriginal perception is strikingly more sensitive than the European. This sensitivity may be associated with the greater familiarity of the Aboriginal assessors with vicissitudes and inconveniences of village life.

Item 10 (criminal) is of special interest. Whereas the European group indicates only one man, who had in fact received prison sentences, the Aboriginal group feels that many of their people would commit petty crimes if they thought they could get away with it. This somewhat surprising consensus seems to the investigators to be realistic, not arising from a sense of unworthiness such as that which an evangelistic Christian education might impart. Nor does it stem from the shame motif sometimes prevalent in Aboriginal psychology. Since several of the informants are councillors, the "criminal" assessment may reflect their frustration at being in the impossible position of having European-style responsibility for law and order, yet not having strong authority to make the villagers comply with regulations.

Item 13 (sex problems) not unexpectedly caused embarrassment. The European informants are aware of some promiscuity, but hesitated to rate it as abnormal. The Aboriginal informants politely declined to discuss sex problems but two spokesmen offered to talk about it privately, afterwards. This opportunity was taken, but it appears that sexual perversion on the island is not so much hidden, as rare. There is a rumor that one young man had expressed homosexual impulses, but this is not confirmed. There are no reported complaints of frigidity or impotence in this community, but the general repression of sex topics calls for further investigation on another occasion.

The response to item 15 (suspicious, blaming) caused us some surprise in that it reveals a recognition by the Aboriginal assessors that a suspicious and blaming outlook is part of the psychological makeup of their people. These Aborigines are aware, to a greater degree than Europeans, of their tendency to assign blame to factors outside themselves.

Item 16 (fears) reveals that Aborigines are much more aware than the Europeans of fears and worries besetting the people. They comment that these customarily take the form of fears of the dark, of ghosts, of solitude, and of being killed. Fears of this kind are so pervasive and common that they can give no estimate of the number of people affected; it is "common." The Europeans were not sensitive to it.

The preponderance of males is less than in the case of the childhood census. This probably reflects the nature of the census rather than the true sex incidence of psychological disturbance. This is because an indirect census directs attention to overt social disturbances and inefficiency rather than to inner discomfort and distress. In Western culture, there is an expectation that males will manifest the former class of psychiatric disorder more than females, and conversely that females will express the latter. This tendency could also have existed in the Aboriginal population, the indirect census instrument being insufficiently sensitive, and not designed, to detect the more introspective types of psychiatric difficulties.

Psychiatric examinations were then carried out on the individuals indicated by the census. This involved interviews with these persons, often with the aid of interpreters, utilizing additional information from other informants where available and physical examinations whenever thought relevant. Using this procedure, many of the individuals indicated by the census were rated by the psychiatrist as not seriously disturbed. The number of people finally determined to be showing the more serious psychiatric disturbances in the opinion of the examiner was 32 out of a risk population of 276 adults. This number is arbitrary, largely influenced by the psychiatrist's own criteria of what constitutes disorders that would normally be of professional concern. The actual number of cases in a population will always depend on such criteria; what is more important is their pattern and their distribution. The distribution of diagnoses among the three population

Table 4. Mornington Island Adult Psychiatric Morbidity Census by Diagnostic Categories

PRIMARY DIAGNOSIS	LARDIL	MAINLAND	KAIADILT	TOTAL
Organic Disorder (with behavior disorder)	1	1		2
Mental Subnormality (mild)	1		1	2
Epilepsy (with behavior disorder)			1	1
Depression			7 [a]	7
Schizophrenia			1	1
Transitory Delusional State	2			2
Personality Disorder	6	4	1	11
Neurosis	4			4
Psychosomatic Disorder	1	1		2
Total	15	6	11	32
Risk Population	142	76	60	276

NOTE: No cases of mania or senile dementia were identified.

a. Significant at the 0.01 level by chi-squared technique using the Yates (1934) correction factor for small numbers.

subgroups—Lardil, mainlanders, and Kaiadilt—is shown in table 4. The diagnostic labels employed in this table are those in regular clinical use in psychiatry. Of these categories, three patterns are of special interest for the Mornington Island epidemiology and are selected here for more detailed comment. These patterns are personality disorders, transitory delusional states, and depressive states.

PERSONALITY DISORDERS

Our previous psychiatric studies among Aborigines had shown that personality disorders are prominent. Among the associated social factors noted are the breakdown of the family as a nurturing system and the economic disadvantages of marginal life leading to enforced dependency upon the state. Some of these factors have been specified in the concept of "marginal personality" by Kerckhoff and McCormick

(1955) after Stonequist (1937); others are by Brody (1966) in his concept of "cultural exclusion." (See chapter 7.) The intrapsychic disturbance noted by us could be categorized in developmental terms as a fixation in oral-dependent activities leading to failure in social maturation. In clinical terms, many of these personality disorders are classified as passive-dependent or inadequate, punctuated by episodic reactions to accumulated frustration expressed by passive-aggressive and overt aggressive means. Dependence upon alcohol where it is available becomes a serious complication in such persons; on Mornington Island alcohol is not yet available, so that aggressive and passive-aggressive personality disorders appear in their unmodified forms.

Sociocultural explanations of personality disorders are not by themselves completely satisfying. While sociocultural factors implicit in such concepts as "marginal man" and "cultural exclusion" play a role in regulating the frequency of these personality disorders, the fact that these disorders are not universal under such circumstances testifies to the importance of individual factors. Factors coming under the general heading of ego-strength serve to regulate individual susceptibility. The following vignettes of personality disorder provide a description of the overt behavior patterns of the sort elicited by the use of our own instrument, but reveal little of the psychodynamic issues involved. A thematic interpretation would require more intimate study.

PERSONALITY PATTERN 1. K. L., LARDIL
This strongly built young man is feared by the community and generally considered mad because of his "wild man" behavior. After drinking methylated spirits he becomes enraged, dances about beating his chest like an ape, and tries to provoke fights. As well as intimidating people he is openly promiscuous sexually—unusual amongst Lardil. Recently he accused an elderly man of sorcery and threatened him with a rifle. The council insisted that something be done in the interests of public safety. Accordingly, he was removed to another settlement on Cape York. This is likely to offer only brief respite, because previously he was removed to yet another settlement for terrorizing his family, particularly his father, a somewhat interfering native practitioner. We were not able to explore the individual developmental difficulties and current frustration underlying his truculence.

PERSONALITY PATTERN 2. Y. W., LARDIL
This physically and socially aggressive young woman with a village notoriety as a trouble-maker is very obese. Her marriage is unsuccessful; her husband, a self-styled native doctor, works on the mainland. She is regularly the center of fights. In one tantrum that we observed, outside the hospital during our visit, she laid about with sticks and

stones and even hurled her weekly meat ration at the missionary. She could not be calmed for several hours. This fight apparently began as a quarrel between children in which the mothers and eventually other relatives joined, reviving old feuds. In other episodes, she has been known to strike out dangerously with a knife that happened to be near at hand. Tantrums are not rare in preschool Aboriginal children and are extreme in form, but they are rare in older age groups. During her hostile episodes she is described as unapproachable and strange. There is no history of epilepsy.

PERSONALITY PATTERN 3. F. L., MAINLANDER

This young man, the eldest son of a leading stockman, exemplifies passive modes of aggression. He has not copied his father's regular habits and reliable character. Although intelligent he appears unmotivated and regularly walks off jobs. He has had opportunities provided for him at many different places but if an argument arises he responds by walking off, and so falls into debt for the air fares that brought him there. He declined one job on the mainland because, he said, his swag (pack) had been lost by the airline company. He accepted another without any intention of taking it up, presumably to frustrate his father and the missionary. The latter had made inquiries in Brisbane in the hope of arranging special trade training but F. L. did not meet the educational requirements. An attempt by the school teacher to supplement his education started well, but the lessons ground to a halt after a few weeks due to his disinterest. The only time that F. L. has shown overt aggression was when "shamed" by the missionary in the presence of his brother and father. He abused the missionary and told him "stick your job up your arse" and found himself in a fight with his brother and father.

TRANSITORY DELUSIONAL STATES

Transitory delusional states are considered by some observers as a variant of schizophrenia but we decided to regard them as a separate group of disorders. They appear especially common in indigenous peoples undergoing Western influences. They are similar to the *bouffée délirante* described by Collomb (1965) as an important feature of African psychiatry, and to the oneiriform psychoses described by Munoz and his coworkers (1966) as forming a substantial part of the functional psychoses of Chilean Mapuches. In the *bouffée délirante* the patient returns to his normal state after the illness, which is said to come on suddenly without preliminary symptoms. A characteristic feature in Collomb's series is the self-identification by the patient with statuses and roles that are higher than his own, and the expression of themes of persecution and megalomania. Ego functions are disorganized, so that there is altered perception of time and space. In the oneiriform psychoses of the Chilean aborigines there were relationships to sex (being a woman), to a low educational level, and to recent migration. At the time of our visit two individuals on Mornington Island had recently undergone episodes showing these general features. Both were women, and both showed derepression of sexual feeling for the missionary during the episodes.

TRANSITORY DELUSIONAL STATE 1. H. N., LARDIL

On her first trip from the island to work at a mainland cattle station this young woman became disturbed shortly after arrival. She told us that she had a nightmare—a big black thing with rolling eyes appeared by her bed and she thought she was dying. She tried to get help by screaming out to her roommate and to the other Aborigines on the station. She had the idea that a white stockman was in love with her and she talked and sang about it incessantly through the night. The station manager took her by car to the doctor in the nearest town but since the doctor's sedatives had no effect she was removed to a larger town where she was given electric convulsive therapy. Sent home to Mornington Island, she showed nothing bizarre or delusional. From her story it seems possible that a white stockman did in fact make sexual approaches to her. With her peers she is vivacious, interested in dancing, and occupied as a hospital aide. But occasionally her behavior emits an echo of her illness: for example, on being permitted to rest in the mission house, she startled the missionary by taking a bath and putting on his wife's clothes. He was unsure how to interpret this, though he made a fair guess.

TRANSITORY DELUSIONAL STATE 2. C. J., LARDIL

This middle-aged woman of high intelligence learned good English from the previous missionary. She was widowed when six Mornington men including her husband were drowned when a boat was wrecked on the way to Burketown at the southern extremity of the Gulf. She then had a series of affairs in which she tried to find a husband, without success. Eventually she became violently disturbed, rushed around naked, savage and animallike. She bit the nursing sister. Shortly afterwards she told the missionary that people were talking about him and herself having a love affair. She herself believed that there was a romance. The village people were upset by the scandal of these ideas. Because of her violence she was removed in a restraining jacket to a mainland hospital. She returned some time later, evidently her normal self, having in the meantime found a husband on the mainland. She now appears reasonably well adjusted. But her son is neglected and is emotionally disturbed; he habitually steals food from the mission, presumably because he is not fed properly at home.

DEPRESSIVE STATES

The census brought to light a number of psychiatric disorders which were classified as depressive. The occurrence of depressive states and of suicide is of considerable interest in view of the conflicting accounts of their frequency in preliterate-primitive tribal societies.[1] The remarkable feature of the cases on Mornington Island is that they occur exclusively in the Kaiadilt subgroup. Of the 60 Kaiadilt adults living on Mornington Island, 7 are classified as having depressive states either at the present time or in the recent past. By contrast, no severe depressive states are diagnosed in the remaining 218 adult Aborigines on Mornington Island, whether of island or mainland extraction. This finding is significant at the 0.01 level of probability. Suicides and attempted suicides are too few in the eighteen-year period of Kaiadilt observation to lend themselves to statistical treatment. There has been one clear "active" suicide, one passive "voodoo"-type death, and several attempted suicides—all occurring within the Kaiadilt subpopulation. Several important questions arise, including the question of definition. Do these Kaiadilt disorders correspond with what Western psychiatrists call depressive states? Discussion of these questions will be reserved until the clinical features of the condition are presented in vignette form.

DEPRESSIVE PATTERN 1. C. Q., KAIADILT

This middle-aged woman was regarded as one of a considerable number of Bentinck Islanders showing mental disturbance after their exodus from their homeland in 1948. She was solitary, unpredictable, and in the habit of "going bush" by herself, whereupon the village would erupt and send out a search party. When her son was drowned off Denham Island in 1958, her agitation mounted. She tried to drown herself in Appel Channel "to meet my son" and had to be restrained. Eventually, several years later, she succeeded in drowning herself.

DEPRESSIVE PATTERN 2. L. T., KAIADILT

This dignified elderly man whose totemic name is Shark figured in a sensational incident locally well known at the time. The launch "Bonny" on a trip in 1940 from Mornington Island to Burketown put in at Allen Island, a fishing outpost of Bentinck Island, where some Kaiadilt including Shark and Rainbow (another totemic name) were

---

1. See Hoskin et al. (1969).

temporarily established with their families. An Aboriginal member of the launch party was speared by the Kaiadilt men and died of his wounds. Police returned to the site and took this Kaiadilt community from Allen Island to Burketown Gaol, where it is alleged that Shark and his companion eviscerated their testicles and passed them out through the bars of the cell. Shark and Rainbow were sent to Aurukun mission where Rainbow died. Shark survived, married there, and returned to Mornington Island in 1952 to rejoin his Kaiadilt community. On examination now, the left testis only is present, a scrotal scar indicating removal of the right. Shark related through an interpreter that he and Rainbow removed their testicles with their finger nails. His story does not make it clear whether they did this in an agreement to kill themselves, or to express sorrow at being removed from their families—Shark himself mentioned both aspects. His behavior has been normal if apathetic since, though he is inactive and seriously unwell with chronic bronchitis. Few histories make the clinician feel the cultural gulf more keenly than Shark's.

DEPRESSIVE PATTERN 3. O. B., KAIADILT

This Kaiadilt man died last year after a chain of events in which the initial occurrence is believed locally to be breach of taboo. He and a companion (Depressive Pattern 4, M. Q.) returned to a taboo site, Wamakurt on Bentinck Island, four years ago, after an absence of ten years. Strong persuasion was applied by a visiting ethnographer to overcome their reluctance to approach Wamakurt. Next day both men complained of pain in the belly and blocked bowels, the traditional penalty for territorial transgression.[2] On return to Mornington Island, O. B. became seriously sick and was evacuated by air to Cloncurry Hospital where surgery revealed a Richter's hernia of the small bowel. He made a slow recovery but two years later again became ill and a surgical operation was required to excise a gangrenous portion of bowel. The surgeon reported that this second operation was successful but that O. B. lacked the will to live. The missionary reported that in the brief remaining period of his life, O. B. was convinced that having committed the sacrilege at Wamakurt he was destined to die.

DEPRESSIVE PATTERN 4. M. Q., KAIADILT

This middle-aged man came from Bentinck to Mornington Island in 1948 with a reputation for status and prowess, but on Mornington he has always been withdrawn and inactive. He commands little support

2. See "*Malgri*: Culture-Specific Disorder," described in *Medicine is the Law* (forthcoming).

from the other Kaiadilt men, a group of whom attacked him the previous year in the course of an argument over children. He was unharmed, but remained a week in hospital, frightened to go home. Six months previously he made five apparently serious gestures at drowning himself in the Appel Channel. Recently he chopped himself about the nose with his tomahawk and the wounds required extensive suturing. He has been subject to traditional ministrations recently, including a penile subincision carried out with incantations by a Lardil practitioner. At present he spends most of his time sitting outside his camp with a woebegone appearance complaining of weak legs, back pain, and blocked bowels. At other times he may be seen atop the plateau overlooking the channel, raving in vernacular that men are going to spear him and take away his wife. On one such occasion a team member approached him on the hill in the company of a Kaiadilt man as interpreter. He told the team member that when he uses a toilet people say that he pollutes it and that if they use it after him they will get sick. He says he is being given *puripuri* by fish bones and feces—that his discarded fish bones are being subjected to this sorcery. He says that he cannot complain to the policemen because they think he is just sick in the head. All he needs, he says, is people to yarn with who do not make fun of him. He wants to be with white people because they understand him better. He frequently attends the hospital on the arms of his two wives. He says he wants to take his life because "long time worry . . . long time head bad . . . maybe blood in the belly, open it up, maybe. . . ." He is preoccupied and frustrated over his relations with his two Kaiadilt wives. He suggests he is ill because he had relations with one during her menstruation. Some of the people express fear that he might kill his children. Since he had to be regarded as a suicidal risk, the team psychiatrist who related to him gave him amitriplytine (anti-depressant) medication and considered arranging a period in a mainland hospital in order to remove him from these difficulties and permit rehabilitation and perhaps trade training. We learned later that the good initial response to the tablets was not sustained after our departure and he had to be sent to the hospital. It was not an ideal solution, but necessary because of the risk associated with his illness. It was what he said he wanted.

The outcome of his illness is described in our epilogue.

DEPRESSIVE PATTERN 5. M. O., KAIADILT
This twenty-four-year-old woman was sent home from her job on a mainland cattle station recently with a note from the manager saying that she was very depressed and had not eaten for nearly a week, since the visit of her sister. On her arrival home she became worse,

neither eating nor talking. The nursing sister at Mornington Island took her into her own house where she spoon-fed her. She sat and stared into space for about five days, not showing any interest. Given tranquilizing medication (chlorpromazine) she changed, burst into tears, and sobbed for days and then recovered. After another month she seemed well and returned to work. She never revealed what she had been troubled about. It was conjectured that she had become ill after hearing about her uncle's self-inflicted injury (see Depressive Pattern 4). Her illness is of interest in that it represents a depressive illness occurring in a Bentinck-Island-born person who emigrated in childhood with the rest of her people.

In chapter 10 a comparative study of the Kaiadilt psychiatric pattern will be made, since unquestionably this subpopulation represents "the sickest society" in the psychiatric sense. It is the little Kaiadilt nation that exemplifies the extremes of rapid exposure to Western influence, ecological hazards, social disintegration, and mental disorder. From a closer examination of Kaiadilt ecology and history we may then determine the relationships that these factors bear one another. In this chapter we are not yet concerned with why the Kaiadilt have the highest incidence of disorders, but with the clinical description of their patterns and in particular with the illnesses in which depression is a feature.

We admittedly called the conditions, of which vignettes have been given, "depressive" for the convenience of our register. We considered that we might equally accurately have designated them "disorders due to gross stress," had that category been a more commonly recognized one in the standard nomenclature of disease. It is true that there are many depressive features. The illnesses were expressed with a depressive affect, in some cases accompanied by self-inflicted injury so severe as to constitute a threat to life. Some were associated with bereavement in which the individuals were heard to express the wish to join the departed one in that other place. These mourners went far beyond the conventional self-mutilation regarded as normal in bereavement by other groups of Aborigines. In a few instances, breach of taboo and family shame were precipitating factors, rather than mourning.

Although depression was a common symptom, one feature that we were inclined to emphasize above others in our discussion of the Kaiadilt was the role of human ecological factors in setting in motion a pathogenic behavioral sequence. We shall consider this more closely in chapter 10. It is a concept about mental disorder that we had not knowingly brought with us when we came, but which we were forced to consider. In this emphasis, there is something of a shift away from the primacy usually accorded intrapsychic events ("adjustment"), or from transactional events ("social adaptation") in human behavior. As we saw, for the Kaiadilt (foreshadowing our discussion in chapter 10), ecological disturbance came first, transactional disturbances followed, and intrapsychic disturbance completed a psychopathological sequence which then reverberated.

But this is to anticipate. When mental health surveys are carried out it is expected that problems will arise with respect to classifying the pathological conditions and interpreting the results. In the transcultural setting additional problems arise concerning the acceptability of the technique used, or even perhaps the acceptability of any survey whatever. Surya and his team, engaged on a survey of psychological disability in Pondicherry (1964), found that over half of the informants interviewed could not or would not admit to knowing anyone falling within the extremely wide scope of the inquiry. No children were mentioned by these informants and no cases of depression. The main reason for the low yield of positive information in Pondicherry was the reluctance of informants to be thought of as informers—hence a tendency to vagueness, use of unidentifiable nicknames and deliberate misinformation. In contrast with the Pondicherry workers, we were the recipients of a good level of confidence on Mornington Island, possibly enhanced by real practical assistance that we were able to supply in the occasional case, but backed by the confidence that the missionary himself seemed to elicit. If there is a serious criticism of the census as a technique, it is not that it failed to elicit cooperation, but that the subjects ascertained tended to comprise those who disrupt social harmony rather than those who suffer from private discomfort. If it were our only indicator, our "twenty questions" census form could bias epidemiology in this direction—just as an individual questionnaire form (for example, the Cornell Medical Index [C.M.I.], a modification of which we employed) could bias it in the other. We now proceeded to the health questionnaire.

six

Others Feel Sick

The Aborigines ascertained to have mental disturbances by the census method (discussed in chapter 5) tended to be those who were socially troublesome rather than those who suffered from private discomfort. The indirect census method is not designed to detect the more introspective types of mental disorder. Yet a distinction between outer and inner expression of mental disturbance is recognized by layman and clinician alike. It is expressed in such clinical dimensions as overt versus hidden, psychopathic versus neurotic, extrapunitive versus intropunitive, alloplastic versus autoplastic. In order to arrive at a rounded view of psychological maladjustment we need an estimate of private discomfort as well as of the more conspicuous disruptions of social harmony.

Information regarding Aborigines' medical complaints is hard to obtain because clinical interviews are hedged by poor communication arising from distances in culture, language, and social class. After years of unsatisfactory transactions, the Aborigine has become inhibited in transcultural settings. The Western doctor has no expectation that he will get an orderly history and full disclosure; unless the symptoms are accompanied by clinical signs he is likely to underdiagnose. Underdiagnosis is a general problem of transcultural medicine. In an American hospital, for example, the de Hoyoses (1965) noted that admission statements of Negro patients averaged two-thirds the length of those of white patients. It was hypothesized that because of social distance there is less doctor-patient interaction; the doctor is less attentive and elicits fewer responses. The Negro patient, being relatively distant from the white resident doctor, has fewer symptoms recorded than the white patient.

Stereotypes rush in where social distance provides a vacuum. There is a popular impression among Australians of European origin that

This chapter originally appeared in slightly different form as "Personal Discomfort in Australian Aborigines," *The Australian & New Zealand Journal of Psychiatry* (1968) 2:69.

Aborigines are "quite happy" and free of psychiatric symptoms. In fact little is known of the distribution of symptoms in Australian Aborigines. In cities and in the fringe settlements of towns they make small use of health services. In missions and other tribally oriented assemblages, Aborigines regularly visit the sick bay for medicine from the nurse in charge, but little detail is volunteered or recorded. It is this class of information that particularly concerned us. To make an estimate of the Mornington Island Aborigines' symptom patterns, and to assess their sense of physical and mental well-being, a questionnaire was used.

We modified the Cornell Medical Index (C.M.I.) Health Questionnaire to suit the Aboriginal situation. The original C.M.I. was designed by Brodman and his colleagues at the New York hospital (Brodman et al., 1949). The respondent is asked to answer "yes" or "no" to 195 simply worded questions on health. A "yes" response is taken to indicate that the particular symptom or complaint is present. The questions fall into eighteen sections numbered alphabetically from A to R, seeking information on the body systems, emotions, and mental states.

Modified versions of the Cornell Medical Index have been employed in previous transcultural studies, for example by Chance (1962) with North Alaskan Eskimos. In such settings it provides a useful inventory of symptoms, rather than a measure of hypothetical personality traits such as introversion or neuroticism. It must be borne in mind that it permits only a partially valid comparison of symptom frequencies across cultural boundaries, for example in comparisons of the mental health of Negro, Puerto Rican, and white populations. This is because the respondent's score is influenced by his culturally regulated "response set." For example, a moderate level of discomfort may be reported positively as a symptom in one culture but not in another. We therefore had no intention of using the questionnaire to compare the medical complaints of Aborigines directly with those of Western populations.

In his Eskimo study, Chance was obliged to omit thirty-eight of the Cornell Medical Index questions. In our study, each section was further reduced. Some questions were omitted as inappropriate to the community. For example, "Do you take two or more alcoholic drinks a day?" does not apply on a "temperance" mission. "Has a doctor ever told you your blood pressure was too high or low?" does not apply where medical transactions are unlikely to be of this nature. The parent questionnaire was mainly abbreviated to facilitate its administration. Most of our subjects were preliterate and their concentration and motivation with a long questionnaire were doubtful. As only one-third of the questions were retained it cannot be claimed that

70

the original C.M.I. was used, merely that it was a source of material, design, and phraseology. This seems of little import when it is appreciated that the original has not been standardized on any population remotely resembling Mornington Island's, and that we did not intend to use it for purposes of cross-cultural comparison. The sixty-five questions finally used were set out in this form.

MODIFIED C.M.I. PSYCHIATRIC FIELD UNIT SURVEY

A. Eyes and Ears

1. Has your eyesight often blacked out completely?
2. Do you often have bad pains in your eyes?
3. Are you hard of hearing?

B. Respiratory

4. Do you have to clear your throat frequently?
5. Do you often catch severe colds?
6. Are you troubled by constant coughing?

C. Cardiovascular

7. Do you have pains in the heart or chest?
8. Are you often bothered by thumping of the heart?
9. Do you often have difficulty in breathing?

D. Gastrointestinal

10. Is your appetite always poor?
11. Do you usually belch a lot after eating?
12. Are you often sick in your stomach?
13. Do you constantly suffer from bad constipation?

E. Musculoskeletal

14. Do your muscles and joints constantly feel stiff?
15. Do pains in the back make it hard for you to keep up with your work?

F. Cutaneous

16. Is your skin very sensitive or tender?
17. Do cuts in your skin usually stay open a long time?
18. Are you often troubled with boils?

G. Neurological

19. Do you suffer badly from frequent severe headaches?
20. Do you often have spells of severe dizziness?
21. Was any part of your body ever paralyzed?
22. Were you ever knocked unconscious?
23. Do you ever have a fit or convulsion (epilepsy)?
24. Are you troubled by stuttering or stammering?

71

25. Are you a sleep walker?
26. Were you a bed wetter between the ages of 8 and 14?

H. Genitourinary

27. *Men Only.* Are your privates often painful or sore?
    Women Only. Have you often felt weak and sick with your periods?
28. *Men Only.* Do you have trouble starting your stream?
    Women Only. Have you usually been tense or jumpy with your periods?
29. During the day, do you usually have to urinate frequently?
30. Do you sometimes lose control of your bladder?

I. Low Energy and Fatigue

31. Does working tire you out completely?
32. Do you usually get up tired and exhausted in the morning?

J. General Ill-Health

33. Are you frequently ill?
34. Do you come from a sickly family?
35. Do you wear yourself out worrying about your health?
36. Are you constantly made miserable by poor health?

K. Operations and Accidents

37. Did you ever have a serious operation?
38. Do you often have small accidents or injuries?

L. Habits, Including Sleep

39. Do you usually have great difficulty in falling asleep or staying asleep?
40. Do you find it impossible to take a regular rest period each day?
41. Do you drink more than six cups of coffee or tea a day?

M. Inadequacy

42. Does your work fall to pieces when the boss is watching you?
43. Does your thinking get mixed up when you have to do things quickly?
44. Do strange people or places make you afraid?
45. Are you scared to be alone when there are no friends near you?
46. Do you wish you always had someone at your side to advise you?

N. Depression

47. Do you usually feel unhappy and depressed?
48. Do you often cry?
49. Do you often wish you were dead and away from it all?

O. Anxiety

50. Does worrying continually get you down?
51. Are you considered a nervous person?
52. Does nervousness run in your family?
53. Did you ever have a nervous breakdown?

P. Sensitivity

54. Are you extremely shy or sensitive?
55. Are your feelings easily hurt?
56. Are you considered a touchy person?

Q. Anger and Irritability

57. Are you easily upset or irritated?
58. Do you go to pieces if you don't constantly control yourself?
59. Does it make you angry to have anyone tell you what to do?
60. Do people often annoy and irritate you?

R. Tension

61. Do you often shake or tremble?
62. Do you become scared at sudden movements or noises at night?
63. Are you often awakened out of your sleep by frightening dreams?
64. Do you often become suddenly scared for no good reason?
65. Do you often break out in a cold sweat?

Administration even of this shorter questionnaire proved a laborious procedure. With the younger Aborigines it was presented in English in a supervised group setting in the church building. The object of the procedure was explained in basic English as an inquiry into health. With the older people the questionnaire was presented individually, using an interpreter speaking Lardil or Kaiadilt ad lib as required. Despite the movements of the people in and out of the village and the island, it was possible in the course of trips around the island to obtain responses from 294 individuals, representing 91 percent of the total population aged fifteen years and over. This response was achieved with some difficulty, even by means of rowing to neighboring islands to locate people away fishing or camping, often in stifling humidity.

The results are presented in table 5 as average scores to show the distribution of medical complaints among the subgroups within the island society: men and women; the various age groups; the various ethnic groups. Because the data to be tabulated were extensive—sixty-five health responses for each of 294 individuals, in addition to sex, age, and ethnic subgroup items, and measures of acculturation—a computer was used.

PATTERNS OF HEALTH QUESTIONNAIRE RESPONSE

In the accompanying figures the data are set out such that the sections of the modified C.M.I. lie along the abscissa of a graph, with average percentage yes response along the ordinate. It is stressed that it is the differences between groups that are of prime interest rather than the absolute figures.

Table 5. Age, Sex, Ethnicity and C.M.I. Scores

CATEGORY	NO. OF SUBJECTS	ALL 65 QUESTIONS (AVERAGE SCORE)	41 "BODY" QUESTIONS (AVERAGE SCORE)	24 "PSYCHE" QUESTIONS (AVERAGE SCORE)
Male and Female by Age				
15–34	152	16.9	9.1	7.7
35–54	99	20.5	12.1	8.3
Over 54	43	21.3	13.0	8.3
Males	146	15.5	9.4	6.0
Kaiadilt	20	18.3	10.9	7.4
Lardil	84	13.6	8.1	5.5
Mainland	38	18.5	12.1	6.3
Part-Aborigine	4	12.2	5.7	6.5
Females	148	22.1	12.1	9.9
Kaiadilt	31	27.2	14.2	13.0
Lardil	83	20.9	11.7	9.2
Mainland	26	20.9	12.1	8.7
Part-Aborigine	8	18.1	8.0	10.1

In figures 2, 3, and 4, the outstanding feature is the existence of five peaks of complaining, in which approximately half of the entire population report positive symptoms. These peaks are in sections B (respiratory complaints), E (musculoskeletal complaints), I (low energy and fatigue complaints), M (complaints related to inadequacy), and Q (complaints related to anger and irritability). The high incidence of complaints related to the respiratory system, to the musculoskeletal system, and to low energy and fatiguability support the clinical observations. These complaints are likely to have a basis in the harsh ecology of village life previously described, such as repeated exposure to cold and wet and hookworm infestation. (See also Lambo, 1965; Tatz, 1966; Dubos, 1966.) Both sexes are affected by complaints in these areas of physical functioning. It is in sections C (cardiovascular), D (gastrointestinal), J (general ill-health), and L (habits, including sleep) that the female excess is most apparent.

SEX AS A VARIABLE

The sex difference is outstanding. (See figure 2.) Scores for women are consistently higher than those for men, with the single exception of F (skin complaints). Whereas the difference is clear and regular in the predominantly physical complaint areas (sections A to L; questions

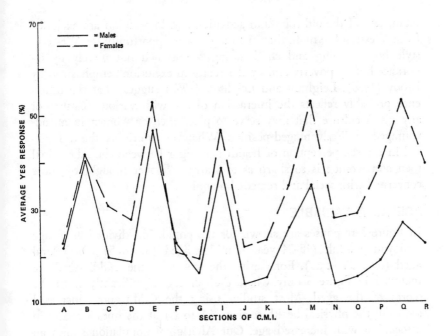

Figure 2. Sex as a Variable in Modified C.M.I. Responses

1 to 41), it is still more marked in the emotional complaint areas (sections M to R; questions 42 to 65). Section H (genitourinary) is omitted from the figures because the questions asked were different for the two sexes.

The excess of affirmatives for females is most noticeable in questions 45 (section M) "Are you scared to be alone when there are no friends near you?" (64 percent versus 31 percent), and 62 (section R) "Do you become scared at sudden movements or noises in the night?" (64 percent versus 25 percent). This fearfulness of Aboriginal women may reflect their exclusion from mastery and self-sufficiency in Aboriginal culture. Most studies using the C.M.I. health questionnaire report higher scores for women than men. Chance (1962) conjectures that the emphasis his Barter Island Eskimo men place on self-reliance may cause them to minimize their physical complaints, but that a more likely explanation is to be found in the differential stress placed on men and women by the rapid introduction of Western technology, with the corresponding loss of Eskimo procedures for gaining status and recognition. This problem was more acute for women than for men, who had more contact with the white man's world and more opportunities for recognition and prestige from working in it. Similar considerations apply to Aboriginal society on Mornington Island, where the women retain few of the old roles and activities, and in addition are excluded from Western life more than the men. Their opportunity for Western-style housekeeping and child-rearing is curtailed not merely by ignorance but by poverty and by the "cultural exclusion" emphasized by Brody (1966). Leighton and Leighton (1967) suggest that the difference probably reflects the interaction of sex with various features of any given culture that may serve to place men or women in an advantaged or disadvantaged position. Whatever its origins, the differential in the self-perception of health and vigor between the Aboriginal men and women is so sharp as to warrant further thought by those concerned with social and remedial planning.

AGE AS A VARIABLE

In figure 3 responses are shown for the population divided as to age into young adult (15–34 years), middle-aged (35 to 54 years), and aged (over 54 years). For clarity, the scores for the middle-aged are included in figure 3 only where they diverge significantly from the scores of the aged. Most studies using the C.M.I. note increased scores in the physical health sections (A to L) of the questionnaire in association with increased age. Our Aboriginal population shows an excess of physical complaints in the aged group. The excess also involves the middle-aged group, though to a lesser extent. The exceptions

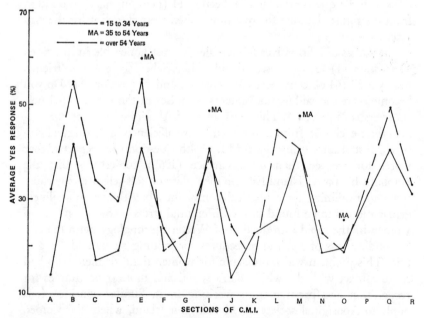

Figure 3. Age as a Variable in Modified C.M.I. Responses

76

are sections F and K which concern accident-proneness and skin trauma respectively, which not unexpectedly have higher scores in the young adult group. The middle-aged group scores highest in section I, concerned with low energy and fatiguability, a result that accords with our clinical impression that many of the middle-aged men are the tired people of the population.

In most studies using the C.M.I., increased scores on the moods and feelings sections have not generally been associated with greater age. In our subjects the differences are not as apparent in these sections as they are in the physical sections. The young adult group reports fewer complaints. A high score in M (inadequacy) and O (anxiety) characterize the middle-aged subjects whereas Q (anger) has an excess in the aged group. The aged more easily get upset or irritated; the middle-aged are more aware of depression; the young adults score highest on only a very few items, the one major difference being that they resent orders (question 59).

ETHNICITY AS A VARIABLE

In figure 4 the four population subgroups are contrasted, the Kaiadilt and Lardil in full, and the mainland Aborigine and part-Aborigine where the disparities are noteworthy. While it is clear that the Kaiadilt —the most poorly integrated of the subgroups—has the highest scores,

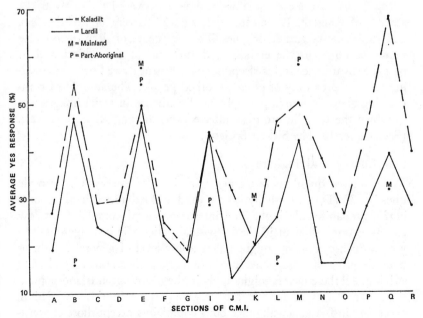

Figure 4. Ethnicity as a Variable in Modified C.M.I. Responses

an analysis of some of the more important complaints and symptom-clusters proves to be rewarding.

Physical Complaints

All subgroups scored heavily for respiratory complaints (frequent throat clearing, severe colds, constant coughing) except the part-Aborigines, who were very much less bothered by these symptoms. It would be interesting to determine why the part-Aborigines have a much greater sense of physical well-being as reflected by these scores. Obvious features of the part-Aborigines' life in this population are that they are better housed, more comfortable in their physical environment, better employed, and have more money to spend. It is possible that they are less likely to make positive responses to the questions when only a mild degree of discomfort is present. There is only one area of physical complaint in which they report symptoms at a level corresponding to the full-blood Aborigines: the musculoskeletal section (muscles and joints constantly stiff; pains in the back making it hard to work).

Insomnia

Difficulty in falling asleep, interrupted sleep, and early morning waking are symptoms commonly found in emotional disorders. Question 39 (Do you usually have great difficulty in falling asleep or staying asleep?) covers these complaints and was answered positively by 27 percent of Kaiadilt, 19 percent of Lardil, 23 percent of mainlanders, and 16 percent of part-Aborigines. The prevalence of sleep disturbance may reflect in part the emotional disturbance of the subject and in part the disturbance in his sleeping environment caused by overcrowding and the proximity of other disturbed people. The amount of complaining about insomnia parallels the disturbance in social integration, in which the Kaiadilt are most affected and the part-Aborigines least. (See chapter 10, The Sickest Society.)

Low Energy and Fatigue

Scores on the questions concerned with level of energy, for example question 32 (Do you usually get up tired and exhausted in the morning?), are uniformly high. The interpretation of complaints of low energy is often difficult in the individual patient; it is dangerous in a group. Such complaints might reflect a low level of general health, or poor sleep, or the neurasthenic concomitant of boredom and blocked striving. All these factors might apply in the Mornington Island population. Complaints of fatigue are very important in this population, exceeding in frequency all other body complaints except those concerning respiratory and musculoskeletal functions. We could not ascertain the direct relationships between lassitude and, say, anaemia, because each individual who answered the C.M.I. was not investigated from the physical point of view. We carried out physical examinations only when it seemed clinically indicated to us.

Inadequacy

Section M in the questionnaire used here contains five questions broadly related to the area that may be characterized as social and personal inadequacy. A high percentage of the population answered yes. When the responses to individual questions by the population subgroups are examined, it is noted that the two otherwise contrasting subgroups—the Kaiadilt and the part-Aborigines—are most aware of feelings of inadequacy. They give the highest affirmative responses to questions 44: Do strange people or places make you afraid?; 45: Are you scared to be alone when there are no friends near you?; and 46: Do you wish you always had someone at your side to advise you? The high score of part-Aborigines to questions 44 and 45 is also consistent with their excessive interest in sorcery compared with the full-blood Aborigines, a feature previously noted. This fearfulness of the part-Aborigines is confirmed by their remarkable 75 percent positive response to question 62: Do you become scared at sudden movements or noises at night?

Depression

The three questions in section N are clearly concerned with symptoms of depression. Question 47 asks: Do you usually feel unhappy and depressed?; 48: Do you often cry?; 49: Do you often wish you were dead and away from it all? Affirmative answers to these questions are commonest in the Kaiadilt. Affirmative answers to the question on crying are very rare in all subgroups save the Kaiadilt. Except in the Kaiadilt, depressive responses were uncommon, a finding in accord with our census and clinical psychiatric examinations previously and independently made (see chapter 5). The possible factors underlying this interesting finding are discussed in chapter 10 in terms of the Kaiadilt's difficulties in the area of human ecology, their history of recent disaster, forced migration, and poor social integration or "anomie." The questionnaire's validity is enhanced by its detection of this high depressive load in the Kaiadilt.

The Other Emotions

The responses to the questions concerned with anxiety, 50 to 53, are comparatively low in all population subgroups. Most of these questions are framed in terms of the lay concept of "worrying" or "nervousness." The responses to questions concerned with sensitivity to criticism and with shyness, questions 54 to 56, are more uniformly affirmative, with the Kaiadilt showing high scores. It is however in the area designated anger and irritability (section Q, questions 57 to 60) that the Kaiadilt show an exceptionally high peak of affirmative responses, though the other subgroups also show high scores. The Kaiadilt appear to be preoccupied with feelings of anger and irritability, and the necessity for their control. It is not unexpected that one finds complaints of irritability and peevishness in the Kaiadilt in association with depression; irritability is evidently not a successful defense against the perception of depression in their case. The gross stress of a noxious environment is probably the common progenitor.

CONCLUSIONS

The information which the scoring of these complaints offers is interesting, though some caution is needed in its interpretation. We have ventured to use it as a basis for comparison between the four Aboriginal subgroups living on Mornington Island. A possible contaminant that may bias these comparisons is the excess of females in the Kaiadilt and the part-Aboriginal populations, contrasted with the excess of males in the mainland group. (An approximate correction may be applied using the details in table 5.) We have been careful not to use the scores as a basis for comparison of symptom levels in Mornington Island Aborigines with those of C.M.I.-standardized populations elsewhere, because of possible differences in the "response set."

Nevertheless some inferences may be made. The first is that these tribally oriented Aborigines perceive personal discomfort and distress at a much higher level than is apparent to the outside observer. This is probably because complaints about health do not find a place in transactions between Aborigines and Westerners, unless the context is a medical one. Even in the medical context, communication is unsatisfactory, and underestimation of Aborigines' discomfort must commonly occur. In addition, many Westerners appear to employ a defense which leads them to perceive the Aborigines they know as happy and contented and to disregard evidence to the contrary.

The information provided by the questionnaire is limited in scope; it has been pointed out that it tends to elicit the more neurotic or personal complaints in contrast to the psychopathic or socially deviant symptoms elicited by the method of indirect census (see chapter 5). The two methods provide complementary information. Further, the questionnaire samples the whole population—or the 91 percent of it that could be located—while the census concentrated on disturbed individuals identified by Aboriginal and European informants. Despite these differences, the data from the two methods are consonant in certain aspects. Each reveals the Kaiadilt subgroup to be the one most troubled. Each shows that depressive symptomatology is a distinctive feature of the Kaiadilt. The questionnaire responses clearly indicate the peaks of physical discomfort that had been ascertained by clinical methods—in the areas of respiratory and musculoskeletal function and in energy level.

TWENTY QUESTIONS TO DETECT PERSONAL DISCOMFORT

Where communication is difficult, as with tradition-oriented or transitional Aborigines, a health questionnaire offers a technique for assessing

Table 6. Twenty Key Items and Sex and Age Effects

C.M.I. ITEM (BY QUESTION AND NUMBER)	CORRELATION WITH PSYCHE QUESTIONS	SEX		AGE		
		M	F	15–34	35–54	OVER 54
Somatic						
7. Chest Pains	.200	29	39	**26**	**44**	**39**
11. Belching	.270	**24**	**35**	26	31	41
13. Constipation	.254	14	21	**11**	**23**	**27**
14. Stiffness	.221	41	45	38	51	44
16. Skin Sensitivity	.211	**19**	**29**	25	26	16
19. Headaches	.300	**45**	**59**	53	50	53
20. Dizziness	.403	**31**	**45**	38	40	34
Exhaustion						
32. Morning Fatigue	.378	39	43	40	45	39
Other						
35. Hypochondria	.459	17	25	**15**	**30**	**25**
39. Insomnia	.308	**16**	**27**	21	17	32
Anxiety						
44. Xenophobia		**43**	**62**	50	58	51
46. Inadequacy		**45**	**61**	45	**60**	**67**
50. Continual Worry		**19**	**33**	24	29	25
54. Shyness		**13**	**26**	21	19	16
61. Shakiness		**26**	**44**	36	33	34
65. Cold Sweating		**17**	**29**	24	19	27
Depression						
47. Depression		**26**	**47**	**30**	**47**	**34**
49. Wish for Death		15	23	21	15	20
Paranoid Irritability						
59. Resentment of Orders		**37**	**64**	55	46	48
60. Frequent Irritability		**41**	**62**	54	46	58

NOTE: Bold type indicates significance at the 5 percent level of chi-squared testing. Also included are the correlations of the ten "body" questions against the summed "psyche" questions (.120 is significant at the 5 percent level).

the amount of physical and psychological discomfort felt by the individual. Without such a technique, it is possible to fail to recognize that health and comfort is of a low order. Indigenes not accustomed to inquiries of this kind should have as brief a questionnaire as would be reliable. Which questions most consistently reveal personal discomfort in Australian Aborigines?

We extracted twenty key questions from our sixty-five–item questionnaire. The questions had to be the simpler and more clinically useful

Table 7. Twenty Key Items and Ethnic Effects

C.M.I. ITEM (BY QUESTION NUMBER)	CORRELATION WITH RETENTION OF BELIEFS SCORE	PERCENTAGE YES RESPONSES					
		FEMALES			MALES		
		K	L	M	K	L	M
Somatic							
7. Chest Pains	.146	29	41	42	20	26	45
11. Belching	.176	39	34	42	50	21	21
13. Constipation	.160	35	17	27	25	7	26
14. Stiffness	.118	52	45	46	30	37	53
16. Skin Sensitivity	.145	32	29	27	10	20	26
19. Headaches	.172	52	65	58	55	39	58
20. Dizziness	.094	42	46	50	20	31	40
Exhaustion							
32. Morning Fatigue	.090	48	43	38	25	40	47
Other							
35. Hypochondria	.155	42	24	15	30	10	32
39. Insomnia	.110	36	27	19	15	13	26
Anxiety							
44. Xenophobia	.028	74	60	46	85	39	32
46. Inadequacy	.091	77	58	54	60	43	42
50. Continual Worry	.083	39	31	35	20	16	29
54. Shyness	.077	39	22	23	20	8	21
61. Shakiness	.184	55	43	39	45	19	34
65. Cold Sweating	.113	32	28	35	10	18	18
Depression							
47. Depression	.014	77	39	39	30	18	45
49. Wish for Death	.095	42	17	27	10	17	16
Paranoid Irritability							
59. Resentment of Orders	.204	84	64	50	55	42	18
60. Frequent Irritability	.162	84	61	46	50	43	32

NOTE: K = Kaiadilt, L = Lardil, and M = Mainland. Significance has been tested here by a chi-squared method due to Rodger (1967); differences are indicated in the text.

ones. In selecting the ten "body" questions we included only those with a correlation of 0.200 or more against the summed "psyche" questions. We tried to avoid questions with a pronounced age effect and favored ones which confirmed ethnic differences observed in the clinical survey. Another guiding policy was to prefer items which correlated significantly with "retention of beliefs" (see chapter 7). This scale was the only one of four culture measures which proved to be a variable influencing mental health. The questions are set out in tables 6 and 7.

Use of this simple technique does not substitute for a clinical psychiatric examination. However, it permits discovery of persons who claim an unusually high level of personal discomfort, who may then be singled out for special attention and for whatever assistance is available or appropriate. Not least, the establishment of groups with high or with low symptom levels can provide clues concerning the aetiology of mental disorders.

seven

Cultural Identity and Mental Health: A Correlation Analysis

Some preliterate peoples seem to have withstood Western technological advance without undue personality disturbance. (See Redfield, 1950; Mead, 1956; Adams, 1959; Chance, 1965.) Australian Aborigines are not among their number and exemplify personality difficulties that may occur during culture contact. The condition of Aborigines forced to give up traditional life and to congregate at the fringes of European settlements was characterized by Elkin (1951) as "pauperism" and "intelligent parasitism." Much anthropological and public attention has been given to Aborigine culture contact since then. The problem has been variously defined, but only recently as one of mental health and morbidity.

Rapid cultural change has been observed to be associated with "social disintegration" which in turn correlates with an increased incidence of psychiatric symptoms. (See Keesing, 1953; Leighton, 1959b; Raman, 1960; Murphy, 1961.) The nature of the link between rapid acculturation and psychiatric morbidity should be specified wherever possible by quantitative techniques. For effective administration, community development, education and health policies we need to appreciate the existence and extent of any correlations between mental disorder and various acculturation processes. Aspects of acculturation under suspicion include the too rapid acquisition of Western ways, the emulation of these ways coupled with exclusion from them, and the retention of traditional activities and beliefs.

In an attempt to determine these relationships we collected by means of questionnaires information from about three hundred adults on Mornington Island. Over sixty health items and over forty cultural items were recorded from each person, amounting to some thirty thousand items of information.

At the outset should be mentioned certain pitfalls inherent in the at-

This chapter originally appeared in slightly different form as "Cultural Identity and Mental Health of Australian Aborigines," *Social Science & Medicine* (1970) 3:371–387.

tempt to isolate by statistical techniques the sociocultural parameters of mental disorder. An obvious danger is to mistake correlations for causes. A correlation between a certain sociocultural context and a high incidence of symptoms need not reflect a causal relationship. A correlation may be statistically and non-spuriously significant yet causally meaningless. Notwithstanding this, the discovery of an association should alert us to the possibility of a causal relationship and make us cautious about discounting it. The causal network in psychiatric disorders is so complex that we did not expect to find a linear relationship between symptoms and any specific social, cultural, or biological factor. Trends and probabilities from the available data were rather what we sought; even this more modest class of information could be very useful for the task at hand.

Another difficulty is the measurement of sociocultural factors in a rapidly altering environment. While it is troublesome in the field to measure the incidence of symptoms, it is even harder to quantify the sociocultural factors accompanying them. The abandonment of Aboriginal and the adoption of Western ways on the island is too fragmentary for its inhabitants to be located either side of an acculturation gap. The trappings of technology do not necessarily imply a significant change in a person's self-identity. The same folk who listen to pop music on transistor radios (though hardly ever to news broadcasts) take part in ceremonial dancing. Men who sail fishing dinghies with outboard motors also use traditional scoop nets and take pride in foraging fruits and animal foods on bush holidays. Women who frequent the hospital for European medicine are very likely preoccupied with the possession syndrome or with sorcery. In fact, increased acceptance of superstitious beliefs by somatically troubled dispensary frequenters has since been verified in another Aboriginal population (Bianchi et al., 1970).

It is inappropriate, in a population such as this, to shape the research model according to the theory of the marginal personality. The concept of marginal man (Park, 1928; Stonequist, 1937) is applied to groups caught between two cultural systems, hence marginal to both. Marginality has been studied in more acculturated Australian Aborigines by Berry (1970), who related it psychometrically to stress factors and to ethnic identification. Berry's population is not comparable with ours, being exposed much longer to Western influence and composed entirely of mixed-ancestry persons who have lost their language and their traditional religious and artistic practices. Berry concerned himself with the psychometric validity of the concept of marginal personality, in the sense of a pattern of traits such as aggression, suspicion, uncertainty, victimization-rejection, anxiety, and lack of solidarity (Kerckhoff and McCormick, 1955; Mann, 1958). But the Mornington Island population does not, racially or culturally, occupy a marginal situation in this meaning of the term, and it was not relevant for us to be concerned with verifying or disproving the concept of marginal personality.

The characteristic of the island's population that creates an opportunity for measurements is the wide individual variation that exists in the adoption of Western ways and the retention of traditional mores. Within each ethnic group for example are people with a high Western self-identification that might be still higher if they were not excluded from fuller participation in Western life by poverty and by group pressures. Other individuals display a preference for traditional ways—and would espouse them more actively were it not for barriers placed in their way. We reasoned that if these behaviors, attitudes, and aspirations could be measured for each individual, they could then be matched against the previously recorded measures of their psychiatric symptoms, and so reveal any dystonic association.

Four basic aspects of the individual's cultural identity were selected by us for measurement: acquisition of Western culture, emulation of Western culture, retention of traditional activities, and retention of traditional beliefs. Questionnaires and scales were developed for each of these variables and administered to small groups or to individuals. Interpreters were employed when the need arose. With perseverance, 294 sets of responses were completed, representing 91 percent of the adult population. The absence of some of the emigrant workers on mainland cattle stations during our intensive "blitz" in June 1966 necessitated a return trip by one of us (J. E. Cawte) in January 1967. The cooperation of this admittedly captive audience was good, permitting this unusually high proportion of completed responses.

The limitations of the questionnaire method are appreciated. With preliterate people it is exceptionally tedious, and when an interpreter is employed he may record the subjects' views through the filter of his own bias. Such limitations must be accepted; if one awaited a perfect methodology one would wait forever, and the opportunity to record ephemeral situations such as exist today on Mornington Island would be lost.

The four instruments to measure cultural identity were prepared from a large number of items using the techniques of Guttman analysis (1950) to reject the unscalable items. The resulting short questionnaires with scoring systems and coefficients of reproducibility (CR) are listed here as a preliminary to the analysis that follows.

The Acquisition of Western Culture Scale
(Individual items score 0–1)

---

1. Do you speak English?
   (Scores 1 if mostly or all the time)
2. Have you ever been to:
   a. a mainland station?
   b. Cloncurry or Mt. Isa?

    c. Townsville?
    d. Thursday Island?
    e. Brisbane?
    (Scores 1 if subject has been to two or more places)
3. Do you often go to the pictures at the mission?
    (Scores 1 if yes)
4. Do you read newspapers or magazines often?
    (Scores 1 if yes)
5. Do you write letters to anyone?
    (Scores 1 if yes)

Scores for acquisition range from 0 to 6. CR = 80 percent.

The acquisition scale was suggested to us by "The Intercultural Contact Scale" developed by N. A. Chance (1965) for use in an Eskimo community. Chance assessed the Eskimos' contact with the European-derived population by their educational level, knowledge of English, residential mobility, hospitalizations, type of employment, access to mass media, and military service. Our scale covers similar areas with modifications. The item concerned with military service is inapplicable in this community. We thought it useful to estimate language preference rather than knowledge of English. The level of education is omitted because in this population it does not scale—the majority have reached the same level (primary grade V) at the mission school and this item differentiates only the older Kaiadilt people.

The acquisition items rejected as unscalable were:

(a) Have you ever had a job on a station or mission?
(b) Have you read a book from the library this year?
(c) Do you need to buy medicines from the store?
(d) Do you attend church regularly?
(e) Do you believe in the God of the Bible?

Question (a) probably failed to scale because the word *other* was omitted from in front of mission. Question (b) was excluded because none of the thirty subjects whose answers were used in the scaling had borrowed a book, though one falsely so claimed. Question (c) is a measure of hypochondria rather than of acquisition; aspirin, cough medicine, and liniment are much in demand even with the most poorly Westernized Aborigines. The rejection of questions (d) and (e) concerning the adoption of Christianity is presumably because these items represent a different subuniverse of acquisition.

The Emulation of Western Culture Scale
(Individual items score 0–1)

If you had the chance to be a baby and to grow up again,
1. What would you like to be: black, brown, or white? (Scores 1 if brown or white)

2. Where would you like to live: Mornington Island, the mainland, a town like Cloncurry, or a big town like Brisbane? (Scores 1 if other than Mornington Island)
3. What sort of house would you like to live in: a bush timber hut, a proper hut, or a house with several rooms? (Scores 1 if house with several rooms)
4. What job would you like to have? (Scores 1 if job is not normally available to Aborigines)
5. Where would you like to go for a holiday? (Scores 1 if place chosen is other than nearby or in the Gulf Country)

Scores for emulation range from 0 to 5. CR = 84 percent.

The emulation scale is a measure of aspiration toward Western-style society. Its projective quality gives respondents a choice of conditions in a hypothetical future. Although Mornington Islanders are excluded by poor economy and education from larger participation in Western-style society, they show varying degrees of aspiration. In his similar scale, Chance (1965) measured Eskimo preference for Western foods, clothing, and hairstyles—indices judged inappropriate in this less-acculturated Aboriginal population.

The Retention of Traditional Activities Scale (Individual items score 0–1)

Is (does) the subject:

1. Clever in the bush? 0, 1, 2, 3. (Scores 1 if rated 3)
2. Use native language? 0, 1, 2, 3. (Scores 1 if rated 3)
3. Believe in native medicine? 0, 1, 2, 3. (Scores 1 if rated 3)
4. Interested in local songs? 0, 1, 2, 3. (Scores 1 if rated 2 or 3)
5. Interested in dancing? 0, 1, 2, 3. (Scores 1 if rated 2 or 3)
6. Know the stories and traditions? 0, 1, 2, 3. (Scores 1 if rated 2 or 3)
7. Make Aboriginal artifacts? 0, 1, 2. (Scores 1 if rated 2)

Scores for retention of activities range from 0 to 7. CR = 87 percent.

We administered the retention of activities scale differently from the others, using a committee of Aboriginal elders to rate the subjects, rather than asking subjects to rate themselves. Because activities in this community are common knowledge, and scoring merely required the committee to assess the degree of participation in them, observer-ratings are likely to be more accurate than self-ratings. The selected male and female informants seemed to enjoy their task and consulted amongst each other about the correct score to assign.

The Retention of Traditional Beliefs Scale
(Individual items score 0–1)

1. Do you think the old native beliefs can help you? (Scores 1 if yes)
2. When you die, do you believe you will go to the spirit home in the east? (Scores 1 if yes)
3. Are heaven and the spirit home in the east the same? (Scores 1 if yes)
4. Do you believe in **malgri**? (Scores 1 if yes)
5. Can **puripuri** hurt people? (Scores 1 if yes)

Scores for retention of beliefs range from 0 to 5. CR = 87 percent.

Malgri is a traditional spirit intrusion syndrome characterized by abdominal pain and distension, headache, drowsiness, and sometimes by vomiting. It occurs in response to a breach of territoriality; a person who enters the sea having omitted to wash his hands after handling land food runs the risk of possession by the serpent or other totemic spirit peculiar to the locality. Two-thirds of the adult population subscribe to this belief and it is reasonable to suppose that those who experience psychosomatic abdominal discomfort will be the more fervent believers in *malgri*.

Puripuri is a term of Papuan or possibly Indonesian origin used in Papua, the Cape York Peninsula, and the Gulf of Carpentaria for sorcery and more precisely for a poisonous substance. The Islanders themselves are more concerned about it than about their own traditional sorcery. One-half of our sample believe that *puripuri* can hurt people. The extent of belief in *malgri* and *puripuri* varies with ethnic subgroup. Thus 63 percent of Kaiadilt expressed belief in *malgri,* 69 percent in *puripuri;* 72 percent of Lardil in *malgri* and 62 percent in *puripuri;* 66 percent of mainlanders in *malgri* and 33 percent in *puripuri.*

The retention of beliefs scale tests the subject's beliefs about the workings of the universe, including his own part in it, covering topics usually included in the concepts of religion, magic, and superstition. It was administered individually so that the respondent's views might be obtained independently of those of his companions. This scale gave subjects more cause for reflection and hesitation than did the other scales and it was noticeable that many would have liked to consult with their companions.

The coefficients of reproducibility for acquisition, emulation, retention of activities, and retention of beliefs are 80, 84, 87, and 87 percent respectively. The coefficient is a measure of whether or not a particular series of items may be usefully regarded as approximating a perfect unidimensional scale. Guttman has set 90 percent as an efficient approximation though this reproducibility is only the principal criterion for scalability. Our least satisfactory scale is acquisition where the coefficient of reproducibility is low at 80 percent and five of the original eleven items did not scale. The best was retention of activities because its coefficient of reproducibility was nearly 90 percent, it contained the most items and it had a number of response categories in each item. This latter is especially important when the total number of items is small. Additional information for readers unfamiliar with scale construction is simply provided by Oppenheim in *Questionnaire Design and Attitude Measurement* (1966).

RESULTS

The effects of age, sex, and ethnic group as variables in the four scales measuring cultural identity are shown in table 8.

Table 8. Average Scores of Measures of Cultural Identity

Population Group	No. of Subjects	Acquisition (Max. score 6)	Emulation (Max. score 5)	Retention of Activities (Max. score 7)	Retention of Beliefs (Max. score 5)
Male and female by age					
15–34	152	4.6	2.2	0.8	2.4
35–54	99	3.7	1.9	3.2	2.6
Over 54	43	2.2	0.9	5.1	3.8
Males	146	3.9	1.9	2.3	2.7
Kaiadilt	20	2.1	0.5	3.6	3.0
Lardil	84	4.1	1.9	2.3	3.0
Mainland	38	4.2	2.3	1.8	2.0
Part-Aborigine	4	5.2	3.0	1.5	1.5
Females	148	4.0	2.0	2.3	2.7
Kaiadilt	31	2.5	1.0	3.4	3.3
Lardil	83	4.4	2.2	1.8	2.7
Mainland	26	4.0	2.1	2.6	2.2
Part-Aborigine	8	4.8	2.8	2.1	1.3

The scores on measures of cultural identity are remarkably even for the two sexes, in contrast to the sex effect on the incidence of symptoms described in chapter 6. The age of the subjects, however, has a clear influence on the scores. The younger people score highest for both acquisition and emulation and lowest for retention of activities and retention of beliefs. Obvious differences are found between the ethnic subgroups. Kaiadilt rank lowest on acquisition and emulation and highest on retention of activities and retention of beliefs, whereas part-Aborigines rank highest on acquisition and emulation and lowest

90

on retention of activities and retention of beliefs; Lardil and mainland groups occupy intermediate positions.

The relationships between acquisition, emulation, retention of activities, and retention of beliefs expressed as correlations are shown below. (The influences of sex, age, and ethnic subgroup have been removed from the correlations.)

Intercorrelations Among the Four Cultural Identity Scales

	ACQUISITION	EMULATION	RETENTION OF ACTIVITIES
Retention of Beliefs	0.085	−0.003	0.062
Retention of Activities	**−0.128**	**−0.157**	
Emulation	**0.181**		

Of the six correlations, the three in boldface achieve significance at beyond the 5 percent level ($r = \pm 0.120$). Retention of beliefs varies independently of the other cultural identity variables and we conclude that neither acquisition nor emulation of Western ways has interfered with the old beliefs.

Our chief object in measuring cultural identity in the culture contact is to examine its relationship to the incidence of psychiatric symptoms. To avoid spuriously high correlations—those stemming not from a connection between culture rating and symptom score but from the fact that each is related to some third variable—the effect of ethnic grouping is excluded and the effects of sex and particularly of age "partialed out" of the correlations.

Of retention of beliefs' correlations against the sixty-five C.M.I. questions used, fifteen achieved significance at the 5 percent level ($r = \pm 0.120$). By contrast, acquisition, emulation, and retention of activities had only a few significant correlations, no more than would be expected by chance variation. The fifteen questions which correlated with retention of beliefs are shown in table 9, with in addition their correlations against acquisition, emulation, and retention of activities.

DISCUSSION

Aborigines Who Acquire Western Culture

Acquisition of Western patterns—represented by reading, writing, and speaking English, by travel, and by interest in radio and cinema—shows no relationship to the incidence of psychiatric symptomatology. Correlations of 0.162 and 0.143 against questions 57 and 59 (irritability and anger) are significant at the 5 percent level but these are only two of sixty-five correlations, no more than might occur by chance alone.

Table 9. Cultural Identity Variables and Psychiatric Symptoms with Significant Retention of Belief Correlations

C.M.I. ITEM (BY QUESTION NUMBER)	ACQUISITION	EMULATION	RETENTION OF ACTIVITIES	RETENTION OF BELIEFS
7. Chest pains	0.006	0.050	0.037	**0.146**
11. Belching	−0.022	0.038	0.025	**0.176**
13. Constipation	−0.025	−0.004	−0.035	**0.160**
16. Tender skin	0.062	**0.124**	0.015	**0.145**
19. Headaches	0.017	−0.028	−0.022	**0.172**
21. Paralysis	−0.025	−0.014	−0.058	**0.136**
23. Convulsion	−0.003	0.000	0.042	**0.123**
28. Urinary hesitancy (men) Menstrual tension (women)	−0.026	0.041	0.001	**0.142**
35. Hypochondria	0.050	−0.030	0.050	**0.155**
36. Always sick	−0.007	0.035	−0.024	**0.165**
38. Accident proneness	0.012	−0.043	0.005	**0.123**
56. Touchiness	0.011	0.109	0.016	**0.134**
59. Angered by orders	**0.143**	0.014	−0.105	**0.204**
60. Irritability	0.043	0.012	−0.021	**0.162**
61. Shakiness	0.086	0.050	−0.064	**0.184**

NOTE: Correlations that achieve significance at the 5 percent level are in boldface.

Acquisition and retention of activities reflect the extent of culture contact and of culture change. Since they have been shown not to influence the extent of psychological disability we are entitled to infer that culture contact of the kind existing on Mornington Island is not a significant causal factor in mental illness. This does not contradict expectations, based on a culture-shock or marginality type of theory, that abrupt Westernization may lead to psychic disequilibrium, because except for the Kaiadilts' more recent exposure to Western influences this culture contact has been proceeding for over fifty years. This is not a rapid change. With the Kaiadilt too, there is evidence that even before their sudden advent to a Westernized existence they were an unhappy, socially disintegrated group beset by bodily preoccupation.

Aborigines Who Emulate Western Culture

Emulation of Western patterns—measured in our scale by preferences with regard to skin color, place and type of housing, work and recreation—are not found to bear a relationship, either positively or negatively, to psychiatric symptomatology. Chance (1965) suggested that while measures of cultural identity taken singly may not show a significant relationship to mental health they may yet do so in combination. For example with Eskimos undergoing rapid culture change he found that a higher degree of modern identification in association with a lower actual contact was accompanied by higher C.M.I. scores. His sample however was small and he did not control for extraneous variables. Chance's Modern-Value Identification Scale refers to actual emulation in the present world, whereas our emulation scale alludes to a hypothetical future, and so is only vaguely comparable.

Table 10. Combinations of Cultural Identity Factors with Average Positive C.M.I. Responses

	EXTENT OF EMULATION	C.M.I. SCORE
"Healthy" Combinations		
Low Acquisition	High Emulation	15.4
High Retention of Activities	High Emulation	16.0
Low Retention of Activities	High Emulation	16.5
"Sick" Combinations		
Low Acquisition	Low Emulation	22.5
Low Acquisition	High Retention of Activities	22.0
Low Emulation	High Retention of Activities	21.6

Table 10 indicates the main "healthy" and "sick" combinations for the three variables: acquisition, emulation, and retention of activities. In each grouping "low" means the lower third and "high" the upper third of cultural identity scores. The average C.M.I. symptom score is shown for each combination. These differences shown in table 10 are to be explained by the fact that the young people have both low C.M.I. scores and high emulation, whereas the old people have high C.M.I. scores and low emulation. Non-recognition of these age-engendered distortions would have encouraged spurious deductions.

Aborigines Who Retain Traditional Beliefs

The extent of retention of beliefs—represented in this retention of beliefs scale by belief in possession, sorcery, the efficacy of native medicine, and the existence of a spirit heaven in the east—is higher in the elderly, in the Kaiadilt subgroup, and in the psychologically ill. The positive correlation of retention of beliefs with occurrence of affirmative responses in the C.M.I. remains, even when contamination by the effects of age, sex, and ethnic subgroup has been removed. The correlations though sometimes highly significant account for only a small part of the variance. Despite this it is worthwhile to conjecture the nature and basis of this relationship.

One possibility is that both the retention of beliefs and C.M.I. scores are measures of neuroticism and therefore not surprisingly covariant. Another is that those with many neurotic and psychosomatic discomforts are more ready to give credence to traditional beliefs. Many of the symptoms correlating with retention of beliefs are those that would be expected to foster belief in the power of *malgri,* sorcery and traditional medicine, viz., pains, belching, constipation, headache, conversion reactions, and accident-proneness. Therefore it may be that when a person is prone to strange somatic events he seeks and accepts superstitious reasons for them and consequently scores high on retention of beliefs. It is likely that holding traditional beliefs and experiencing psychophysiological turmoil are mutually reinforcing, rather than that there is a one-way linear relationship.

The most striking finding in this study is that none of the parameters of cultural identity used by us are importantly associated with symptom levels. Indeed, with the exception of the retention of traditional beliefs scale they appear unrelated, even when studied in combination. Therefore, in seeking links between mental health and cultural identity it seems likely that one may be asking the wrong questions. The links with mental health may not be directly with the individual's various cultural activities, interests, and aspirations, so much as with his social and interpersonal difficulties.

The finding that retention of traditional beliefs was the only aspect of cultural identity measured by us associated with high symptom scores may lend support to this conclusion. In the clinical study of this population reported in chapter 6, an association was found between belief in *malgri* and *puripuri,* interpersonal tensions and manipulations and psychiatric illnesses. We do not know how disruptive the possession-sorcery component of belief may have been in traditional culture, where conceivably it had some regulating or integrative functions; possibly it has become more pathogenic with increased exposure to strangers and with the social fragmentation of settlement life.

One implication for social policy is that it may be warranted to discount the acceptance of *malgri, puripuri,* and other "sick" beliefs in this transitional culture. This would require an educational program aimed not so much at indoctrinating as at increasing the understanding—on both Aboriginal and Western sides of the cultural interface—of traditional Aboriginal beliefs. The relationship between retention of traditional beliefs and psychological disability merits further examination.

The other psychometric study of Aborigines to which we alluded earlier (Berry, 1970) was carried out in a more acculturated community (Storm Cove) but lends further support to this relationship. Berry's analysis showed a pattern of more marginality, more deviance, and more stress, for those rejecting the dominant white society. At Storm Cove, the traditional orientation took the form of a reaffirmation of traditional values rather than a retention—it was too late for this. Personal discomfort and turmoil seem to be present at Storm Cove until people resolve the conflict not by reacting and rejecting but by assuming an "Australian" (Western) identity. Berry suggests that if this rather unsatisfactory situation holds true generally, then minority groups searching for their own identity and values may be doomed to further psychological discomfort. If it does not hold true, then either retention or reaffirmation of traditional ways (and the acceptance of these by the dominant group) may yet provide a path to satisfying personal and intergroup relations in plural societies.

PRINCIPAL COMPONENTS ANALYSES

To remove its vitiating effect upon the interpretation of C.M.I. scores, age was partialed out of a correlation matrix of twenty variables leaving nineteen which include: male or female, the four ethnic subgroups, the four ratings of cultural identity (acquisition, emulation, retention of activities, retention of beliefs), seven individual items, and three Cornell Medical Index scores (total score, psychological sections [M to R] score, and section J [familial and personal sick roles] score).

The seven individual items were:

Do you attend church regularly?
Do you believe in *malgri*?
Can *puripuri* hurt people?
Would you like to look after youself and be out of *The Act?*
Would you like the mission to look after everything?
Rating of interest in local songs.
Rating of interest in traditional dancing.

A principal components analysis, unity in the leading diagonal, was performed. Unrotated factors I and II contribute 31.7 percent of the variance (16.8 percent and 14.9 percent respectively). Item saturations above ±0.300 are reported. They are the only two factors with large saturations on the C.M.I. scores.

Factor I		Factor II	
Total C.M.I.	0.647	Total C.M.I.	0.568
C.M.I., M–R	0.625	C.M.I., M–R	0.525
C.M.I., J	0.566	C.M.I., J	0.445
Kaiadilt	0.595	Mainland	0.364
Mainland	−0.325	Lardil	−0.306
Retention of Beliefs		Retention of Activities	
Score	0.564	Score	−0.668
(puripuri)	(0.590)		
(malgri)	(0.337)	Emulation Score	0.333
Emulation Score	−0.456		
Acquisition Score	−0.402		
Retention of Activities			
Score	0.376	Female	0.321

The first unrotated factor represents a combination which if translated into a description of a paradigmatic subject would read: "She is a Kaiadilt, not a mainlander, and scores high on the retention of beliefs scale particularly assenting to the belief that *puripuri* can hurt people. In line with these she has low acquisition of Western values and does not emulate Western ways, clinging to the old ways." Neurosis plagues the subject. This after all is what the data showed with different analyses.

The second unrotated factor defines a subject again "more likely female, and troubled by neurosis. This woman has low retention of traditional activities and emulates her white sisters. She is more often mainlander than Lardil." This factor suggests a person discontented with life on an "alien" island who desires the advantages of an unavailable Western life. Under this load she develops psychological distress. Notice that the indigenous Lardil are not similarly troubled.

Unrotated factor III contrasts the "acculturated" Lardil and the "primitive" Kaiadilt.

Unrotated factor IV (8.8 percent of the variance) is reported for its relevance to Aborigines' attitudes to "paternalism."

Factor IV

Would prefer to be out of "The Act"		0.454
Would prefer the mission to look after everything		−0.388
Acquisition Score		0.345
Emulation Score		0.419
Retention of Activities Score	(songs 0.396)	
	(dancing 0.485)	0.394
Regular church attendance		0.366
Total C.M.I.		0.299
Kaiadilt		−0.274

Were there a typical example of a person scoring high on this factor, he (or she) would be any of the island's inhabitants, other than a

Kaiadilt, with the desire for increased self-government and less imposition of Western control. In accord with this wish for a less controlled status he has a hope for the benefits of Western civilization and has acquired Western ways (and goes to church regularly), while retaining his own practices. These conflicts between desire and reality are manifested in some tendency to higher C.M.I. scores. The less acculturated Kaiadilt accepts the status quo.

Further factors beyond the fourth contribute little to the variance and are not pursued here. Rotation was not beneficial in this instance, though the first rotated factor demonstrates the predisposition of females to neurosis. The factor has high saturations for C.M.I. scores and for being female.

Guttman and Factor Analyses

There is sometimes value in performing both Guttman and factor analyses; as the Gullahorns (1968) say "performing both analyses appears worthwhile for exploring diverse relationships and implications in one's data." The thirty-two variables chosen to tap cultural identity and attitude were subjected to a principal components analysis. In this instance the results of a varimax rotation give the most simplified factors.

Some new light is shed on emulation which it will be recalled had a low coefficient of reproducibility (84 percent). It comes out as saturations on many factors, for example:

The holiday item gathers with acquisition variables, as do the preferments for a superior house and job. These last two also appear on a factor indicating the desire to be out of *The Act* and an antagonism to mission control. Emulation of the white man's color does not cluster with the other emulation items but associates with pro-government and anti-mission attitudes. (Prefers to be white 0.706, pro-government 0.486, pro-mission —0.303.) The pro-government question was "Would you like the government to look after everything?"

The Retention of Beliefs Items Split into Two Factors

A		B	
Old beliefs helpful	0.530	Old beliefs helpful	0.412
Malgri	0.758	Spirit home	0.821
Puripuri	0.794	Spirit home = Heaven	0.846

The retention of activities items hold together very closely and, interestingly, song ability which scaled perfectly on Guttman analysis has the highest of the seven item saturations. The acquisition scale is also preserved but takes on the new accretions of some emulation items and a negative loading on use of native language.

TRADITIONAL CHILD-REARING PRACTICES AMONGST THE LARDIL

The children's specialist of the team, in order to make a survey of emotional disturbances of childhood on the island, had first to make a closer examination of child-rearing practices. From the Lardil child's point of view the most important adult figures in his life were his mother, her co-wives, and his father, his maternal grandparents, and maternal uncle and aunt. The eight-subsection system, of the kind associated with the Walbiri of central Australia, has been recently introduced, perhaps within three to four generations (see chapter 4). The Kaiadilt people have only recently been introduced to this system through their contact with the Lardil. Although greatly admired by the Aborigines, the system has real difficulties in practical application to small populations. A fuller comprehension of the complexity of formal family relationships awaits anthropological investigation. Sufficient information was gained, however, to present an account of the child's development.

Pregnancy, heralded by amenorrhea and pelvic sensations, was confirmed by omen if the father had a stroke of good fortune or met with an unusual incident such as the spearing of many fish in shallow water. The relationship between coitus and conception was recognized to the extent that it was believed that a man must have sexual intercourse at least several times with a woman to prepare the way for entry of the spirit child. The *goamanda* (literally, bubble-people) or spirit children were thought to dwell in the worm holes found in sand at low tide. Contraception or induced abortion was not practiced. It was believed that the father brought the child to the mother and that there was no question of maternal choice. Pregnant women observed various food taboos. It was believed that the eating of deep-sea fish might cause stillbirth, difficult labor, poor milk supply, or perhaps penile deformity in the male child. Other foods were thought to facilitate delivery.

Infertility was regarded as an affliction. A mother with several children might take pity on an infertile relative and allow her to adopt one of her own children. Twins were unwelcome and the mother free to choose which of them she would preserve. Illegitimate pregnancy is said to have been uncommon, and its occurrence the cause of remonstrance and argument. The offending man was sometimes compelled to marry, although the acquisition of a sexual and economic partner must often have been welcome in a society where women were unequally distributed. "Wrong-head" unions—those contrary to the sanctions of the subsection system—were frowned on but often eventually accepted; however, there is some suggestion that marriage laws are even more strictly applied amongst the Lardil today than in earlier generations.

When her labor pains began the mother went to a sacred spot (Warra Warra amongst the Windward Lardil). Assisted by the maternal grandmother and other female kinfolk, she knelt, thighs abducted, grasping a digging-stick. Her relatives pressed from behind upon her womb, supporting her back as she strained, all singing

> *Burra burra nggidi dja nggidi dja.*
> Baby come forth quickly.

After birth the umbilical cord was severed by biting. The placenta was buried, but the proximal part of the cord, after its natural separation, was preserved in a decorative amulet wrapped around by grass string and bedecked with bird feathers (*yirri*). The mother wore this as a necklace during her child's infancy to aid it in finding the breast and as a charm against excessive crying. It was then transferred to the maternal grandfather until formally presented along with other gifts in middle childhood.

The lying-in period lasted about a week and the father was prohibited from visiting during that time. He provided special foods, delivered by female relatives. The newborn child was nursed and fed in a bark coolamon (*djumud*) which could be slung across the back for carrying. Breast-feeding was on demand, used often for pacification and continued for varying periods up to and sometimes beyond the birth of the next child. Wild roots, goanna, sugarbag (wild honey), and white clay applications were regarded as lactagogues.

Although generally tolerant the parents might punish an older child for severe infractions; but they would resent others, apart from the maternal uncle and grandfather, who usurped their function in this regard. Toilet training was permissive; the child when sufficiently advanced taught himself by imitation of other children to defecate away from the camp and to cover his excreta with earth. The major developmental crisis would appear to have occurred at this time with weaning and, frequently, displacement from the breast by a newborn sibling.

Child-rearing, traditional and contemporary   **99**

Children were probably physically and emotionally most vulnerable at this age, a period of tantrums and maternal exasperation.

Boys and girls played freely together until the increasing awareness of prepubertal years led to social differentiation. Many of the activities were based on identification with adults. The boys ranged up in opposing factions based, for example, on family affiliation and battled with grass spears (*dilmir*). An episode recounted by Jacko, an elderly traditionalist, shows how a childhood squabble sometimes snowballed into a camp quarrel.

One boy he bin spearim me too hard. I get angry so I bitim one side my spear (to sharpen it). I hit him good and he bleed in the leg. This boy got a fish bone spear and got me in the foot. I go home and cry to my father and mother. My father give this boy a hiding. Then his father fightim my father. My mother fightim there too for me. (How did it all finish?) Someone bin stop the fight—my brother want to finish it, stop him.

It is instructive to compare the traditional Lardil games of childhood with those of European origin. Girls and boys might build a small seaweed windbreak or humpy with fireplace. Here they could enact family scenes after the fashion of "mothers and fathers." A mangrove seed (*bordul*) served as a doll baby, nursed in a small coolamon, and fed with toy breasts hung from the girl's neck, fashioned from the pods of the cotton tree (*dalnjit*). Land or sea food was hunted with small spears and spear-throwers, or nets made from the branches of the pandanus tree. Other games included slippery-slide (*dirrul*), hide-and-go-seek and find-the-object (*djirbaldi*), catches using a ball fashioned from an old fish net (*buldjit*), and competitive running. Drawing in the soil or sand to learn animal tracks, and building model fish traps from sand occupied much of the time.

By preadolescence more time was spent by the boy with his father and especially his maternal uncle and maternal grandfather, learning to hunt and preparing for circumcision. The girl was trained by the maternal aunt and grandmother in handcraft and food gathering. Most girls had already been promised to their prospective husbands by the age of five. The relative openness of camp society ensured that the child could not remain sexually ignorant, and it appears that sexual experimentation was common although officially frowned upon by adults. The same ambivalence applied to premarital coitus after menarche. Masturbation in boys was considered dangerous and a sign that marriage must be arranged since penile damage was a possible outcome.

The onset of menstruation or breast development indicated marriageability. Menstruation was related to the myth of the haughty Dugong woman who, fed uncooked pandanus fruit by her punitive male kin-folk, developed abdominal pains and bled per vaginam (the harpooned young female dugong is said to lose blood vaginally). It is said to be connected with the curse of the male rainbow serpent Thuwathu who, burnt by his vengeful sister Bulthugoo, swam up the Dugong River pouring imprecations upon her (see chapter 3). The menstruating woman was expected to remain apart from the main camp. She was prohibited from bathing in the sea lest salt get inside her and cause *malgri*. Should her husband have coitus with her at this time he would be liable to such mischance as shark-bite or illness.

When his facial hair grew the young man was ready for initiation, an occasion for gathering of the scattered family hordes, for celebrations and the formal exchange of gifts. The first operation was that of circumcision, involving removal of the youth's prepuce with a sting-ray barb while he lay supine across the backs of his brothers-in-law. There is no record that female introcision was performed.

It appears that sorcery (*lababridi* or *puripuri*) was not directed against children, apart from the occasional case where a man's whole family was included in a *midjil* or *mulya* curse. The mother avoided losing breast milk into the sea since her nurseling might develop *malgri*. Older children were also at risk from this illness for the same reasons as an adult.[1] The neonate was prevented from being carried over a river or creek lest illness ensue. Massage of the baby's chest or legs with milk or excrement was thought to ensure strength and rapid growth. If the nursing mother ate too much sugarbag (wild honey) or deep-sea fish it was thought that her child would develop vomiting and weakness. Skin lesions were related to mud or sand abrasions and treated with ashes. The sick child might be treated by rubbing with body sweat, blood drawn from a subincision, or exposure to the smoke of burning leaves or grass.

The death of a small child might be regarded as a mere misfortune but in many cases the mother would blame herself, reinforced in this by the father's accusations. The death of an older child was regarded as the responsibility of both parents who were beaten by the maternal uncle and maternal grandfather. The mourning mother would lacerate herself and often had to be restrained by her relatives from doing herself more injury. Larger children were buried in the earth and smaller children interred in a hollow log where visiting by the grieving mother was possible. Thus, the significance of a child's death was different from that of an adult. An inquest was always held after the death of an adult to determine whether death was caused by sorcery

1. See *Medicine is the Law* (forthcoming) for an account of the *malgri* illness, a culture-bound psychiatric disorder.

and who the culprit was. For the death of children blame and guilt rested firmly with the parents, particularly the mother.

The social practices of the Kaiadilt people are broadly similar to those of the Lardil. The young girl was promised in marriage at the age of five or six. Similar taboos applied to menarche, menstruation, childbirth, and pregnancy. The umbilical cord was severed by the maternal uncle flush with the abdominal wall and had no ceremonial significance. When twins were born the father selected the one he wished to keep, accusing his wife of having slept with another man to produce the second child. Breast-feeding continued for a comparable length of time and weaning was sometimes forced by coating the nipples with the bitter juice of a vine. Various informants insist that there was no attempt by either adults or children to defecate away from the immediate area of the camp. It is possible however that this habit was a result of physical debility and general disorientation when the Kaiadilt first came to Mornington Island. Rubbing of the child with excrement to ensure strength and growth was practiced on Bentinck Island also. There were different initiation rites. The initial circumcision was performed by the maternal uncle at about fourteen years of age with a stingray barb. Subincision was carried out shortly afterwards by the individual using a sharpened stone on himself. The subincision could be pricked with a bream-fin barb when blood was required for medicinal or ceremonial purposes.

In general it appears that the Kaiadilt lacked the richness of the Lardil material and artistic culture. This may have been due in part to their isolation and the lack of infusion of stimulation from the mainland. Their own culture has been swamped since the 1948 migration to Mornington Island by the more viable heritage of the indigenous people.

Themes are discernible in the account of child-rearing given by the people of Mornington Island. The child was primarily part of a hunting group of perhaps six adults and their families, held together by kinship ties. The primary hunting groups of the Leeward and the Windward shores of Mornington Island met for ceremony and celebrations several times a year over a week-long period. By virtue of his birth the Lardil man shared proprietary rights to a section of the littoral and its hinterland, and gained membership in the corresponding totemic group. The sea was the major source of sustenance and was not to be offended by contamination with material belonging to the land; if offended it might rise up and invade or enter man or his land territory. Man and land were subject to the changing and sometimes unpredictable moods of the element which surrounded them. Significantly the spirits of his unborn children came from the biotic zone between the tidal margins.

Children were highly valued and probably indulged in their early years. It was the responsibility of the parents, particularly the mother, to care for and protect them. Failure to do so would arouse the wrath of the maternal grandparents, and maternal uncle and aunt who also had special obligations toward the child. Descriptions of bereaved mothers leave little doubt as to the intensity of intropunitive behavior resulting from loss.

Breast-feeding was prolonged. Body contact was intense and as the infant became more mobile spread beyond the mother to the extended family. Discipline, like toilet training, was permissive though subject to vicissitudes in parental mood. The child was exposed early to the intimacies and dissensions of family and social life generally and reflected these in his play. Intrapersonal privacy must have been precarious and the child vulnerable to narcissistic hurt by ridicule, shaming, or social failure. The taboo on brother-sister incest was a potent one. A certain ambivalence toward childhood and premarital adolescent sexual experimentation became more evident at puberty. Psychosexual differentiation was socially formalized at this time when the boy, through the initiation ceremonies, gained access to the secret world of men, and the girl by virtue of her menarche to the subordinate sphere of women. The indulgent nurture of infancy and childhood gave way to the more serious training and higher expectations associated with adolescence and young adulthood.

CONTEMPORARY CHILD-REARING PRACTICES

Information on the social environment and child-rearing customs of the present day was gathered by direct observation and from interviews with European staff of the mission and with the Aboriginal people.

The most striking feature of child-rearing imposed by the missionaries was called the "dormitory system." For about twenty-five years, until 1951, children were reared in dormitories segregated by sex. This system aimed to encourage a more rapid abandonment of peripatetic tribal life, the better learning of English and basic Western skills and customs, and to protect the girls from early sexual exposure and pregnancy. Needless to say, the dormitory system has been the subject of much contention amongst missionaries and others. Although abandoned now, we cannot think that it was as pathogenic as its opponents claim. Whatever the cost to some individuals in terms of affective deprivation, social dislocation, or confusion of identificatory models, the system has provided an influential group of adults. The youngest of these on the island is now over twenty years old. They use English as their basic language, adopt European models of industry and of dress and hygiene, and teach their children accordingly. The dormitory graduates include a number of children who were admitted from the mainland and the general cohesiveness of this now middle-aged group has probably been a major factor in promoting the acceptance and assimilation of later arrivals from Bentinck Island and elsewhere.

A social consequence of overcrowding is the early emancipation of children from parental authority, with transfer of allegiance to the peer group—a germinal situation for adolescent delinquent behavior. The disciplinary problem is intensified by the absence of many of the younger fathers who are away at work on the mainland. In some cases both parents are away and the children who have returned to go to school are cared for by relatives. Approximately 50 percent of the population is under the age of fifteen, an indication of the relatively large family size. (For the remainder of the Australian population the proportion under fifteen years is little more than 30 percent.) Some of the more sophisticated women have heard of contraception. None has access to it.

Economic factors are basic to these problems. An extreme case is that of one mother who is unmarried, has two illegitimate children, and lives on two dollars per week from child endowment and the charity of her extended family. An increasing number of homes have radios but newspapers are seldom purchased and few own or read books and magazines. The social environment by Western standards is culturally deprived.

An insistence by the older group on "straight-head" marriages often prevents the union of marriageable people. Young single girls, particularly those from the Kaiadilt enclave where there is a relative shortage of young men, go out to the mainland to work as domestics on cattle stations and are prone to pregnancy. This may be due to the difficulty of adopting an independent self-restraint when separated from the supportive family group. Many of the young people disclaim respect for the old subsection laws but few with strong ties to their birthplace are able to ignore them.

The traditional belief in omens of pregnancy persists. A woman's pregnancy is also regarded as a potential cause of dissension in the community. After one serious village quarrel the nurse was asked to examine the wife of a prominent combatant to determine if she were with child. In such a way the community can project and rationalize the blame for disintegrative forces within it.

Antenatal care is provided at a small but reasonably well-equipped hospital, and modern medicine has entirely supplanted traditional obstetric practices. There are no longer any bush deliveries. The less sophisticated women are too shy to make a direct approach until they are about five months pregnant, but by this time the rumor has filtered through to the nursing sister who takes the initiative in calling the woman for examination. To a large extent the taboo against the father's presence at the time of delivery and afterwards still applies.

Serious obstetrical complications are handled when required at the mainland base hospital at Mt. Isa. Over a period of thirty months from December 1963 to June 1966 there were fifty-two deliveries. Ten of the neonates weighed under five-and-one-half pounds, a high incidence of dysmaturity. There were two stillbirths, five cases of postpartum hemorrhage, but none of puerperal infection. The traditional custom of preserving the umbilical cord has completely died out, although the formal exchange of gifts when the child reaches five years is retained.

The duration of breast-feeding varies with the degree of acculturation. Some wean at about nine months introducing semisolids in the form of canned baby food, fish, rice, or "damper" (a type of biscuit). Most continue until the child is four or five years. Bottle feeding when necessary is supplied through the hospital. The breast is often provided as a pacifier for children of three or four years. Much the same general permissiveness applies to toilet training. A few of the more acculturated mothers institute training at about twelve months.

The situation concerning discipline, control, and punishment is mixed. Several of the European staff complain that many mothers are too inert to stop their younger children from interfering with mission equipment until aware that someone disapproves. One mother with high aspiration toward Western values told with some pride that she had begun to smack her children when they were two years old "to make them good." She mentioned swearing and aggression toward other children as occasions requiring firm handling. Application of physical punishment often appears related more to vicissitudes in parental mood and patience, the child receiving a cuff for behavior which might well be ignored in another context or at another time. Some parents show remarkable indulgence of their child's aggressiveness. One father was noticed to tolerate a long period during which his four-year-old son hit him repeatedly in the face while he was watching a dance. Aggressive retaliation sometimes seems an afterthought to appease Europeans who happen to be present. Excessively firm punishment on the other hand seemed to correlate well with character disorder of an aggressive type in the parents. As one might expect from the Aboriginal concept of the good man, fathers are more tolerant and permissive than mothers. This disparity may become the cause of marital quarreling; the father hits the mother because the latter has struck the child.

Special mention must be made of the use of ridicule by adults and also older siblings, children, and peers. A child who transgresses or irritates may be derogated as "a bloody big-nose" with emphasis on physical clumsiness or ugliness. One mother spoke of this with distaste as a manifestation of the values of lower-class village families. Children are universally vulnerable to loss of self-esteem and teasing is very much a part of their life in the peer group. One is impressed with the ubiquity of the phenomenon in the mission school situation and with the violence of the reaction by some of the victims. The teacher remarked on the disciplinary problem that arose on this account. Despite these observations there was little evidence of peer discrimination against children of mixed blood, of non-Lardil parents, or from irregular or illegitimate parent unions.

The nagging wife is familiar in any ethnic group, but cultural transition has given rise to special stress in interparental relationships. Where the father by virtue of lack of talent or inertia has been unable to lift his family above subsistence level, and the wife has strong aspirations toward European values, the whole family is affected by parental role-reversal, submission or self-deprecation of the father and emasculation of paternal authority. One outcome is the sexual acting out by the adolescent sons of their basic hostilities toward females, combined with efforts to avoid the responsibility of lasting emotional ties.

Supervised sports are available for the older children at school but there is a lack of communal organization and external challenge sufficient to generate organized team games amongst adolescents. To some extent bushcraft, hunting and fishing with spear and line, fulfills this role, although the first of these skills is dying rapidly. Most are expert anglers by middle childhood. Of the traditional artistic pursuits, singing and dancing alone have retained the interest of the younger people. The most popular Western art forms are country-style music and cowboy films, a reflection of the aspirations of most young men.

Children commence their formal education at the age of five years when they attend the preschool for half-days in company with six- and seven-year-old first graders. There are two trained teachers, the headmaster and his assistant, for 125 pupils including preschool children. Their work is assisted by three untrained but responsible female Aboriginal monitors. Virtually no individual remedial work is possible. Provision is made for brighter children in later school grades to attend boarding school on the mainland. Observation of the classroom suggests a general distractability and "squirminess" more intense than in the comparable Western situation. This necessitates rapid variations of subject material by the teacher in order to sustain interest and concentration.

Few seem able to coordinate pencil and paper for drawing until the age of eight years or later. The major area of difficulty is in the acquisition of number concepts. Basic reading skills and the learning of songs and tables are comparatively satisfactory but few surmount the difficulty associated with hypothetical arithmetic. As a consequence many are educationally retarded and must repeat years in the basic grades. To some extent the recently introduced Cuisenaire method of teaching arithmetic has helped.

The children from the Bentinck enclave form a distinct group. Apart from their bilinguality, they are noticeably timid, shy, and fearful. Not long ago the teacher proposed a launch trip for the junior classes. The rest of the children boarded the boat with eagerness but the Bentinck Island children refused. Some were afraid even to go out on the jetty —surprising behavior in view of the traditional association of the Kaiadilt with the sea. Some of the adolescent Kaiadilt schoolboys have shown tendencies to form an exclusive gang which has been involved in minor episodes of entering and stealing from mission property. The infants' school teacher also suggested that there was a reluctance by Lardil and Kaiadilt children to sit together in class. He commented too on a tendency of children born to mainland parents to regard themselves as of somewhat lower status and to be more provocative, quarrelsome, and attention-seeking at school.

In the playground choice of playmate is based on sex, from the youngest to the more senior children. Boys play with boys and girls with girls. Kaiadilt children tend to cohere. There is no evidence that the dominant Lardil group has intentionally excluded mainland or Kaiadilt children.

As a test of the children's aspirations, thirty-nine of the older children, ranging in age from ten to fourteen years, were asked to write answers to the following questions:

(1) If you could make a wish, what job would you have when you grow up?
(2) What job do you think you will really do when you grow up?

The answers divided the subjects into three groups:

(a) Five children who gave disparate answers to the two questions.
(b) Thirty-two who gave answers which were the same.
(c) Two children who gave answers which were the same but had the quality of wish fulfilment—"pilot" and "lady doctor" respectively.

The children in group (a) with disparate answers did not show grossly unrealistic aspirations. The fantasied occupations were nurse (2), and sailor, stockman, teacher (each 1).

The children in the largest group (b) showed the following distributions: stockman 9, nurse 6, carpenter 4, mechanic 4, sailor 3, housegirl 2, office girl 1, typist 1, gardener 1, railway worker 1.

All the above occupations are within reasonable limits of aspiration, although few will attain an educational level adequate for vocations such as stenography or nursing.

The two children in group (c) are interesting. The girl, aged twelve, appears to have had a school phobia in 1964. Her father died six months before our visit in 1966 and the mother had lost an infant child within the last three years. The boy, aged fourteen, is an aggressive and provocative youth at school and in the village. Both children were indicated by European informants, independently of the case-finding questions, to show behavioral disturbances (see cases 18 and 23, chapter 9).

The low aspiration level and the lack of disparity between fantasy and realistic expectancy are impressive. This low horizon has been created by cultural deprivation, leading to lack of experience of a variety of people in different occupations, and by economic stress, with resultant group expectation of an early school-leaving age and of employment in work regarded by Europeans as of low status. Low motivation and low aspiration, low parental expectancy, cultural deprivation, and environmental hindrances to study and reading independently of school all contribute to a network that entraps the child in a generally poor school performance.

The one important social organization catering to adolescents is the church fellowship. Apart from its religious purpose the fellowship aims to encourage cohesion and group interaction. The work of the group leaders is made difficult by the mutual shyness of the two sexes in this age group. Few adolescents seem able to sustain conversation for long and the intersexual tension, already evident in late childhood, continues into young adulthood.

The difficulties associated with the subsection or "skin" system have been described. They have affected the Kaiadilt especially, since there is a shortage of unmarried men. It undoubtedly has something to do with the high illegitimacy rate amongst young females of this group, for marriage has not occurred between the Kaiadilt and their neighbors. In any event it is doubtful if Lardil people would encourage intermarriage with what they consider a lower caste group.

Children who grow up in the human warmth and contact of village life could not remain sexually ignorant. By adolescence, all have a knowledge of the basic facts of external anatomical differences, pregnancy, childbirth, and menstruation. One suspects that the growth of sexual understanding remains at the level of concreteness and action. There is a reticence to discuss these matters both between the sexes and between older and unmarried people. Some mothers fob their inquiring children off with a fable of the pelican—an adaptation of the stork story—to inhibit questions about pregnancy and childbirth.

108

It is in this area of sexual education that gaps left by the passing of the traditional initiation system can be detected. The older methods related basic factual knowledge to the more abstract values of a coherent tribal society. At the present time, what amounts to pre-verbal concepts must await adolescent peer group discussion for validation. Some time ago films on sex education were shown to segregated audiences. They were well received, particularly by the parents who had been struggling with problems of communication.

Sweetheart relationships in adolescence and serious courting are hampered for various reasons. Even if the parents approve of the relationship the young couple may have to keep tryst on the beach or in the bush. There is nowhere for them to go in the village, and a public display of affection would arouse the ridicule of the onlookers. For these reasons the superintendent endeavored to arrange for couples intending marriage to meet in his living room; unfortunately it was found that the young people spent miserable, speechless, self-conscious evenings together. They felt apparently even more exposed than before and lacked the conversational expertise to carry off the situation.

In summary, generalizations emerge from these observations and need to be kept in mind in the ensuing presentation of the patterns of psychological disturbance in this community. The child-rearing environment is characterized by close population, lack of privacy, large family size, and a tendency for childhood peer groups to cohere beyond the control of overtaxed parents. This problem is intensified by the enforced absence of some of the fathers. Basic subsistence is ensured by Australian authority, communal sharing, support of the extended family, and the abundance of fish. Economic privation is probably most felt where aspirations to acquire the material benefits of the surrounding European culture are highest. The community is loosely cohesive but in times of stress tends to fragment into factions, the Windward and Leeward Lardil and the two out-groups, the mainland outsiders and the relatively exclusive and primitive Bentinck Islanders. Despite the existence of Aboriginal councillors and policemen there is a relative absence of authoritative leadership. There is a general acceptance of and dependence upon Western medical and obstetrical methods. Breast-feeding tends to be relatively prolonged. It is provided on demand and is used mainly for pacification.

Children are handled indulgently, permissively, and with warmth. There is little parental check on emotional expression. Physical punishment, when used at all, tends to be inconsistent. Behavior controls are predominantly social. Ridicule and shame appear more prominent than internalized conscience and guilt. There is a marked interpersonal sensitivity and vulnerability.

Education is hampered initially by poor acquisition of language and later by difficulties in adopting an abstract attitude to number concept and hypothetical arithmetic. Rote learning is unimpaired. These results are probably related to cultural deprivation in the preschool years, and in Piaget's (1957) terms, to a delay in transition from the preoperational level of cognitive development to the level of concrete operations. More speculatively it may be hypothesized that rudimentary development of internal controls leads to poor tolerance of frustration and delay in gratification. Without these, abstract thinking is greatly impaired. Occupational aspirations tend to be low and formal education to finish at the statutory school-leaving age. Most are destined to work on the mainland. There is an absence of spontaneously evolved community organizations for adolescents. The old bushcraft skills are dying; fishing, singing, and dancing retain only token interest.

Intersexual relationships, during adolescence and early adulthood, are characterized by distance, separation, and tension. Basic sexual knowledge is not related to wider social values, although the traditional marriage and kinship laws are still applied in the transitional context. This may represent a reactionary attempt on the part of older people to hold fast to some immutables in a changing society.

THEORETICAL PROBLEMS IN TRANSCULTURAL CHILD PSYCHIATRY

The interest that has been shown in the influence of child-rearing practices, both normative and deviant, on the personality of the child in various societies has been prompted largely by psychoanalysis. It is of central importance in dynamic psychiatry. It has been a major stimulus to developments in anthropology, sociology, and education. On the other hand there have been few transcultural studies of psychiatric disorder in children; indeed prevalence studies amongst the children of Western societies are notably few.

Why is transcultural child psychiatry so undeveloped? The reasons are various. Not least of them is the undeveloped state of child psychiatry, which established its identity during the past fifty years and is still in a stage of formulation. There is indecision over the conceptualization of the syndromes of psychological disturbance during the stages of early childhood. Here one is faced with the relativity of many disorders. What upsets one parent or subculture may be of no concern to another. What is a severe deviation at one level of development may be normal, even desirable at another. In addition, indirect methods of communication are necessitated with younger children and reliance must be placed on the report of observers. All these difficulties are accentuated when transcultural studies are attempted.

From a theoretical viewpoint the criteria for psychological disturbance may come from five sources: the child (unlikely); the parents, especially the mother; an informant belonging to the same transcultural society, such as a native practitioner; a transcultural observer highly involved in the society, such as a mission superintendent; a trained transcultural observer less highly involved in the society, such as a psychiatrist or anthropologist. In other words the criteria, which

This chapter originally appeared in slightly different form as "Patterns of Behaviour Disorder amongst the Children of an Aboriginal Population," *The Australian & New Zealand Journal of Psychiatry* (1967) 1:119.

may be individual, familial, societal, or transcultural, tend to emphasize disorders involving action (such as over-aggressiveness, stealing, sexual delinquency) or inhibition of action (such as gross withdrawal, marked timidity) at the expense of those causing private stress without remarkable overt manifestation (such as obsessional neurosis).

Observations on cultural relativity notwithstanding, it is likely that some disorders will be recognized universally as pathological. Amongst these are severe intellectual retardation, organic brain damage, failure of acquisition of speech, severe convulsive disorder, psychosis of childhood, and severe psychosomatic disability. A highly permissive society may, on the other hand, be able to tolerate such deviations as late acquisition of habit control, frequent temper tantrums, or social timidity of a degree insupportable by Western parents.

When a society is in a state of cultural change the relativity problem becomes more complex. Some parents or subgroups may have identified partially or wholly with Western values. On Mornington Island where the Western medical approach is highly regarded, particularly in the field of obstetrics and infant care, the more "responsible" parents —usually those with the highest degree of acculturation—had no difficulty in indicating children who had nocturnal enuresis, poor school achievement, breathholding attacks, or who were either too aggressive and disobedient, or excessively shy, shrinking, and immature.

Experience shows that clinical disease entities and the usual criteria for their diagnosis cannot be used conclusively in transcultural studies of mental disorder. Because of difficulties engendered by Western systems of classification, some transcultural psychiatrists utilize an anthropological classification adapted to the culture, or try to utilize a transcultural psychopathological classification. But these systems refer to adults; the special needs of children have received less attention. The major patterns of behavior which cause concern to parents or society have been summarized by Sherwin and Schoelly (1965) and in the Group for the Advancement of Psychiatry (G.A.P.) publication, "Psychopathological Disorders in Childhood" (1966).

There are two polar approaches to fieldwork. One may wait and by gradual stages learn something of the indigenous concept of what represents psychopathology. This is time-consuming and by no means free of contamination by the very fact of participant observation. On the other hand one may work by taking a census of morbidity from various observers who act as cross-referent checks on one another, confirming this by interview with the children and parents indicated. The latter approach was employed in the Mornington Island study.

The diagnosis of psychiatric disorder in childhood relies upon information from several sources: the nature and development of the presenting complaint to the clinician; the developmental history of the

112

disorder; the patterns of interparental and parent-child interaction and of the relationship between the family and the wider society; and an examination of the child, both physical and psychological, sometimes with the aid of special tests. An ideal diagnostic formulation would integrate the data from all these sources and communicate the following information: the major symptom-complex; the aetiological factors; the degree to which the disorder is reactive and reversible or, on the other hand, internalized and self-perpetuating; the degree of impairment; and lastly, the prognosis. The classification should also be appropriate to the society in which the child is living. A purely descriptive label is inadequate and must be deepened and extended by a dynamic and genetic formulation.

In order to assist our observations on Mornington Island the following nosology was developed, utilizing where appropriate the categories suggested by the G.A.P. (1966).

(a) *Healthy Responses.* Referring to normal, adaptive, transient, and self-limited behavioral responses to developmental or accidental stress.

(b) *Reactive Disorders.* Characterized by pathological, maladaptive behavioral responses to acute or chronic psychological stress, responses which are potentially reversible if the stress is removed or modified.

(c) *Developmental Deviations.* A group of disorders, often with an important biological component, involving a pathological delay in, acceleration of, or deviation from, all or specific aspects of normal development.

(d) *Anxiety-Inhibition Syndromes.* Characterized by marked shyness, inhibition of motor action or initiative, tenseness or apprehension in new situations, and proneness to view the environment as threatening. These children may remain dependent, clinging, and infantile into the school years. In many cases they retain anachronistic infantile habits as well.

(e) *Tension-Discharge Syndromes.* Characterized by chronic behavioral patterns involving the expression of aggressive, acquisitive, or sexual impulses which conflict with the norms of society. These children tend to act impulsively in frustrating circumstances, exhibiting poor inner controls without marked overt anxiety, and to be repeatedly in conflict with parental or social authority.

(f) *Personality Disorders.* A diagnosis restricted to preadolescent children and continuous with (d) and (e), often developing out of earlier behavioral patterns which are less organized. It refers to a variety of chronic, pervasive, and fixed pathological trends ingrained in personality structure and often not recognized as deviant or distressing by the child himself.

(g) *Psychoneurotic Disorders.* Structured psychological disorders

The children in difficulties   113

involving unconscious internal conflict and tending to constellate into a number of subclasses: anxiety, phobic, conversion, dissociative, obsessive-compulsive, and depressive.

(h) *Psychophysiologic Disorders.* Involving chronic dysfunction and eventual structural damage to organ systems and in which there is a major psychogenic component.

(i) *Psychotic Disorders.* Characterized by severe delay in, or fragmentation of, ego development, and gross incapacity or deviation in the development of object relationships.

(j) *Brain Syndromes.* A variety of behavioral responses to acute or chronic impairment of brain tissue function.

(k) *Educational Retardation.* Children who are scholastically two or more grades retarded, according to chronological age.

(l) *Severe Mental Retardation.* Severe impairment of intellectual functioning.

(m) *Traditional Disorder.* Children known to have suffered from a disorder ascribed to the traditional system of pathology (see *malgri*).[1]

This type of diagnostic formulation does not provide the complexity and depth of a full psychodynamic understanding. It does however involve the beginning of an aetiological conceptualization. All the above categories imply something about causation although not to the same degree. All offer some precision as to phenomenological presentation.

In cases where psychogenic factors are important one must investigate the patterns of relationship between mother and child and in particular possible interruptions in that relationship. Information is required also of the interaction between father and child, between the parents themselves, and of the functioning of the family unit in transaction with the wider society. Beyond this one must comprehend the characteristics of the culture, the ideals and values shared by the whole society. All these influences find a final common path in the child-rearing practices of the individual family and will be reflected in the world-view of the child himself.

The task is even more challenging when the society is exposed to Western influence or is in some conflict with a surrounding dominant culture. In this case the traditional values and the values acquired from the other culture interact in an equilibrium of varying stability. It is imperative that an attempt be made to reconstruct the traditional methods of child-rearing. Without such understanding current practices can be appreciated only in a foreshortened and imperfect way. Markedly deviant individual child-rearing practices then assume a new meaning; so also may socially "normative" practices which are deleterious or even pathogenic to Western eyes.

1. This culture-specific disorder is described in *Medicine is the Law* (forthcoming).

Transcultural child psychiatry is likely to yield information with various applications. It offers an immediate practical utility to a country which is beginning to come to terms with the problems of incorporating an ethnic minority group. Beyond this, it opens up theoretical questions of basic importance to psychiatry. Psychological disorder in adulthood is the terminus of a longitudinal development, the result of interaction between inherited and biological factors, characteristics acquired as the result of experience during childhood and adolescence, and stresses encountered in later life. In many syndromes the relative importance of these factors is a matter of controversy. As Murphy and Leighton (1965) suggest, the objective of transcultural psychiatry is no longer to prove that culture is a major cause, but rather to ask what kind of cause it is.

The patterns of behavioral choice available to a human being are not infinite in number. It is for this reason that clinicians are able to define various syndromes or diagnostic entities. The transcultural psychiatrist may investigate and compare the characteristics of these syndromes in different societies. He must find which syndromes are universally valid. He will note the disorders that have a universal prevalence. He will remark those that have high incidence such as anxiety-inhibition syndromes amongst Kaiadilt children, or a low incidence, such as psychoneurotic disorders on Mornington Island. He is especially interested in syndromes which are specific to the culture, such as *malgri*. These observations form the basis for further studies designed to elucidate causes.

If longitudinal studies commence at an early age they will lead to a clearer understanding of the manner in which sociocultural factors contribute to psychological disorder. The family is a microcosm of society. The child's experiences within it lay a foundation for his relationship with the wider community, his identity as an adult, and his view of the world. His development is the path upon which inherited, biological, interpersonal, and social influences converge. It is here that the operation of these influences can be viewed with greatest clarity.

THE CHILDHOOD PSYCHIATRIC MORBIDITY CENSUS

A list of common symptoms, described simply and by intention rather imprecisely, was prepared for presentation to various members of the European staff and to a council of the leading men and women of the indigenous population. (See table 11.) The list was prepared on the basis of previous field experience with Aborigines and corresponds with a similar list for adults (see chapter 5). The children who were indicated by this procedure, and their parents, were interviewed by the child psychiatrist. Knowledge of the family background was augmented by information from the mission staff.

Table 11. The Childhood (to Age 15) Psychiatric Morbidity Census

SYMPTOMS	INDICATED BY ABORIGINAL INFORMANTS	INDICATED BY EUROPEAN INFORMANTS
1. DULL, backward, slow learner	10	10
2. CONFUSED, forgetful, gets lost	—	—
3. EPILEPTIC, takes fits, has blackouts	2	4
breath-holder	6	—
4. OVERACTIVE, restless	8	—
5. CRIPPLED, paralyzed, many burns, blind, deaf, deformed	4	2
6. SPEECH DIFFICULTIES, stammer, dumb, baby talk	4	6
7. QUARRELSOME, many fights with play-mates, tantrums	8	7
8. DISOBEDIENT to parents or teachers, very cheeky	7	4
9. TRUANT, refuses to go to school	3	3
10. THIEF	7	8
11. RUNS AWAY, has to be found	2	—
12. BABYISH, won't compete, won't defend himself, cry baby	6	3
13. POOR CONTROL OF BLADDER OR BOWEL	5	6
14. CHILDISH HABITS, thumbsucking, nail biting, hair pulling	1	5
15. EATING PROBLEMS, too much, too little	2	1
16. FEARFUL, shy, timid, afraid	3	5
17. COMPLAINING, many aches and pains	1	4
18. SLEEP PROBLEMS, nightmares, sleep walking, insomnia	3	1
19. MAGIC, reputedly suffers from	2	2
20. WITHDRAWN, does not play with others	5	—
21. MISCELLANEOUS	—	3
Total	64[a]	58[b]

a. 46 males; 18 females.
b. 36 males; 22 females.

European and Aboriginal informants indicated roughly equal numbers of children. The totals given in table 11 exclude cases indicated more than once. There is a high degree of concordance between them for individuals designated as showing some forms of behavior difficulty. The major differences are as follows:

Aboriginal informants in item 3 named as "taking fits" six children who are in fact breath-holders. None of these was known to the

Europeans. Aboriginal informants named eight children (six boys and two girls) who are restless and cause problems to the wider community because of their overactivity. These were not indicated by the Europeans.

In items 8 (disobedient), 12 (babyish), and 20 (withdrawn), Aboriginal informants named roughly twice as many children as did Europeans. These differences can probably be accounted for on the basis of greater familiarity by the Aborigines with the behavior of the children in the village.

In items 6 (speech difficulties), 14 (childish habits), and 17 (complaining), Europeans in the school and hospital situation showed more sensitivity to the children's behavior.

In item 21 (miscellaneous), the headmaster indicated three children who did not fit any of the prescribed categories. Two are children prone to daydream excessively in school and one is an effeminate boy.

The preponderance of boys, more marked in the cases named by Aboriginal informants, is related to the clustering of males in items 4 (overactive), 7 (quarrelsome), and 8 (disobedient). There is a considerable overlap among these three categories.

Some general comments can be made about the indirect census method. The response by both European and Aboriginal informants was extremely good. The latter proved the more sensitive, in some areas particularly. Psychiatric examination of the children and an assessment of family background generally confirmed the opinions of both sets of informants. Amongst the Europeans the most sensitive were the nursing sister and the school teachers. The preponderance of males bears out the experience of most child psychiatric services, where the ratio of males to females is about 2 : 1. This leads to the observation that indirect census methods are more likely to indicate those disorders of behavior which cause concern in the wider community. In some degree individual problems or problems of concern to the immediate family will be overlooked. This is partially offset by the communal sharing of problems and the lack of privacy in the village, compared with a middle-class European community.

After individual children were indicated by informants, they were interviewed together with one or both parents. They were physically examined and where appropriate the parent was invited to discuss the child's behavior. Parental responses varied; some were unable to communicate, some seemed oblivious of the alleged difficulty, some were resistant and denying while still others were eager to seek help for what they themselves recognized as a problem. Information as to family background was obtained from the European staff. Diagnoses were then assigned (see tables 12 and 13). In the time available it was possible to examine fifty-three children. Three were excluded as not abnormal, for example two three-year-old bed-wetters.

Physical examination revealed a high incidence of chronic upper respiratory tract infection. Four cases of partial deafness resulting from otitis media were discovered. There is no doubt that special techniques would uncover more cases of hearing deficit.

In all cases a primary diagnosis was essayed. It proved rather arbitrary in a small number of children with multiple deviations. An example will indicate the type of difficulty.

CASE 1. L. O., AGE 5 YEARS, KAIADILT

This boy's father, B. O., died tragically in late 1965, at the end of a period of depression and decline ascribed by his people to the breach of a powerful taboo. The mother, aged thirty years, is a dependent woman regarded as an incompetent housewife by the mission staff. She is supported by a widow's pension administered by the missionary. The maternal grandmother is supportive and has tended to infantilize L. O.; her overprotectiveness has probably been intensified since the father's death. L. O. has always been a sickly child. Chronic upper respiratory tract infection with recurrent otitis media has resulted in partial deafness. For about two years he has had frequent hospital admissions following grand mal convulsions. He is timid and shrinking, having little speech which appears to be used only with his near family. A chronic thumb-sucker and bed-wetter, he is grossly immature in comparison with his peers. A primary diagnosis of brain syndrome (epilepsy) was made. In addition to this he has a hearing deficit and developmental deviations (thumb-sucking, enuresis) which are part of a more extensive anxiety-inhibition syndrome. One might have diagnosed him primarily in this category, adding further to the marked Kaiadilt tendency to exhibit this behavioral pattern (see table 12).

It is appropriate at this stage to give further clinical illustrations of how primary diagnoses were derived.

Reactive Disorders

This category refers to those pathological behavior patterns which are a response to stress either acute or cumulative, and which tend to be reversible when the stress is relieved or eliminated.

CASE 2. K. U., AGE 11 YEARS, LARDIL

The U. family underwent a series of difficulties during 1964 and 1965. The oldest daughter became illegitimately pregnant to another Islander. Marriage was prevented by the rigid adherence of the families to the kinship system. In the same period there were two more misadventures. The mother had a stillbirth and in late 1965 her youngest child died. K. became hypochondriacal during this period. She complained

118

frequently of aches and pains during the day. There were several attacks of acute abdominal pain in the morning before going to school and K. was reluctant to separate from her mother. These complaints have disappeared during the past six months and she presents no overt behavior problem at present. Mrs. U. is regarded as a responsible and competent woman. She became violent and hostile while concerned about her oldest daughter. Mr. U. died recently. He is described as having been stolid, taciturn, and prone to avoid work. Despite this recent loss the family has regained cohesion. Mrs. U. impresses as a sensitive and intelligent person. K. is charming and friendly at interview although she says little. According to the mother she is well now.

The data in this case indicate severe environmental stress affecting a whole family, and concomitant behavioral disturbance in the child which proved reversible. Improvement has been maintained despite recent difficulty.

Developmental Deviations

Cases in this category showed speech disorder, nocturnal enuresis, and chronic thumb-sucking. There was one case of mild stammering. The remainder of the speech cases showed dyslalia.

CASE 3. J. D., AGE 6 YEARS, LARDIL

This boy was indicated by the school teacher as having poor acquisition of English and being hampered by poor pronunciation. Examination revealed a hand-sucking child with a multiple dyslalia of infantile quality. He is the youngest of a large family. Both parents are middle-aged and considered either dull or of low competence. The father does no work. Cognitive testing suggested dullness. The family lives by child endowment, the help of relatives, and desultory fishing.

In those cases where the developmental deviation is only one of a broad constellation of behavioral symptoms the primary diagnosis should refer to the more inclusive disorder.

Anxiety-Inhibition Syndrome

This term refers to a behavioral pattern of anxiety, social timidity, inhibition of initiative, and protracted dependency.

CASE 4. H. H., AGE 6 YEARS, KAIADILT

This child was born on Mornington Island to Bentinck Island parents. She was brought to the teacher's attention because of her refusal to separate from her mother when first commencing school. She has remained timid, fearful, almost mute, and lacking in initiative. She seems afraid of new situations and strangers. The father is poorly assimilated culturally, but skilled in handcraft, aggressive, and something of a leader amongst his own people. He recently hit the mother on the cheek with an axe during a quarrel. The mother is tribally oriented, very hard to make emotional contact with, and apparently timid and withdrawing. Three of her five pregnancies ended in miscarriage or stillbirth due to preeclamptic toxemia.

CASE 5. M. H., AGE 7 YEARS, LARDIL

M. refused to go to school during his first year and had a period when threatened separation from the mother led to recurrent abdominal pains. He repeated grade I and is now settled in grade II although often dreamy, "far away," and self-absorbed. He mixes poorly and avoids competitive or aggressive play. The father is an expert didjeridoo (dronepipe) player who has otherwise not been successful. He is a moody sensitive man who reproaches himself for not being able to raise the economic level of his family. The mother is a querulous person beset by the problems of a large family. M. is the youngest of eight children. He was delivered by caesarian section, in the mother's middle age, because of breech presentation and preeclamptic toxemia.

Tension-Discharge Syndrome

The considerable variety of cases in this category shows uncontrolled aggressive outbursts and/or chronic thieving as the dominant behavioral pattern. These children are characterized by the "acting out" of impulsive drives with little tolerance for delay in gratification and little overt anxiety.

CASE 6. B. C., AGE 6 YEARS, MAINLAND

This child was described by the teacher as very attention-seeking. She is aggressive and provocative to other children and indignant if they react in kind, tending to tell tales and hold grudges. She is a nail-biter. She is said to be rejected by other children partially because of her low status as a "mainlander." The parents are young and recently arrived back at Mornington Island after being unable to hold their own economically on the mainland. They are cared for by elderly kinfolk. The young mother is probably dull, certainly inadequate to cope with the responsibilities of independent life but generally attentive to her children and dependent on her husband. Two siblings died as a result of pelvic obstruction during labor. This child's speech and pronunciation are poor. Cognitive testing confirmed the clinical suspicion of dullness.

CASE 7. S. U., AGE 14 YEARS, MAINLAND

A defiant and aggressive boy who has been verbally abusive to female teachers or monitors who thwart him. In many ways he seems reliable and well adjusted but he harbors a grudge against "white bastards." He is regarded by the village community as a disobedient "tearaway." There is marked interparental conflict in this family. The father is abnormally sexually jealous, cranky, and morose. He often accuses his wife of infidelity and maligns her in front of the family.

CASE 8. B. S., AGE 13 YEARS, MAINLAND

This boy was mentioned by European staff and Aboriginal informants as a chronic and compulsive thief. His ten-year-old sister is also regarded as unreliable in this way. B. S.'s mother was first widowed in 1946. She developed a psychotic illness after this but recovered with residual neurotic symptomatology. She had two illegitimate children before a second marriage to a man who died in 1961. She is regarded as an intelligent woman with strong erotic and dependent needs. Four years ago Mrs. S. married an older man who is described as a "cunning and lazy old manipulator." He does no work and relies on his kinfolk for support. At examination B. proved to have a unilateral deafness. He was aloof, sullen, and downcast. Later contact on the beach and in the school yard revealed unsuspected facets of spontaneity, charm, and desire for contact with an adult male figure. This boy's conduct disorder is probably related to affectional and maternal deprivation beginning at a time when the mother was severely disturbed and in need of external emotional support and continuing up to the present. Cognitive testing revealed an ability well above the average despite his poor school progress.

CASE 9. O. M., AGE 11 YEARS, KAIADILT

This boy was born of Bentinck parents on Mornington Island. His father suffers from a chronic depressive disorder. His mother is subdued, withdrawn, and unable to supervise her older children. O. M. in company with a gang of other Bentinck lads ranges over the island much more widely than his parents and has been involved in several episodes of entering and stealing from mission property. He is beyond the effective control of his parents.

CASE 10. F. K., AGE 7 YEARS, MAINLAND

The teacher described F. as very bright but quarrelsome, teasing, provocative, and spiteful. She is intensely competitive and resentful of anyone who does better at school. The mother was born on the mainland but was separated from her own mother when an infant and reared in the Mornington Island dormitories. F. is the third of three illegitimate children born before the mother's marriage. Two more children have been born since the marriage. Mrs. K. is a mercurial and vivacious woman liable to become abusive, hostile, and hypochondriacal under stress. There has been periodic interparental conflict with mutual accusations of adultery. This child's above-average intelligence was confirmed by cognitive testing. Her aggressiveness is probably derived in part from identification with parental behavior patterns and also possibly from sibling rivalry problems in the immediate family.

Personality Disorder

This category is used where the behavioral deviation has become chronic, pervasive, and ingrained.

CASE 11. D. O., AGE 11 YEARS, LARDIL

Described by the head teacher as attention-craving, effeminate, preferring to play with girls rather than boys, sometimes dressing in female attire, this child is apt to linger around the mission doing small things for the European staff rather than to range farther afield with his peers. At interview D. is an oddly genteel boy with softly modulated speech. He made good verbal contact. He and his younger brother are the last of seven siblings. The father, a blind man, died three years ago. The mother remarried a year ago and has been absent from her children for three years working on the mainland. They are cared for by a friend of the family who considers D. "a good boy" but says he misses his mother very much and "frets himself sick." This boy's personality deviation shows a confusion of psychosexual identity and depression following separation from both parents.

CASE 12. D. M., AGE 11 YEARS, LARDIL

D. M. is known as a "cry baby," a target for teasing, and as unable to defend herself; nevertheless she seldom seeks the teacher's protection. Her mother has been known to take up cudgels on her behalf. Mrs. M. is a formidable and aggressive woman. She is abnormally sexually jealous, and there are many quarrels between the parents. Apart from this she is an attentive, conscientious, and competent parent. The father is an amiable, rather irresponsible man. At interview D. was mute, shrinking, and withdrawn. Physical examination revealed an asymptomatic cardiac valvular lesion, probably rheumatic in origin. She has a passive-dependent personality, aggression-inhibited, and regressive. The dynamics are uncertain, but the overprotection of a dominant mother is probably a significant factor.

122

CASE 13. W. C., AGE 12 YEARS, LARDIL

Although not dull this girl often appears backward due to her lethargy, lack of vivacity, and periods of vacancy and daydreaming. She has withdrawn from her peers to some extent, avoids competition, and is described by her father as timid, fearful, and suffering from nightmares. The father is a respected and intelligent man, but taciturn and rather morose. He keeps his temper under control although often inwardly irritated by his workmates. The mother has poor emotional control and a reputation for promiscuity which has been the cause of much interparental conflict. Mrs. C. said that W. had always been nervous and is still afraid of animals and old people. She is so disobedient in a passive-aggressive way that she is seldom asked to do anything to help. This girl has the rudiments of a schizoid personality. Both parents have certain schizoid characteristics. There is a suggestion of poor and conflict-laden affective communication between family members.

Psychoneurotic Disorder

This term embraces a variety of structured psychological disorders characterized in the main by a defense against anxiety. Anxiety is however a frequent concomitant. The symptoms are intensified whenever anxiety increases.

CASE 14. Q. C., AGE 7 YEARS, MAINLAND and CASE 15. N. C.,
AGE 12 YEARS, MAINLAND

This brother and sister are quarrelsome children. They are well known to the teachers and nursing sister for their numerous physical complaints and tendency to exaggerate bodily discomfort. Q. C. has recurrent chest pain which was exacerbated at the time of a recent measles epidemic. N. C. has attacks of abdominal cramps when there is trouble at home. Another brother H. C. (11 years) makes much of pain in an ankle which was once injured and presents a discipline problem. The father is absent working on the mainland for most of the year. It is asserted that he seems to prefer this arrangement. The mother is an intelligent woman but regarded as dramatic, exhibitionistic, and promiscuous. Her last child was the result of an extramarital liaison. For some years she has been subject to hysterical paralyses of the limbs and seizures in time of stress, and for this reason she was forced to discontinue work on the mainland and return to Mornington Island. The two older brothers N. C. and H. C. prefer to live with another family who cared for them previously in their parents' absence. They shuttle between the two households when the restrictions or stresses in one or other become intolerable. At interview the mother seemed intelligent and affectionate but said the children were too much for her. Her most recent hysterical attack coincided with the realization that she was once again pregnant as the result of her husband's return on his Christmas vacation. She was self-preoccupied and gave an involved account of her symptoms. When her children present complaints to her she tells them to go off to see the nursing sister. She added, "I don't know if they get there or not." Both mother and children demonstrate recurrent psychoneurotic episodes of hysterical nature. These can be interpreted as resulting from the conversion of anxiety into physical symptoms. There is a substantial secondary gain, and evidence of identification by the children with the mother's behavior while under stress, in a milieu where the basic needs of all family members are chronically unmet.

Psychophysiologic Disorder

This term refers to dysfunction of bodily systems resulting from an interaction between somatic and psychological components. It is to be distinguished from conversion or hysterical reactions which tend to involve voluntary muscle or special sensory systems and to have a symbolic communicatory significance.

CASE 16. K. E., AGE 14 YEARS, LARDIL

K. was the only obese child in the school. He was subjected to much teasing on this account but was popular owing to his unvarying passive good nature. Several European staff members mentioned that he loved to care for smaller children and was unusually protective toward them. It was suspected that an endocrine abnormality might underly his obesity but this is excluded by the normal development of his genitalia and secondary sexual characteristics. He has a voracious and undiscriminating appetite. His mother is a large, kindly, and maternal woman, still mourning the recent death of her older daughter. Her husband died when K. was about six months of age. She cared for the boy, who is the youngest of the family, until he was eight years of age. At this time economic pressures forced her to leave him in the care of his older sister while she sought work on the mainland. Investigation revealed that he was kept as a knee-child and breast-fed for a prolonged period until her departure—a subject of merriment to his peers at the time. It was after his mother's departure that K. began to overeat and gain weight. At the examination, K. was giggly, immature, and prone to suck his forefingers rather than answer questions despite Mrs. E.'s proddings to "speak up for the doctor." Some months later, during a follow-on visit by another of the team, the boy was suddenly reported ill with a paralyzed left arm and leg. A great fuss was made in the village and he was brought to the hospital where the paralysis proved to be hysterical. It was the day before school was to have recommenced after the long summer vacation. The next night there was a film showing and when the missionary suggested K. could attend he "made it" unaided. In an interview he said he wanted to continue with school and blamed his injury on football. The diagnosis in this case is psychophysiologic disorder: psychogenic overeating and obesity in a passive-dependent adolescent with episodes of conversion hysteria. There are marked oral-dependent fixations related to his mother's infantilization of him until middle childhood. Her overprotection probably arose from her depression at the time of the father's death and from narcissistic identification with K. as a special child. The overeating and obesity may have been a reaction to the breaking of the symbiotic tie in middle childhood.

Educational Retardation

A proportion of the children indicated as retarded at school was examined by the means of the Queensland Test of cognitive functioning (McElwain, Kearney, and Ord, 1970). It is sufficient to state here that school and Queensland Test performances correlated well in the extreme examples given of the brightest and dullest children. No severely mentally defective children were seen nor were any found to be suffering from cerebral palsy or childhood psychosis.

This psychiatric survey though incomplete indicates the major areas of behavior disturbance. It also demonstrates strikingly low incidence or total absence of certain conditions from the diagnostic categories discovered. From the incidence of disorder as tabulated in table 12 some conclusions can be drawn. There is a relatively high incidence of educational retardation. Although this appears to affect the Lardil group most severely, the difference between the groups does not reach statistical significance. No cases of severe mental deficiency were found. There is a concentration of those with tension-discharge disorder in the mainland group, reaching a 0.01 level of statistical significance. In other words there is a distinct tendency for disturbed mainland children to be aggressive, quarrelsome, provocative, and disobedient. There is a striking tendency for Kaiadilt children to show the anxiety-inhibition syndrome, to be timid, shy, fearful, and withdrawing. The difference here reached a 0.01 level of statistical significance. When the more specifically psychogenic disorders are pooled (see table 13) it is shown that mainland and Kaiadilt contribute a disproportionate number of the total (reaching a 0.01 level of significance). Of the total number (280), 27 children (9.7 percent) show some form of psychogenic disorder (see table 13). This appears to be a high level of incidence although figures for the Australian population generally are not available. It is to be noted that this figure excludes educational retardation, epilepsy, sensory defect, and speech disorder.

Table 12. Childhood (to Age 15) Psychiatric Morbidity Census: Diagnostic Categories of Ascertained Cases

PRIMARY DIAGNOSIS	LARDIL	MAINLAND	KAIADILT	TOTAL
Reactive Disorders	1	—	—	1
Developmental Deviations	4	1	—	5
Anxiety-Inhibition Syndrome	1	1	5[a]	7
Tension-Discharge Syndrome	2	9[a]	2	13
Aggressive	2	7	—	9
Acquisitive	—	2	2	4
Sexual	—	—	—	—
Personality Disorder	1	2	—	3
Psychoneurotic Disorder	—	2	—	2
Psychophysiologic Disorder	1	—	—	1
Psychotic Disorder	—	—	—	—
Brain Syndromes (epilepsy)	2	—	—	2
Educational Retardation	14	—	—	14
Severe Mental Retardation	—	—	—	—
Traditional Disorders	—	—	—	2
Total	26	15	7	50
Risk Population	197	45	38	280

a. Significant at the 0.01 level by chi-squared technique using the Yates (1934) correction factor for small numbers.

No cases ascribable to the organic hyperkinetic syndrome were found. This observation is questionable in view of the superficiality of the survey and the lack of neuro-diagnostic aids. There are no cases of psychosis in infancy and childhood, using this term to include such syndromes as early infantile autism, symbiotic psychosis, and childhood or juvenile schizophrenia. This group of conditions is in any case uncommon.

Although there is a small number of children with disorders referable to some degree of emotional deprivation in early life, there are no cases

Table 13. Childhood (to Age 15) Psychiatric Morbidity Census: Psychogenic Disorder in Population Subgroups

PRIMARY DIAGNOSIS	LARDIL	MAINLAND	KAIADILT	TOTAL
Psychogenic Disorder[a]	6	14[b]	7[b]	27
Risk Population	197	45	38	280

a. Includes diagnostic categories: reactive disorders; anxiety-inhibition syndrome; tension-discharge syndrome; personality disorder; psychoneurotic disorder; psychophysiologic disorder.

b. Significant at 0.01 level by chi-squared technique using the Yates (1934) correction factor for small numbers.

126

of the affectionless psychopathy described by Bowlby (1952). Most striking of all is the scarcity of disorders with overt psychoneurotic symptomatology. Most of the tension-discharge, anxiety-inhibition, and personality disorders show the rudiments of psychoneurosis, but there are no individuals with well-evolved obsessive-compulsive, phobic, or dissociative syndromes or with free-floating anxiety states.

While these observations warrant further investigation and testing, it is justifiable at this stage to offer some tentative hypotheses. The clustering of psychogenic syndromes amongst the mainland and Kaiadilt children is predictable in view of the background of these two minority groups. The mainlanders who are much more diverse in origin are less cohesive, seeking recognition by means of more individual techniques. In some cases the social reasons for family migration from mainland to Mornington are "pathological," for example alcoholism, inability to cope economically, family disintegration. There is evidence that many feel vulnerable to rejection by the dominant Lardil group and threatened by the periodic internecine strife between Windward and Leeward factions. The appearance of conduct disorders amongst the mainland children may therefore be the expression of a need to rely on egocentric aggressive and attention-seeking maneuvers, characteristic of the mainland group generally.

By the same token, the striking incidence of pre-neurotic behavior disorder with timidity, fearfulness, and resistance to change amongst Kaiadilt children seems to arise from the social climate of the Bentinck enclave. The unique history of this group has been described: overpopulation, adverse climatic conditions, and eventual inundation by tidal wave were associated with starvation, killing between hordes, social disintegration, and evacuation from home territory. The family groups surviving the catastrophe cling together in mutual dependency, unable to care for their children without European aid, turning away from a confusing and potentially hostile outer world.

The apparent absence of severe mental deficiency is difficult to explain except in terms of chance in a relatively small risk population (280). The infant mortality rate in the last three years (approximately 4 percent) which is possibly lower than previously may amount in part for this finding. It is very doubtful whether cases of striking mental retardation could have been overlooked by the survey. The high incidence of educational retardation has already been discussed in the section on current child-rearing practices (see chapter 8).

The absence of affectionless psychopathy is probably a tribute to the close attention and contact normally given to their children in early life by Aboriginal mothers, and to the availability of the extended family in cases where separation has occurred through maternal death, desertion, or absence. From a theoretical point of view the relative absence of distinctive psychoneurotic syndromes is highly interesting. These disorders seem very much a part of middle-class Western upbringing, although there is a tendency for the more diffuse personality disorders to replace them. Psychoanalytic theory suggests that psychoneurosis is the result of premature exposure to, or premature suppression of, internal drives in the family context. An unsteady repression of these forces is maintained by an unbalanced development of the superego, which itself is based on identification with certain aspects of the parents. The precarious nature of the repression is revealed by a continuing vulnerability and proneness to anxiety and guilt whenever internal or external stimuli impinge too directly on proscribed areas of the personality. The early development of concepts of goodness, badness, sin, and individual responsibility is a corollary of the high level of self-awareness and superego development in the nuclear middle-class family.

The characteristic Aboriginal tolerance of behavior which would be regarded by Westerners as in need of correction has already been mentioned. By Western standards, internal controls are delayed and possibly based to a large extent on peer identification. Guilt and self-blame are less prominent than shame and social ridicule. Another possible factor is the relative diffusion of identification over a greater number of adult models. The relationship between delay in the development of internal controls and retardation of conceptual thinking has already been described.

We regard this as a pilot study in transcultural child psychiatry. It demonstrates the possibility of identifying children with behavioral disturbances in the field. A nosological system has been devised which may prove to have a wider applicability. The patterns of disturbance which were investigated do not appear qualitatively different from those characteristic of Western society. The major distinction appears to be in the increased prevalence, in this transitional people, of three broad groups of disorders: educational retardation, tension-discharge syndrome, and anxiety-inhibition syndrome.

The same observation very likely applies to other minority groups or emergent societies throughout the world. The evidence suggests that these disorders are related to the effect upon family interrelationships of a breakdown in traditional cultural values following the impact of external acculturation pressures. Further work could focus with profit on the deviant family in a context of cultural change. In such a way child psychiatry can contribute to bridging gaps between anthropology and sociology. It throws light on theoretical issues of great importance to psychiatry. It may also lay a foundation for future practical attempts to meet a growing challenge.

The Sickest Society: The Search for Determinants

ten

We are now in a position to utilize the experiment that nature endowed. The numerical and statistical findings indicate which population has the highest incidence of disorders; this has now to be matched against the environmental factors. In this way a relationship between mental disorder and its environmental determinants may be established: the object of epidemiological research. Since the data place the Kaiadilt at one extreme as the most severely affected subgroup of this population, according to most of the measures we used, their environmental experience becomes the focus.

Not only do the Kaiadilt show a high total incidence of serious mental disorder, they show characteristic varieties and patterns that significantly differ from those of the Lardil and the mainlanders. We may briefly recall those germane to the present purposes. In the census that we conducted, 11 out of the Kaiadilt population of 60 adults were ascertained to have psychiatric disorders of at least moderate severity, compared with 6 mainlanders out of the total of 76 and 15 Lardil out of the total of 142. The initial ascertainments were made by committees of Aboriginal and European assessors and the ascertained individuals then were given psychiatric examinations. The most striking differential that emerged in the patterns of illness was that there were seven cases that could be classified as depressive disorder in the entire population, and all came from the Kaiadilt group—a difference significant at the 0.01 level of probability.

The high incidence of Kaiadilt mental disorder carries through into the new generation, as the separate census of children under fifteen reveals. Of the total of 38 Kaiadilt children 7 show a psychogenic disorder. The mainland children have a still higher incidence; 14 out of the total of 45 manifest a psychogenic disorder. The adjustment of Lardil children is in striking contrast: only 6 out of 197 show a psychogenic disorder. These differences are significant at the 0.01 level of probability.

Although the Kaiadilt and mainland children are conspicuously

129

maladjusted their disorders are of a different kind. Children of the mainland group show predominantly a tension-discharge syndrome characterized by chronic patterns expressing aggressive and acquisitive impulses at odds with the norms of society. The children act impulsively in frustrating circumstances and are repeatedly in conflict with authority. The Kaiadilt children on the other hand display an anxiety-inhibition syndrome characterized by extreme shyness, inhibition of initiative, and apprehension in new situations. The children tend to remain dependent, clinging, and timid into the school years. They are by no means among the duller scholars; if anything, dullness in school is the characteristic of the apparently emotionally adjusted Lardil child.

A comparison of the three populations by means of the census is reliable for the overtly disturbed members of society, but might overlook the neurotic individuals who suffer more privately and create little or no disturbance socially. To detect this group we adapted the Cornell Medical Index for use in the adult population. The questions test whether individuals consider themselves to be suffering from symptoms in the main areas of bodily and psychological functioning. Here, too, the questionnaire indicates the highest level of complaints to be in the Kaiadilt community.

Having established these basic epidemiological data and turning our attention to the environmental setting, we note three broad areas where causal determinants are commonly sought in such situations:

1. Constitutional (genetic) factors.
2. Cultural change pressures coming from without.
3. Social influences ("disintegration") operating from within.

Few suggest, of course, that these classes of information are mutually exclusive, or that causation in psychiatry acts from one sector in a linear way. It is rather a question of where the emphasis should fall. To these areas, arising from our experience of Aboriginal adaptation and its vicissitudes, we would add for consideration a fourth:

4. Human ecology and its stresses.

In examining Kaiadilt epidemiology we shall try to indicate where the emphasis might be placed amongst the four classes or systems of information: genetic, cultural, social, ecological. Before doing so, it is necessary to round out the salient features of the Kaiadilt history.

The recorded history of the Kaiadilt is remarkable but brief. It begins with Lt. Matthew Flinders who, by a chance that he regarded as most unfortunate, made a more extended observation of them than of any other Aboriginal tribe (Flinders, 1814). In the course of his exploration of the Australian coastline in 1802 Flinders had reached the southern waters of the Gulf of Carpentaria when H.M.S. *Investigator* began to leak alarmingly. He was forced to beach the ship for inspection in what is now called Investigator Roads, between Bentinck and Sweers Islands (see map 1). A large number of the planks proved to be in a rotting condition, casting doubt on H.M.S. *Investigator*'s capacity to withstand rough weather. In the days of dismay that followed, Flinders adapted his plans to two complications: his ship's unseaworthiness and the scurvy that afflicted himself and his crew. He abandoned his survey and returned to Sydney via Timor. Meanwhile he delayed long enough to have time ashore on the low coastal islands and to have brief encounters with the natives, who on the whole declined invitations to approach him. These experiences confirmed Carstens' view: "altogether thinly peopled by divers cruel, poor and brutal nations." There may be subtle differences in English vocabulary usage between the eighteenth century and the present; cruel may have had a connotation of crude or indifferent to suffering; brutal of brutish or animal-like. But there is no mistaking the general character of the description.

A comment on Flinders and his times is relevant to this judgment of the Kaiadilt and their congeners. His journal *A Voyage to Terra Australis* is perhaps the best and most scientifically precise account of any great voyage of discovery, of his, or any other era. Judgments of culture and social character were not of a class that Flinders was equipped to make; indeed the existence of a culture among Australian Aborigines as it is appreciated today eluded European observers for generations. Thus, a description of the Kaiadilt as "cruel, poor and brutal" might conceivably be regarded as the casual opinion of an ethnocentric and uninformed European. On the other hand, it is also probable that some human characteristics are universally valid as indicators of success in adaptation. Were the Kaiadilt cruel, poor, and brutal by any standards? Some judges consider them the most primitive people ever encountered on Earth. Certainly they must rank high among the most isolated and excluded, being the last group of coastal Aborigines to come into regular contact with Western society, and being strikingly restricted also in their contacts with other Aborigines, as the genetic study shows.

Flinders' own world was not free of the qualities imputed to the Kaiadilt. On his voyage home with the data of the survey of the Great South Land, he called for provisions at the French island of Mauritius, expecting that his passport would ensure a free passage, only to be interned for seven years. Some of his logs were confiscated. Demoralized by frustration and broken in health, Flinders' eventual homecoming passed unnoticed in the jubilation that followed England's victory in the Napoleonic Wars. Far from receiving acclaim for his achievement he was pensioned so inadequately as to make the preparation of his work for publication a matter of doubt. In good public service tradition he was required to pay the cost of vegetables on which he had fed his scorbutic crew in Timor, and of the cabin lights he had installed for his naturalist and artist. His suggestion for the name of the South Land—Australia—was at the time refused. The great work *A Voyage to Terra Australis,* complete with its astonishing accuracy of cartographic detail, was placed in his hands a few days before his death.

The existence of poverty, cruelty, and brutality in a culture of superior technology is of relevance to its existence in one of inferior technology in that it seems to illustrate its occurrence as a universal condition of mankind. There are cruel, poor, and brutal nations and there are cruel, rich, and brutal nations. Society has made amends to Flinders, the scientist-explorer who named Australia. The new university in South Australia bears his name. The town in Eyre's Peninsula, on the west coast of South Australia where the writer spent his childhood, is usually known by the name Flinders gave it, Streaky Bay; on the map it may be seen more formally as Flinders.

What of the Kaiadilt?

The strategic factor of Kaiadilt human ecology was the difficulty of navigating a raft when no land is visible on the horizon. Although Bentinck Island is part of the Wellesley group, of which Mornington is the largest, it lies over the horizon, separated by a distance of more than twenty miles from Mornington Island and the convenient chain of smaller land masses joining Mornington with the mainland. Voyage by raft between Mornington Island and the mainland could be accomplished without undue loss of life. Voyage by raft from Bentinck Island is a much more difficult and dangerous undertaking, with no land on the horizon to steer by when the strong winds prevailing in the Gulf of Carpentaria blow the raft off course. Consequently the Kaiadilt were more rigorously confined to their homeland in uneasy equilibrium with its natural resources. They were subject to the phenomenon of fluctuating abundance in which periods of plenty and population increase were succeeded by periods of drought and famine when the resources of the island failed to sustain the population that had increased in better times. Overpopulation was controlled at such times by death from starvation or by killing between the hordes in competition for the available food. At a rough estimate the natural resources of Bentinck Island, exploited by the existing technology, could not safely have supported many more than 100 people, certainly less than 150. Without emigration, the Kaiadilt nation was restricted to this size.

The situation of the Kaiadilt thus differed from that of the mainland Aboriginal tribes by the enforced isolation inferred from a consideration of the geography, the limitation of artistic and material culture, and the absence of the dog. The absence of the dog could of course be interpreted in two ways: either they never had any, or the dog succumbed during a previous period of famine. In a land where no large marsupials survived the dog was of no value in the hunt. The extent of this isolation is illustrated by genetic studies as indicated in chapter 2. The Kaiadilt possess no blood group A gene but are rich in the B gene. The converse is true for the Lardil of Mornington Island: unmixed Lardil lack blood group B. Fingerprint patterns show similar differences. Possible explanations for the development of such unusual gene frequencies in adjacent populations must be sought in terms of effective isolation and micro-evolution. If ever a hungry man managed to navigate his raft to the neighboring island it is certain that he rarely managed to leave his genes there.

Kaiadilt isolation continued until after World War II. They recall being terrified by air traffic from the war base established on the mainland at nearby Karumba. At this time they were preoccupied by their own warfare, arising from the subsistence conflict on a drought-stricken island. The women and children foraged the zone between the tide marks for crabs, oysters, and other shellfish. The men speared the larger fish from the edges of reefs and sandbars and peddled their rafts of dried mangrove stems in hunts for dugong and turtle. During the drought the diminished run-off of fresh water may have affected the habits and availability of some of these species. The sparse woodland yielded less yam, water-lily root, lizard, and frog. So they lived through the period when their Lardil neighbors were being exposed to European society in the form of the Presbyterian mission, to some extent protected from the effects of nature's fluctuations.

It is not accurate to say that the Kaiadilt were entirely without Western contact, but it was brief. A fever of unknown origin, "Gulf Fever," seized Burketown around 1870, in the early years of European settlement. About half the population died and survivors took refuge on Sweers Island, across Investigator Roads from Bentinck Island. Here they made what appears on old maps as a town laid out in streets and squares, but which in reality was a briefly occupied quarantine station. In the early years of the century, within living memory of a few Kaiadilt, a white man made an attempt to settle on Bentinck Island with some mainland Aboriginal helpers and to operate a lime kiln. His psychiatric state is open to question. He is remembered for riding around on a horse and shooting at the Kaiadilt with a rifle before he abandoned the island. An incident in 1948 contributed to the Kaiadilt's reputation as a wild, unapproachable, and primitive people. The two Kaiadilt men who were removed by police to Burketown jail tore out their testicles with their fingernails and passed them through the bars of the prison cell (see chapter 5).

In 1947 the missionary from Mornington Island visited Bentinck in response to a request from a Lardil man, Gully Peters, who had been engaged in collecting trepang (*bêche-de-mer*) from Bentinck waters. Gully and his wife Cora had established a relationship with the inhabitants while camped ashore, and had learned their language. They knew that the Kaiadilt were in physical and mental distress. They appeared to be dying out due to killing amongst the bands, inflamed by hunger during the prolonged drought. Gully reported that a man coming back at night from fishing on a reef might be killed for his catch. The band might then kill and eat the dead man's children. The missionary reported subnutrition, dysentery, and chronic chest disease.

The culminating catastrophe came in 1948 in the form of a tidal wave or freak high tide that contaminated the coastal waterholes and made survival so precarious that the missionary decided to remove the Kaiadilt to Mornington Island. This gathering together and evacuation of a frightened, hostile, and disorganized population was accomplished through the diplomacy of Gully and his wife Cora. While an era of regular Western contact began for the Kaiadilt, for Bentinck Island it meant the succession, in the ecological sense, of the human species. Today one may fly low over Bentinck Island in a light aircraft and the only life to be seen is birds: the sea eagles and gannets. The island is deserted and it is hard to imagine it ever supported human life. It seems likely that but for the intervention of Gully Peters and the Presbyterian mission, the Kaiadilt could be as extinct as many other Australian nations including the Tasmanian. Of those evacuated from Bentinck Island, many died shortly after arrival on Mornington Island.

The Kaiadilt enclave on Mornington Island has been described, in physical appearance and in its relationship with the rest of the village, in chapters 2 and 3. (See also fig. 1.) It will be sufficient to say here that it is a motley collection of huts, shelters, and shades, constructed in an impermanent manner from a variety of materials that happened to be at hand. It lines a sandridge between the main Lardil village and the sea, facing down the channel in the general direction of the homeland. Poverty and economic inequality, low Western acculturation and education are most evident from its configuration.

THE FIRST DETERMINANT: CONSTITUTIONAL AND GENETIC FACTORS

The importance of genetic factors for behavioral disturbance is undisputed in entities known to be inherited such as Huntington's chorea, phenylketonuria, and the XYY sex chromosome constitution. The importance of a genetic factor in manic-depressive disorder is fairly widely recognized, and to a lesser extent accepted for some of the conditions contained in the mixed bag clinically labelled as schizophrenia. After this, divergences of opinion in psychopathology become noticeable. Divergences of opinion about the importance of genes in psychiatry have themselves a cultural coloring. Continental European countries, in particular Germany, give them much emphasis together with the delineation of disease-syndromes as the most scientific approach to the raw material of psychiatry. This emphasis is less in North America, where there is more interest in reaction-types and intermediate forms than in disease-entities, and in general a stronger emphasis upon psychodynamic factors in causation.

We have amongst our data observations that the Kaiadilt have distinctive gene frequencies, revealed by the two most direct measures available, blood groups and fingerprints. These indices permit a complete separation of their genotype from that of the Lardil and the mainlanders in this population. We have furthermore in our data the observations that their phenotype, resulting from the interaction of their genotype with the environment, is distinctive and also separates them from the Lardil, on the basis of emotional instability, variously expressed. We must therefore pose the question of whether the Kaiadilt genotype has led to a phenotype characterized by temperamental instability, easy arousal, and poor emotional control, perhaps with a tendency toward quarreling and depression.

This question could have been answered if we were confident that the environmental experience of Kaiadilt and Lardil were comparable. If the two groups of Aborigines had comparable environments, their distinctive phenotypic temperaments could be incriminated as related to their different genotypes. But Mornington and Bentinck islands are in effect different worlds, offering contrasting environmental experiences. Indeed, our problem throws into high relief the whole question of the significance of blood groups and other genetic markers. Are they, as they might seem, infallible guides to human phylogeny, not subject to the environment? This is an assumption commonly made when the distinctive blood groups of Australian Aborigines and Papuans, for example, are taken as evidence of their different origins. Or are persons of certain blood groups more vulnerable to certain diseases or death, with lessened viability on a physical or temperamental (central nervous system) basis?

From our data the possibility that the Kaiadilt genotype is an important factor in their instability cannot be excluded, though it seems unlikely. We have recorded elsewhere an Aboriginal group of comparable size[1] and high incidence of mental morbidity. The Yowera drew their members from surrounding tribes within the past two

1. The Yowera, of east-central Australia, are discussed in *Medicine is the Law* (forthcoming).

generations and are unlikely to have distinctive genotype. (No genetic markers were taken.) On the other hand, they have undergone environmental stresses of the severity that might be classified "community disaster"—as have the Kaiadilt. In the case of the Yowera, their special and gross stresses seem sufficient explanation of their social disintegration and psychiatric morbidity rate.

The distinctive gene frequencies of the Kaiadilt are a reminder to those seeking to understand personality wholly in terms of culture that genetic factors cannot be overlooked. Their distinctive genotype warrants no direct inference of a relationship to their adaptation. But if it had not been distinctive and had in fact resembled that of the Lardil, the position of the environmentalist or culturalist would have been a little more comfortable.

THE SECOND DETERMINANT: CULTURAL CHANGE PRESSURES FROM WITHOUT

During the planning phase of our expedition, before the visit to Mornington Island, we were more interested in the influence of Western culture upon the Aborigines than in other variables in mental morbidity. Culture contact is the influence most emphasized in the Australian literature describing the present condition of the Aborigines (Rowley, 1970). Our acceptance of this point of view at the outset of our work is reflected in our plan to measure various aspects of cultural identity. It was anticipated that certain forms of cultural identity might be found associated with mental ill-health.

We carried out a fairly elaborate attempt to measure cultural identity. We rated all the adults on four scales: acquisition of Western culture, emulation of Western culture, retention of traditional activities, and retention of traditional beliefs. This required computer analysis (see chapter 7) and the results are interesting theoretically for transcultural psychiatry. Some correlations were detected. Acquisition of Western culture was associated with a low incidence of symptoms. Emulation of Western culture was less strongly negatively correlated with symptoms, although in combination with other factors its importance for adjustment emerged. Retention of traditional activities was too closely influenced by age—more marked in old people—for a clear correlation with adjustment to emerge. Retention of traditional beliefs, however, emerged as an important variable in mental health.

The Kaiadilt are characterized by low Western acculturation, but also by high social disintegration. If we restricted our focus to the Kaiadilt we should be unable to determine whether low acculturation or social disintegration was the operative factor for mental disorder. Comparison between Lardil and mainlanders provides a clue here. Their levels of acculturation are similar in duration and extent, but

136

it is the more socially disintegrated mainland community that suffers the higher incidence of mental disorder. This suggests that measures of cultural change such as we made are less specific for mental health, and that the important variables are concerned with social disintegration. Measures of cultural change are interesting and important in that they suggest aspects of cultural change that are salutary, others that are detrimental for mental health.

In the case of the Kaiadilt, as if to confirm the priority to be accorded to factors other than Western cultural influence, we recall that their history indicates that they were sick and socially disintegrated before contact with Western culture. It is different in the case of the displaced and rootless people we called mainlanders. Their symptoms, both individual and social, can obviously be traced more directly to the incursions of Western influence into Aboriginal society.

THE THIRD DETERMINANT: SOCIAL INFLUENCES (DISINTEGRATION) OPERATING FROM WITHIN

It was agreed by all observers on Mornington Island that the subpopulations could be ranked in descending order of social disintegration, with the small group of part-Aborigines at the top (least disintegrated) followed by the Lardil, with the mainland immigrants next and the Kaiadilt far down at the bottom (most disintegrated). The term "social disintegration" is used here in the sense employed and explained by Leighton and Harding et al. (1963) in their analysis of psychiatric symptoms in selected communities. "Social disorganization" or "social fragmentation" are the terms preferred by some anthropologists.

Social disintegration is a reality that may be readily observed even though its components are too complex to quantify easily. It is reflected by certain factors separately and in combination: poor housing, lack of conjoint effort at self-help, lack of a social credit network in which one good turn begets another, unemployment or irregular employment, loss of roles, loss of values, loss of the normal structure of leadership and followership, cultural exclusion as a member of a subordinate minority, racial discrimination—all these factors contribute. In a settled society in which statistics are kept one might look for measures—such as the rates for divorce, delinquency, illegitimacy, suicide, attempted suicide, infant mortality, crimes of violence, failure to cooperate in public health activities, industrial absenteeism—which taken together give a measure of social disintegration. In preliterate society we have evidence that the prevalence of sorcery accusations also gives a measure of social disintegration; it was noted, for example, that sorcery is commoner in dislocated mainland Aborigines than in the more settled Lardil population.

Examples illustrate the Kaiadilt position at the bottom of the scale of social disintegration on Mornington Island. A large proportion of the population is unemployed, though attempts have been made to incorporate them into the available work. Consequently there is hardly any income apart from the normal government pensions for the aged and for child endowment. Kaiadilt housing is the poorest, consisting chiefly of humpies of bark, burlap, and tin a few feet high that blow down in high winds but are easily re-erected. Information is not available on the traditional shades and shelters used by the Kaiadilt on Bentinck Island but it is safe to assume that they bore little resemblance to their humpies on Mornington Island, either in materials or construction, and above all in the permanence with which they are occupied on the same piece of ground. The humpies in the village are therefore an expression of extreme poverty as much as of traditional culture and technology. A few of the Kaiadilt who have found regular employment in the mission have graduated to iron huts erected with carpenter's tools. The humpies are not used by the Kaiadilt by preference; a questionnaire reveals that almost all would rather live in a proper hut.

Although the Kaiadilt are cohesive in the sense that they live together in their enclave surrounded by foreign territory occupied by the Lardil, within their enclave self-help is at a low ebb. Sick members of their group are usually visited and fed by Lardil people and neglected by their own. The social credit network is bankrupt or even on the debit side of the ledger. This is not entirely due to the persistence of vendettas and hostilities from Bentinck Island. Parents have been just too disorganized and demoralized to care for their children after infancy. Until recently Kaiadilt children had to attend a special kitchen in the village; if their feeding were left to their parents they went hungry.

The social disintegration of the immigrant mainland group is intermediate between the Lardil and Kaiadilt. They are heterogeneous in origin and although identified as "mainlanders" by everybody on the island, they do not see themselves as a group; they are social isolates who identify with the dominant Lardil to some degree. Thus their houses occupy peripheral positions in the village, but are randomly distributed with respect to each other. They form no enclave within Lardil territory and this circumstance protects them from being treated as outsiders and scapegoats of Lardil society. It is the Kaiadilt who occupy this role. On the other hand the mainlanders' lack of the Lardil tongue and of territorial associations precludes them from attaining a really successful level of identification with the dominant society.

It should not be assumed that there is a simple causal relationship beginning with social disintegration and leading to mental disorder. Leighton (1965) suggests that mental disorder may also have a *retroflexive* effect on the level of social integration. A high rate of mental disorder might make a population vulnerable to disintegration, the two conditions reinforcing one another in a downward spiral of malfunctioning.

The existence of a "spiral of disintegration" can be readily demonstrated by observations of social interaction in these populations. When one spends time in the Kaiadilt enclave of the Mornington Island village, one learns that mentally disordered individuals can and do contribute retroflexively to the disintegration of their group. Two examples must suffice to remind us here. We frequently encountered O., a strong Kaiadilt in his mid-forties, sitting morosely outside his hut, looking at the ground and muttering to himself. His two wives, resigned in appearance, attended him from within earshot. O. was recovering from a self-inflicted blow in the face with a tomahawk. Some months previously he had tried to drown himself in the channel. Sometimes we observed him standing atop a sandhill, shouting and cursing in his vernacular, too angry to be approached. As the history of his disorder emerged we grasped the implications that it had for his group. One of his wives was formerly—on Bentinck Island, before the exodus—married to a man whom O. killed. She had been taken by O. as a co-wife. After they moved to Mornington Island, O. had been expected to give her up and to live with one wife in the Christian manner. He had no wish to live monogamously but the second wife took advantage of the situation to rebuff his husbandly demands. Constant tension arose when O., dependent and regressed, insisted on the attention of both wives. The family was terrorized by his demands, complaints, and accusations. Nobody in that family worked.

At the far edge of the Kaiadilt enclave we often spoke with blind Q. in front of his bark shelter. Q. appears to be in his mid-sixties; he is now mostly quiet and is given tranquillizing medication when he is not. He hears the voices of women promising to come to him; they approach but go away. He hears the voices of men threatening to kill him and he shouts back at them. For a time he was so noisy and destructive that he could not be tolerated in the village and had to be marooned on a nearby island. There he was provided regularly with food but otherwise left in isolation. Now restored to the village, he is normally calm unless the children tease him. He thinks he is suffering from sorcery.

These are examples of gross psychiatric disturbances that have further disorganized life in the Kaiadilt community. Milder disturbances such as convictions of weakness and ill health are prevalent and deter the individual from taking part in work or entering into wider social relationships. The depressive ideas that are found in the Kaiadilt adults and the anxiety-inhibition syndromes prevalent in Kaiadilt children have an effect on social cohesion and mastery in this group. There are strong indications that the syndrome of anxiety-inhibition in Kaiadilt children is related to the emotional climate of upbringing. Assuming that the depressive ideation of the parents is related to the disasters they have undergone, it is reasonable to think that the children's condition is a response to parental withdrawal, self-concern, and acute awareness of the potential life holds for disaster. How else would the children of a fishing and rafting people be scared to walk on the jetty?

THE FOURTH DETERMINANT: HUMAN ECOLOGY AND ITS STRESSES

Important as social disorganization is conceded to be for the mental health of the Kaiadilt, we are still left with the question of its origins.

It would be easy for the casual observer mistakenly to attribute Kaiadilt social disintegration to the stresses of forsaking traditional life and rapid exposure to Western society. This is a common interpretation of the decline of the Australian Aboriginal race. Our reconstruction of Kaiadilt history before their 1948 exodus shows that in their case social disintegration was already present on an ecological and territorial basis. Robbery, murder, abduction, and acts of revenge were prominent, arising from overpopulation and the struggle for survival. Social disintegration associated with fluctuating seasonal abundance was a periodical reality for the Kaiadilt. The conventional impression of Aborigines as sociological geniuses, governed by elaborate kinship rules and finely regulated by complex sanctions and taboos, hardly applies under these circumstances. Indeed, the association we infer to exist between social integration and fluctuating abundance raises the question as to how far it was a reality for other groups of the Aboriginal people as well.

From the human geographical or ecological points of view, Bentinck Island provides an example of zonation and succession of man. The Kaiadilt, with their distinctive genotype and their human isolation, illustrate the zonation of a species in relation to the natural environment. The fluctuating abundance of their relationship, enforced by seasonal cycles characteristic of Australia, appears to have led to overpopulation followed by periods of self-destruction. In one of these ecologically unsuccessful periods the self-destruction may have risked complete extinction, to be followed by the succession of species of lower orders in the animal kingdom better adapted to that environment. This may well have happened to other human communities in prehistory. In the case of the Kaiadilt, the succession from Bentinck

Island was accelerated through the agency of other men, the Kaiadilt strain being transplanted elsewhere.

If we are to translate the ecological process into psychiatric terms—for these are men—we must turn to the concept of gross stress. The Kaiadilt situation of famine and sickness may be viewed as a community or civil disaster comparable to those produced by flood, tidal wave, volcano, or fire. In the case of the Kaiadilt it was not a single calamity but a repeated or sustained threat. In the period of which we have knowledge, only limited resources were available to meet it and adapt to it; the Kaiadilt survived in what must be presumed to be a state of chronic stress and anxiety.

In their present post-traumatic phase, their psychological adjustment bears resemblances to that reported by Eitinger (1964) in the survivors of concentration camps. The captivity of these survivors was characterized by painful trauma, year after year, with threats and starvation, with fear-provoking situations constantly repeated and not discharged. In the post-traumatic phase, psychiatric symptoms are found in about half the cases, bearing high correlations with psychic disturbances during the imprisonment, with the severity of torture, and with the severity of weight loss during captivity. The greater the sum of these psychophysiological stresses to which the prisoners were subjected, the greater the immediate psychopathological reaction and the greater the incidence of chronic reactions. In the aetiology of these symptoms the premorbid personality was relatively subordinate in importance to the massive psychophysical traumatizations. Some analogy between the concentration camp survivors and the Kaiadilt appears to be acceptable, though in the Kaiadilt the basis of the stress is more immediately the unsatisfactory state of the ecology.

The Kaiadilt provide a model for psychiatry that is immediate and direct. In their case, we are impressed with the role of human-ecological and geographical factors in setting in motion a disturbed psychiatric pattern. It is suggested that ecological disturbance came first, interpersonal disturbances followed, and intrapsychic disturbances completed the psychopathological sequence which then reverberated retroflexively throughout the society and down the generation.

If such conclusions have any generality at all, they suggest that if psychiatry moves out from the confines of affluent Western societies that have formed the basis for most of its knowledge, the change may require it to modify some of its preconceptions as to what fundamentally matters in psychological adjustment.

eleven

Implementation: The Psychiatric Field Unit

We must now lower the focus of the microscope for an overview of the Islanders, and of the alien contact in general. We see the Aborigine as the exemplar of man's first economy, of the hunting, fishing, food-collecting type, regulated by social institutions and modes of thought characteristic of this way of life. We see him confronted by man's most evolved economy, the occidental economy, exemplified by European Australians. By an accident of history he is asked to condense the progress of millennia into a few generations—historically speaking, overnight. Most peoples of the earth have progressed in more or less gradual stages through food-collecting economies to pastoral and herding economies, to simple cultivation, to sedentary cultivation with varied crops, emerging finally either as the advanced agrarian civilizations of the Orient or as the occidental economies of the kind represented by Europe, North America, and Australia. Some of Earth's peoples have made rapid advances through social and technological innovations, but the Aborigine is unique in the apparent opportunity to span human economic and geographic evolution at a single step.

Some of the characteristics of these two economies are juxtaposed in table 14. It should be borne in mind in reviewing this table that it is no mere academic comparison, but portrays a dynamic interface of economies that are juxtaposed in real life. Any social order may be viewed as a system constantly interacting with ecological, economic, political, moral, and medical orders. But in this social order the interaction is fantastically accelerated; an analogy with a chemical reaction heated by a flame over a platinum grid might not be farfetched. In such an intensive interaction it is not surprising that the heat and the conflict lead to faltering adaptations and to downright maladaptations of serious consequence for the people. This is the field of transcultural psychiatry. We would prefer to designate it economic, or ecological, or interface, psychiatry if it were not for the proliferation of terms already present in this field.

Table 14. The Economies of Aboriginal- and European-Australians

ABORIGINAL-AUSTRALIAN ECONOMY	EUROPEAN-AUSTRALIAN ECONOMY
Use of Natural Resources	
Fish, dugong, turtle, eggs, shellfish. Birds, marsupials, reptiles, roots, fruit, honey. Balanced but intermittent diet. No agriculture or animal husbandry. No metals, pottery, permanent building. No trade or writing, little counting or measuring.	Cultivation of "Western" cereals and domestic animals. Irrigation in arid zones; plantations in tropics; mechanical power used for industry, agriculture, food preservation. Forest and grassland replaced by cultivation and pastures. Ploughing and overgrazing lead to erosion. Destruction of forests for timber and pulp. Mining, quarrying.
Land Division and Settlement	
Nomadic or semi-nomadic search for food leads to sparse occupation, no villages. Territory divided into estates protected by tradition, social or medical concepts such as **Malgri**, or by fighting between hordes.	Sparse in pastoral areas (cattle or sheep stations); higher in cultivated lands (towns), but population mostly in industrial seaport cities. Complex patterns of settlement of rural and urban areas. Private ownership of land usual.
Communications	
Tracks mark foraging routes. Language distinct from neighboring tribes.	Network of roads, rails, and airways. Transoceanic shipping. Mass media: newspapers, radio, telephone, television.
Sociopolitical Organization	
Basic unit: the horde or a few families. Wider tribal linkage through language and strong kinship. No chiefs or central government. Rule by seniority, status, tradition ("The Dreaming"), and negotiation or dispute.	Basic unit: the conjugal family; kinship ties and credit network weakened. Local, state, and federal governmental levels. Public service and military supported by taxes. International trade, alliances, tensions, wars.
Moral and Medical Order	
"The Dreaming" totemic-religious repository of tradition, behavior, ideas of causation. Medicine man influential, exploits sickness as an inducement to social conformity. "Sorcery" and "possession" concepts. Myth and ritual important.	Christianity (rather desultory). Individual competitiveness. Accumulation of possessions ("Jones" ethos). Increasing social welfare, education, pensions. Technological advances in medicine with specialization and hospitals, lessening of personal and family support of general practitioners.

NOTE: This table is intended to demonstrate the several orders of the relationship between the two Australian cultures and their environments. It has been suggested by the systematic analysis of the economies of mankind by Lebon (1966).

We looked at the alien contact[1] in its historical, ecological, economic, and social contexts and, as became clinicians, we sought symptoms. Since we are physicians of an occidental culture, we tried to form estimates of their nature, frequency, and severity. We did this within the limitations imposed by our methodology and time restrictions. Commentaries on the health of marginal societies are plentiful in the literature of culture contact but in most cases they have been made by broad and general observations. The more specific inquiry that we carried out entitles us and perhaps obliges us to offer some conclusions on how medical behavioral science may assist the Aborigines. We do this in humility, fully aware of the difficulty and unpredictability of the Aboriginal task of adapting to Western society while preserving some cultural aspects that ought not fade from man's heritage. We offer recommendations because information we gathered forms a part of the total information that concerns an isolated, emerging, and troubled people.

Modern psychiatry is a characteristic development of Western twentieth-century medicine. With the growing technological specialization of other branches of medicine making ever greater demands on the physician's technical knowledge and expertise, psychiatry has become the branch of medicine responsible not merely for mental alienation but for the personal adaptational and emotional aspects of medicine. It is the branch of medicine that makes the most detailed study of the individual life, and it creates the closest emotional relationship with the patient. What rapport, in the sense of mutual interest and assistance, is possible between those who practice it and Australian Aborigines?

This problem concerned us emotionally, in our internal struggle to achieve the "detached concern" that is an objective of our profession. Any satisfaction that we felt from our encounter and our work on the island was tempered by the reflection that it was not a beginning but an ending, a personal disaffiliation from the island community. The demands of our regular practice and training duties in the city will make it hard to come back. The members of our field team have different training and values, but none finds much satisfaction in the kind of medical practice in which the clinical picture commands exclusive respect, in which data are just data and conclusions are deduced from what the subject looks like, says, does, or puts down on his questionnaire. Such an approach neglects direct involvement in the future, in the health and growth of the people and of their children. None

1. So far as we can tell, "cultural contact" is the term commonly encountered in the British literature, whereas "acculturation" may be preferred in the American; there are several nuances here. When we have tried in this book to view the problems from the indigenous point of view, we have used the term "alien contact."

144

of us cares to practice our vocation exclusively in this way. Psychiatry without the possibility of a continuing relationship may be compared with minerals engineering that prospects without being interested in problems of mining and refining the ore.

Concentration upon the future presupposes a wish to be intruded upon and a wish to intrude. Did the Islanders find enough pleasure and profit in us to want us back? Or do they echo the La Perouse settlement resident in Sydney who complained "we have had the arse surveyed off us recently" (Smee, 1966)? This citizen belonged to a group of fringe-dwelling Aborigines with a long history of exclusion and subordination. The full-blood tribally oriented Aborigines with whom we are here concerned enjoy visitors and try to retain them. Our welcome was not in question on the island. Our role as physicians may have provided an entree into sickness and private information, and our experience of Western and Aboriginal medicine may have accredited us and led more quickly to the heart of things. But most people respond in kind to courtesy, interest, and appreciation, and these factors probably assisted our relationship more than did any magic of our medicine.

An observation of the pioneering Australian anthropologist Baldwin Spencer (1914, p. x), noted for his work with the central Australian Aranda, is of special interest fifty years later. "Amongst all the tribes I have found it of very great advantage to be able to show them that I am well acquainted with the customs and secret matters of other tribes. As soon as they understand this it is wonderful how they open up, and it is also equally remarkable how they close in the presence of anyone who is uncongenial to them." One suspects that Spencer's familiarity with customs and secret matters stemmed from some personal interest and respect; the latter qualities made him congenial rather than his mere erudition in lore. Aborigines and anybody else discriminate between a genuine interest and a transitory interest sparked by novelty, and on this distinction is rapport founded.

Our own reminiscence is apposite in this matter. When we recall the help given in the tedious parts of our survey, the sociability and recreation that lightened our work, culminating in our special corroboree when we departed, we cannot believe we are unwelcome intruders. The tones of our own musical instrument—it happened to be the Indian sarode of our geneticist—harmonized with the Aboriginal instruments of the dance. The fun was real. With the people sitting on blankets around the arena by the windmill in the late evening, Dick Roughsey formally presented a decorated dronepipe and charming Edna Adams laid our table with a cake she baked. This was a public affirmation; but chiefly we recall those private moments when both sides struggled to communicate and to establish the nature of the bedevilling problems. Aborigines in their own community are usually depicted as expressive people with emotions close to the surface, yet in the alien contact there are the grave inhibitions. Some have learned the art of not talking. Smiles sometimes express not so much pleasure as ingratiation or timidity. Inhibited children baulk not only in classroom self-expression but seemingly in the business of preparation for life. Women are apathetic, static, hard to communicate with. Do we find compensation enough in the discussion with the confident informative men—Gully Peters, Prince Escott, Henry Peters, Lindsay and Dick Roughsey, Pompey Wilson and their like? Or in their activities—the oral literature, the dances of sea serpent and tide, and their voyages around the island? Or in the missionary's reflective commentary on the verandah before the electric generator cuts out for the night? Or in the island's own personality—Birri beach hushed with soughing casuarinas, turtle eggs in the sand, the Sandalwood River (in Gully's sea-eagle country) teeming with fish that one may actually catch?

Because of the field program we set ourselves, it was like this last year with the Walbiri people of central Australia; next year it may be the same with people in Arnhem Land. Our program samples rather than provides a service, and makes medical relationships only to break them. This is a policy calculated to accomplish research, but it frustrates the aims of medical care. And we are well aware that on our return home we shall encounter some anthropologists—only some— who have not read our findings but who will point at us the finger of "cultural relativism" or "psychiatric imperialism."

In what follows we suggest a plan adapted to the needs of Australia. With suitable modifications it may have applicability in other countries having communities undergoing Western influences without psychiatric services. In order to develop services adapted to the psychological needs of Australian communities we should contemplate a ring of psychiatric ecologists or field units around the margins of the outback. A psychiatric ecologist is one who gains a working knowledge of the human hazards of his spatial zone. He provides some individual treatment, but his major role is to carry out mental health consultation with the helping professions such as school teachers, doctors, nurses, welfare officers, clergy, police, and magistrates to enable them, within their limitations, to act to advantage in mental health. There are as yet no psychiatrists trained to carry out this dual role in Australia; but the profession is young.

The psychiatric needs of a scattered community cannot be met by the present practice of stationing a psychiatrist to receive referrals in the nearest base or city hospital. This psychiatrist is not likely to come to grips with social disturbances some hundreds of miles away, when only the identified patient is removed to his care. He is not part of the community, does not directly contribute to it, may not even identify with it nor understand it, and may well be ignored by it.

A region that contains a population of fifteen thousand or more approximates to the social geographer's concept of a self-sustaining community: one that polarizes around a center capable of providing reasonable services for education, health, and recreation, thus giving opportunities for reasonable social adjustment to the normal range of personality types. A ring of such communities runs around outback Australia through Mt. Isa, Charleville, Longreach, Bourke, Broken Hill, Mildura, Port Augusta, Kalgoorlie, Port Hedland, Derby, Darwin, and possibly Alice Springs. Psychiatry should be included as a logical part of the technology of developing such communities, but only if it is ecologically sensitive psychiatry, organized in field units.

The term "human ecology" as we have used it in connection with the adaptation of people in particular spatial environments contains a hint of euphemism. It evades the term "psychiatry." This is justified because the term "psychiatry" is defensively perceived by some people as relating only to the lunatic asylum and its accompaniments in that epoch. The human ecology team or psychiatric field unit that we advocate in this book consists of a general psychiatrist, a child psychiatrist, and an anthropologist or social psychologist with clinical experience, each applying his knowledge to the problems of health. Let us suppose for purposes of illustration that regular visits to the Mornington Island community form part of the schedule of such a team. To what topics would it direct its attention in its work with this community, and how would it articulate with the Australian community at large?

PSYCHIATRIC FIRST AID

Psychiatric first aid can suppress disturbed symptoms of disturbance regardless of their origin. Some symptoms are self-evident to the layman, as in over-excited, restless, interfering behavior, or in depressed, withdrawn, uncontributing behavior, or in deluded, suspicious, unreasonable behavior. Frequently, however, psychiatric symptoms are camouflaged by a wide range of disturbances of conduct or by complaints of physical ill-health. In this book we have noted how a society fragmented by rapid social change, forced emigration, low levels of health and economy, or by natural disasters may expect a higher incidence of symptoms, both overt and concealed. We have noted that these disturbances can produce in a retroflexive manner further disruptive effects on family or village life. The Kaiadilt illustrate how social fragmentation begets mental disturbance, and how mental disturbance begets more social fragmentation in a runaway spiral of malfunctioning. Yet many of these symptoms benefit from medication. The tranquillizer and antidepressant preparations of the past decade surpass in efficacy anything previously available, and we have seen them interrupt these runaway spirals. Their very efficacy, like that of the surgeon's knife, contains a danger; it should hardly be necessary to add they cannot be prescribed casually, without adequate knowledge of the individual, family, and social group. Because of the scattered nature of the outback, it is obvious that these drug preparations must sometimes be placed in the hands of those who are not strictly qualified to use them, and who therefore need in their use the regular supervision of a psychiatric field unit.

MENTAL HEALTH CONSULTATION

The mission on Mornington Island has trained individuals in the supervision of village sanitation and similar matters. To what extent might councillors, police, or others of status be active in mental hygiene as well? We noticed several opportunities during our sojourn. The undercurrent of sorcery (*puripuri*) and spirit intrusion (*malgri*) provides one example of an opportunity for mental health consultation. We found that strong belief in these supernatural events correlates with neurotic symptoms. Aborigines are not the only ones with a literal belief in these complaints. One of the Europeans at a neighboring mission attempts to counteract Aboriginal magic and supernatural with its early Christian counterpart; sorcery victims are constrained to hold the New Testament, kneel, and pray—logical behavior if sorcery is thought to be supernatural. Readers of accounts of sorcery in popular literature might have gained a similar misunderstanding.

In every complaint of sorcery there is an opportunity to discover the victim's grievance or sickness. Some Aborigines need only minimal prompting and encouragement to perceive the human problems that underlie the supernatural complaint. If this opportunity is taken regularly and with understanding over a period of time by those Aborigines and Westerners capable of doing so, it is probable many sick people will get treatment and that adherence to sorcery will weaken. Banishment tactics merely reinforce it, driving it underground where it flourishes and exerts a more disruptive influence on the society.

Council meetings designed to foster political awareness and experience provide another opportunity. At the council meetings on the island we saw ad hoc mental health consultations on collective problems, though it was not of course identified in these terms. An example was the subordinate position of the Kaiadilt, who are socially disadvantaged and often discriminated against, described by the Lardil indigenes of Mornington Island with the familiar epithets heard in Western society about its ethnic minorities. Most Lardil of the island do not see their problem primarily as one of assimilation of Kaiadilt to Lardil. After a

148

characteristic "race riot" Prince Escott proposed that everybody stop talking about "Bentinck people" and use instead the term "New Mornington Islanders." Council discussed how to deal with racism on the island. It seemed to us that the separate enclave of the Kaiadilt at the edge of the main village encouraged scapegoating and discrimination. A rearrangement of housing might offer a partial solution without further disorganizing the Kaiadilt. The existing gain in group cohesiveness amongst the Kaiadilt from this spacing behavior was minimal anyway. It was worth a judicious trial. Such pragmatic considerations form the agenda of mental health consultation which could be promoted by a psychiatric field unit.

We had the cooperation of the Europeans connected with the community in various capacities. The European nursing sister stationed at the mission contributed an experience of local personality and adjustment problems that greatly assisted the clinical examination phase of the survey. She expressed gratification at the improvement in insight and management she had been able to achieve as the result of her participation in the survey. The aerial medical officer for the region, stationed at Mt. Isa Base Hospital about three hundred miles to the south, was in radio contact. This permitted discussion of individuals suffering from disorders amenable to simple measures of the type that we have called psychiatric first aid. As an instance of collaboration between a field team and the Aerial Medical Service, an item of correspondence will serve.

The Aerial Medical Officer,
Mount Isa Base Hospital,
MOUNT ISA. Queensland.

Dear Dr.:

This is a running report of findings in the survey of the Mornington Island community. We are chiefly concerned to find out something about the psychological adjustment of the people as a whole and to correlate this with cultural and economic circumstances. We are carrying out examining, questionnaires and inventories, and will let you have a copy of this material when completed. We would then appreciate any comments you may have to make.

A few individuals were found this week suffering from psychiatric disturbances of a kind likely to be helped by simple pharmacological measures. Following the radio conversation with you we prescribed in some of these cases. Here is a list for your records.

T.C.: Paranoid schizophrenia with nocturnal disturbances occasioned by fears and hallucinations. He benefits from Stelazine mgm. 2 nocte.

Q.M.: Depressive state with hypochondriacal and suicidal preoccupations. Seems to be benefitting from amitriptyline 50 mgm. t.d.s. If he still cannot be involved in some constructive activity (the Superintendent will make a special effort) we can arrange a period in Brisbane for protection and rehabilitation-training.

I.O.: Epilepsy, observed in a grand mal seizure by one of us. Given Epanutin 30 mgm. b.d.

N.H.: Transitory delusional state following first visit to mainland last year, said there to be schizophrenic. No evidence of schizophrenia in her present adjustment. Largactil reduced from 400 to 100 mgm. daily and could be suspended if she remains well on your next visit.

E.C.: Episodes of limb paralysis, undoubtedly conversion hysteria. The present conflict centers around domesticity, childbearing and the present unwanted pregnancy. She could have oral contraceptive under Sister's supervision before her husband's next annual visit.

U.B.: Eleven-year-old boy, regular bedwetter, likely to benefit from Imipramine 25 mgm. nocte, could be raised to 50 mgm. if necessary.

M.U.: Four-year-old child, diagnosed epileptic, given Epanutin, 30 mgm. b.d.

There are several periodically disturbed women whose fertility has outrun their mothering and general coping capacity. In the city we would normally prescribe oral contraceptive tablets. We discussed the situation with Sister and the Superintendent, and with their approval sent samples from drug houses, about 24 months' supply in all. These women include S.M. and F.C. Regular supervision of tablet taking is of course the problem. You might consider other family planning methods.

Yours sincerely,

(Signed)

Important as the relay of information between physicians undoubtedly is, it was even more important to impart orientation, guidance, and instruction to the staff of the mission, including the school teachers. It was the staff who remained in daily contact with the people and who had the best opportunity of acting to the psychiatric advantage of the community. This is the service of mental health consultation that a visiting field unit might be expected to provide.

ANTI-INSTITUTIONALISM

An aspect of island society highlighted by the council meetings and of special interest to human ecology is its institutionalism, using the term in its medical connotation. The community is institutionalized in the manner of mental hospitals, prisoner-of-war camps, and sanatoria for chronic illnesses such as tuberculosis and leprosy. Effects on the personalities of inmates include apathy, loss of initiative, and regression from attempts at self-sufficiency. Rowley (1966) points out that concentration of Aborigines under authoritarian control in missions, government stations, and settlements serves the purposes of getting unwanted minorities out of the way, affording them protection from immoral

150

influences outside, and influencing their attitudes and conduct within. He considers that the institution system possesses great inertia because managers of such institutions, forced to look to head office for advancement and promotion, follow the objectives of frugality, avoidance of "trouble," and optimistic reports, rather than of the initiative and independence of the inmates.

Psychiatry is slowly and on the whole successfully engaged in overcoming its own institutionalization associated with the asylums of a previous era, abolishing these establishments and where this is not yet economically possible employing special social techniques inside and outside. These techniques include group development through meetings and activities, with augmented contact with the community at large. The experience could speed the process for Aborigines. On the island, for example, it is important to determine whether the alternating pattern that we noted of avoidance of confrontation and periodical riots is an Aboriginal characteristic, or the expected result of nomadic factions learning to live in a village setting, or an artifact of institutionalism.

MOTHER AND CHILD

Fundamental to the development of character are the early transactions between mother and child. The relationship between mother and child on the island is affectionate and indulgent but, in the conditions prevailing, insufficiently organized around the child's informal instruction. It affords poor socialization and preparation for school and industrial life. Preschool training is desirable if the child is to gain more from this crucial period. Young mothers and their infants form a diad that should have the opportunity of being involved together in drawing, reading, writing, and spoken English. Infants in this way might receive better reinforcement than at present, with less regressive pull by the family away from Westernization. Conduct of the kindergarten should be the task of young Lardil women trained in Montessori work at the nearest center. This training should be carried out in groups because experience shows that island girls sent away singly for training are threatened by the cultural upheaval and by nostalgia and some have been subject to psychiatric breakdown.

Aboriginal wives and mothers face many difficulties in their status climb relative to husbands and in their occupational change, but none more threatening than their fecundity, recently acquired from improved health care and nutrition. Where we have succeeded in the medical setting in breaking the barrier to communication we find that women resent their fertility and would prefer to control it. The impression gained by Westerners that settlement women enjoy having another baby every year is a defensive fable. For Aboriginal women, contraceptive assistance should be available on request as it is to their Western sisters, bearing in mind that oral hormones require daily supervision and that insertion of contraceptive intra-uterine devices is a more practicable though more fallible method.

The interest of the field unit child psychiatrist is not confined to the preschool years. He is in a position to sharpen the teacher's sensitivity to individual differences. One of his tasks is to detect among the children the innovator or emulator, the somewhat rare Aboriginal personality type that can tolerate or accept change. Our tests show that this trait exists in varying degrees; once the flame is found it must be fanned. Two contrasting techniques of teaching involve respectively the criticism of errors and the reinforcement of successes. Our strong impression is that Aboriginal children tolerate the former technique very poorly. Yet it is the method one frequently hears in Aboriginal classrooms. The angry criticism and sarcasm of the teacher are probably less a technique to achieve compliance and increased effort than his response to overwhelming burdens imposed by his task. It seems to us that Aboriginal classes should be only half the size of Western ones, not twice as large as is often the case in our experience. Teachers then might be able to concentrate better on teacher support/approve behavior than desist/disapprove behavior. In such an atmosphere of award, student attentiveness should increase.

TRAINING TRANSCULTURAL WORKERS

Application of mental health principles is limited by the availability of trained workers. Psychiatry has been effectively represented in most Australian universities in the past decade or less. It takes at least ten years to train a matriculated student to be a psychiatrist—more for a child psychiatrist. It is not surprising if transcultural psychiatry is as yet poorly represented, because it involves further anthropological experience and regional exposure.

Those few who work in this field have the obligation to ensure that their knowledge and experience is transmitted in university teaching. We have already stated our view that transcultural psychiatry is part of the technology of social change; these social changes involve not Aborigines alone but the entire interface of culture contact in this part of the world. The dominant white society needs education and information just as much as the subordinate minority. These activities must be part of the program of a modern university, and of other centers for the training of potential fieldworkers such as teachers' colleges, police colleges, and technological (trade-training) institutes. At the present time in Australia many university curricula appear to represent almost any exotic area of study in preference to transcultural psychiatry. Perhaps because the discipline is midway between psychiatry and anthropology, university departments of psychiatry and anthropology have each left the responsibility to the other. By all accounts, psychiatry and anthropology in Australia are in urgent need of cross-fertilization.

RACIST WHITE ATTITUDES

Racial prejudice by whites toward Aborigines is as old as the alien contact itself. The explorer Matthew Flinders' description of the tribes of the Gulf of Carpentaria as "cruel, poor and brutal nations" so typifies white reaction that we chose it for our text. Prejudice is not a disease; it is a complex behavioral pattern that has several dimensions, ranging from adaptive to psychopathological, from altruism to sadism, from science to ignorance. Its tenacity is illustrated by comparing mid-nineteenth century prejudice with attitudes found in present-day Australia. The following is extracted from *The Illustrated London News*.

"A Black Camp" in New South Wales, after the Annual Gift of Blankets from the Governor

The Blacks of Australia are, with the exception of the Bosjesmen, the lowest and most irreclaimable of the native tribes with which we are acquainted. After strenuous efforts, commencing sixty-four years since, they are now exactly what they were when first discovered. They speak a little English, some have even been taught to read and write well; but, although occasional instances of affection and fidelity are found among them, just as we meet with tame foxes and pheasants, they are as a race truly irreclaimable.

The illustration upon the preceding page represents the Camp of a party of New South Wales Blacks after they have received the annual gift of blankets which it is usual to present to them on her Majesty's birthday. The tent-shaped erection is a gunyah, the nearest approach to a dwelling at which the Blacks of this region have arrived. It is formed of a few branches of wood, covered with sheets of the bark of the gum tree, which they strip off with remarkable ingenuity. The men are armed with spears, or the boomerang—that curious weapon which thrown at an enemy or game flies in an excentric direction, returning if required after striking to the feet of the thrower. This was long considered to be peculiar to Australia, until the discoveries at Nineveh proved that it was known to Nimrod and the Assyrians. The club, in native language a nullah-nullah, is equally employed in smashing out the brains of a fallen enemy and correcting a lazy or refractory wife. Bows and arrows are unknown to them.

Those tribes which are not in receipt of blankets from the Government, still continue to manufacture very warm and beautiful cloaks of opossum skin, which they wear with the hair side inwards, the other side ornamented with geometrical patterns drawn with wonderful accuracy. The opossum is to the Black what the raindeer is to the Laplander: the flesh is their food, the sinews make thread, and the skins are used not only for cloaks but for buckets or water-bags used in crossing deserts.

The Correspondent who has favoured us with the preceding Sketch appends the following well-timed reflections: "The mysterious and wonderful arrangements of Divine Providence are brought forcibly to our minds on viewing the modes of life of this peculiar people, existing without a wish beyond hunting the forests, and living precariously on food which they obtain by climbing the immense gum-trees, wholly ignorant that at their roots the most precious metal has been concealed for thousands of years; generation after generation of aborigines has passed away, unconscious of the riches concealed beneath the surface of their native hunting-grounds, perchance sufficient to have made them the most powerful race under the sun."

Some fine specimens of gold from Australia have, we learn, been transmitted by Mr. Robert Cook to the British Museum and the Museum of the Geological Society, where they have attracted much attention. (April 24, 1852, p. 314.)

Better information is needed on the present extent and influence of racial prejudice in Australia. Many prejudicial ideas persist but are offset by a growing spirit of liberalism and interest in alternative hypotheses. Some may fade with better public education. One would for example expect that the "dying race" misconception of Aborigines, widely accepted before World War II, cannot survive many more years in the face of published population statistics, and of tourists' observations of central and northern communities where the rate of growth is so fast. The "quite happy and healthy" misconception of Aborigines is in part a defensive denial of problems by Europeans, but has in part been fostered by the Aborigines' capacity for spontaneous gaiety and their apparent unconcern with middle-class values; it can scarcely withstand information of the sort available in this book. The "send them back to the bush" idea should die, if only because there is no bush left to which to send them. The truth is that there is no possible return to the Aboriginal culture for Aborigines, and if health and growth is the aim there is no standing still in the present marginal society. The "lazy, unreliable, gone walkabout off the job" idea associates the undeniable industrial inefficiency with nomadism, in which hard work is intermittent between periods of idleness. The better substantiated hypothesis is that industrial inefficiency is associated with poor education and the values imparted by the culture of poverty, and that personality traits in general have much to do with training and environmental opportunity so limited for Aborigines.

Racial prejudice is infinite in variety. The "biologically inferior" conviction interprets the "childlike mind" and social evidence of inferiority as arising from biological endowment rather than from

154

social circumstances. The fact is that there has been very little scientific study of racial differences in performance or in potential. Even the term "primitive" conveys to ethnocentric people the idea that Aborigines represent in an evolutionary sense some lower species of Homo sapiens. The more reasonable hypothesis is that the Australian Aborigine is modern man, whose technological retardation is accounted for by millennia of isolation from the remainder of mankind and by the poor natural opportunities for the development of a settled economy offered by the Australian continent. This "biological equality" hypothesis is admittedly more acceptable to those who have had the opportunity to live with tribally oriented people and to admire the complexity of their environmental knowledge and their systems of art, religion, and kinship. Man for man, such Aborigines often have a greater knowledge and involvement in the arts than the Westerners having the chance to observe them.

MENTAL HEALTH IMPLICATIONS OF "ASSIMILATION"

Whenever and however "the Aboriginal problem" is aired a comment on the official Australian policy of "assimilation" is inevitable. The official policy toward Aborigines, stated in 1951 and fairly widely accepted by the community, has an objective described as assimilation and is intended to insure that "all Aborigines and part-Aborigines are expected eventually to attain the same manner of living as other Australians and to live as members of a single Australian community, enjoying the same rights and privileges, accepting the same responsibilities, observing the same customs, influenced by the same beliefs, hopes and loyalties as other Australians."

This policy statement has been more widely quoted in Australia than anything else concerning Aborigines, yet incredible as it may appear, there is no public documentation of it to which reference can be made. In 1951, the Hon. Paul Hasluck, minister for territories (at present governor-general of Australia), arranged a meeting in Canberra of ministers concerned with Aboriginal welfare in all states and the Northern Territory. The frequently quoted statement defining "assimilation" comes from the ministers' confidential report, and is presumably part of a press release. Because the original source of the statement is not available, and because the statement as issued gave rise to controversy over an implied forceful removal of Aboriginal identity, we sought the actual wording from the Office of Aboriginal Affairs, Prime Minister's Department, Canberra. As supplied it reads:

Assimilation is the objective of native welfare measures. This means that the Aborigines and persons of mixed blood are expected eventually to attain to the same manner of living and to the same privileges of citizenship as white Australians and to live, if they choose to do so, as members of a single Australian community, observing the same customs and influenced by the same beliefs, hopes and loyalties as other Australians. Their education and training and the provisions in regard to their housing, health and employment will be graduated according to their progress towards this eventual goal. Any discrimination between the treatment of the white and the coloured person is to be regarded as a temporary measure based, not upon colour, but existing needs for the guardianship and tutelage and is to be removed as soon as the need for it disappears.

The policy of assimilation is based on the expectations that gradually the tribal structure will be weakened and will disappear and that gradually the Aborigines and persons of mixed blood will be drawn more closely into association with the white community. Administration should not seek to resist or impede such change, but rather to regulate the course of change and to guard individual natives or groups of natives against the ill effects of sudden change and to assist them to make the transition from one stage to another in such a way as will be favourable to their further social advancement.

It is clear that this 1951 statement of assimilation, as quoted here, includes the possibility of choice by Aborigines—the grounds for objection to it made by Aborigines and others. These objections became heated in some quarters because the assimilation statement, as made available to the public, was taken to mean that Aborigines would perforce lose their identity, culture and pride of race.

The protagonists of what was thought the alternative policy of "integration," sought support for the idea that Aborigines should retain their identity by continuing to live in their own groupings but seeking to raise their educational and economic status to that of white Australian society. The debate between "assimilation" and "integration" became heavily charged with theoretical and semantic difficulties, much of which might have been averted by a more detailed publication of the policy officially determined in 1951.

Upon inquiry directed to the Office of Aboriginal Affairs as to the source of the 1951 policy statement, quoted above, the reply was received giving a direction that the office considered that the definition and explanation of assimilation was contained in the booklet *The Australian Aborigines,* published by the Department of Territories in July 1967. The foreword to this booklet indicates that a major part of it is the work of Emeritus Professor A. P. Elkin, C.M.G.

The policy of assimilation is a clear repudiation of any official intention of apartheid. But the debate between assimilation and integration tended to obscure for a time that what is really taking place in much of Australia is the third alternative—segregation. Instead of assimilation or integration we are witnessing the growth of disadvantaged, culturally deprived, and subordinate communities in rural

156

areas. Aborigines who have been flocking out of rural areas into the cities since the 1950s in search of work form communities with ghetto characteristics. A large part of the members of the communities is without the skills or opportunity for satisfactory employment or social betterment.

The policies of assimilation or integration could be considered satisfactory from the point of view of the mental health of Aborigines, if either were attainable. The same cannot be said for the actuality—segregation, fraught with the dangers of social tension. Australian society might reapply the warning of Harvard's James B. Conant (1964) concerning the underemployment of early school leavers and their subsequent life in the slums, that we are allowing social dynamite to accumulate in our cities. If segregation is taking place it is because economic and social reality is frustrating the intentions of the official policy of assimilation. Economic and social reality determine that the Aborigine does not in fact possess freedom of choice to assimilate into European society. This has led to earnest criticism of the official policy: "If we couch our policy in wide and glowing terms but at the same time refuse to extend to the Aboriginal people the means by which they may accomplish the same objectives as other Australians, then the policy may be rightly written off as a sham." (Stevens, 1966, p. 282.)

The mental health implications of the Aborigines' property rights and economic status are far-reaching but take us beyond the intention of the present work. Analyses by economists and others leave no doubt of the seriousness of the situation. The point of remedial application is sometimes placed at the population level, sometimes at the level of national policy. Thus Long sees the problem of mental pauperization on missions and settlements as a need for administration "constantly directed towards making either the community as a whole, or all the individual inmates, independent of management" (1970, p. 184). Rowley (1962) sees it as a fundamental gap in the background, purpose, and intention of our native policy which, if not closed, will continue to frustrate all those engaged in native welfare programs. Writing in 1970, he comments that the frontier days are over. "There are many political and economic reasons why an increasing gap between respective living standards cannot be accepted by government" (p. 340). Schapper (1968) sees the centralization of Aboriginal welfare duties within a single government department as a terrible mistake which will delay advancement and the narrowing of the socioeconomic gap. Such centralization conveniently removes onus and initiative from powerful government departments such as Health, Education, Labor, and Social Services.

AFTER MEDICINE, THE LAW

It is true that some of the more powerful social institutions in the European-Australian order have scarcely begun to think about the culture contact. Psychiatry has a contribution, but as with the other welfare institutions, efforts will be ephemeral without the vigorous and energetic direction of the law of the land. Loss of property rights and economic, educational, and social disadvantages have arisen from inadequate legal safeguards for the native occupants of Australia in the early phases of colonization. It seems now that nothing but radical and imaginative legislation can redress the situation. Tasks of this magnitude in health, education, and economic opportunity require the active and informal support of the country as a whole; in Western society this is only likely to be expressed through legal enactment.

Psychiatrists have been little interested in the psychiatry of culture contact, and possibly for this reason feel free to point the finger at another professional group that until recently has been almost as undistinguished. With some notable exceptions, the legal profession—especially those lawyers who are also legislators or influence legislators—have not espoused the cause of this disadvantaged minority. Mr. D. A. Dunstan (1966), a lawyer who has been premier of the State of South Australia, caused to be enacted legislation likely to improve Aboriginal land title and employment in that state. In this way an attempt was made to retrieve the original intentions of the South Australian Company to provide a political expression of J. S. Mill's moral philosophy.[1] While each state and territory of Australia has its own policy, work is done piecemeal through a variety of organizations—political, social welfare, trade union, church, and cultural. The Federal Council for the Advancement of Aborigines represents a majority of these organizations, but not necessarily Aboriginal opinion. Aboriginal opinion is not necessarily developed or cohesive. At present the scope and activity of the government Office of Aboriginal Affairs, created after the 1966 Referendum on Aborigines, is awaited with

---

1. The promoters of the colony (the experimental philosophers as they were sarcastically termed in London) had given much thought to their experiment in the art of colonization, including the design of safeguards for the Aboriginal inhabitants. Their ideals were of course frustrated by unruly colonists. An early historian, Blacket (1911, p. 46) writes: "Alas! such good advice in relation to a few of the colonists was thrown away. The aborigines suffered much from their contact with some unprincipled and lecherous whites. They soon learned to drink, swear, gamble, and to commit baser sins. While as yet the first settlers dwelt in tents and bough booths on the shores of Holdfast Bay, notices were fastened to the gum-trees offering a reward for information as to the persons who supplied drink to the aborigines. To the shame of our race we have to acknowledge that one of the first cases tried in the infant settlement in South Australia was that in which two whites were charged with stealing a jacket and some spears and waddies from the aborigines. To-day they are a weak, degraded, decimated race, doomed to speedy extinction."

hope. Whatever the organization, legislation to promote the positive advantage of Aborigines, in health, education, and economy, is needed to retrieve their lowly status and the growing social problem it presents.

An arrangement useful to individual Aborigines is a nationwide legal aid bureau, conducted by lawyers along the lines of the voluntary service in Sydney developed by Professor J. H. Wootten. An ombudsman to study the growing complaints against officialdom would serve a purpose. The active interest of the legal profession would materially assist Aborigines and the small army of workers trying to pave the way for this ancient, reprieved, but collapsing people. But without strong laws to redress present disadvantages, nothing will avail. Psychiatry itself is but a social institution, operating with an array of medical techniques employed by socially sanctioned experts, but needing the patronage of the social institution of law to prosper.

The world is full of crusaders. Effective social reform depends upon the study of the problem in breadth and depth. It is our view that the field psychiatric unit has demonstrated that it can contribute an essential element to this study. Its role has been described in forceful terms by Margetts in Canada. "Apart from the interest and study value offered by clinical psychiatry in faraway lands, the tabulation of our psychological knowledge about all peoples has two practical aims. The first is the *promotion* of improved methods of case-finding and clinical care around the world. The second is an emphasis on how to stay healthy, and even alive. Unchecked individual and secondary mass psychopathology could destroy the human race." (1965, p. 79.)

From the Edge of Annihilation

In 1970 Virginia Huffer, M.D., of the University of Maryland Psychiatric Institute, on her sabbatical leave, joined the transcultural program of the University of New South Wales School of Psychiatry. One of her projects was to go to Mornington Island to investigate the personal adjustments of traditionally oriented women during cultural change.[1] This is a subject in which there are critical gaps in information and in understanding. A team member visited Mornington Island in December 1970, to assist Dr. Huffer. He had the opportunity to assess changes in that community since our visit and to judge the effectiveness of intervention by the psychiatric team three years previously.

A large part of the community had been evacuated from the village because of an epidemic of infectious hepatitis and the shortage of water at the end of the dry season (normally March to December). School was in any case dismissed for the long Christmas vacation, and many families had taken their children across the Appel Channel to Denham Island, or up the east coast of Mornington Island to Birri. At each of these sites new buildings—a prawn-processing plant at Denham, and the cattle station headquarters at Birri, neither at the stage of economic functioning—indicated the advance of activities there since our survey. Mornington village itself looked the same, except that it was now traversed by an electric light wire. A row of Western-style houses was being erected adjacent to the airstrip.

The first concern was to see how the Kaiadilt were faring, since this group had been identified as "the sickest society" in our survey. Had the psychiatric team brought them any advantage? It was hoped that the antecedents of the Kaiadilt disintegration and the associated maladjustment and maladaptation could be traced further, since this situation provides an "experiment of nature" of considerable theo-

1. See Huffer, Virginia (forthcoming). *The Sweetness of the Fig: Aboriginal Woman as a Transitional Figure.* Monograph for the Australian Institute of Aboriginal Studies, Canberra, and the University of New South Wales School of Psychiatry, Sydney.

160

retical interest to the study of psychiatry and of acculturation. No further quantitative measurements were carried out. It was not even possible to see the community functioning in its usual way because of the temporary evacuation. But judging by clinical impressions, the Kaiadilt level of adaptation stood a little higher than before.

Kaiadilt youngsters continue to perform comparatively well in school and in job training, a trend we had previously noted. A group of Kaiadilt lads is working on the housing project near the airstrip. A Kaiadilt girl works as a store assistant; another has been working in the mission office but left just recently, the village policeman reports, because of "teasing." These adaptational successes are in spite of—or because of—the manifest Kaiadilt timidity and anxiety, as compared with the more comfortable Lardil youngsters. Kaiadilt girls continue to have a succession of babies when they go outside their group, mostly to mainland Aborigines or white men, though in one case to a Lardil boy in a "sponsoring" family in the village. Marriage is not seriously contemplated in any of these cases. There seems in fact some pressure against these marriages from the girls' rather dependent parents, keeping the young mothers attached to their original households. Bringing home an illegitimate child after working outside is acceptable, but deserting the family of origin is not.

The Kaiadilt enclave of the village looks as poverty-stricken as ever. Because so many people were evacuated it was impossible to judge whether the racial tension and discrimination between Kaiadilt and Lardil was in any way relaxed. It is the general opinion that the internal dissension among the Kaiadilt is less severe now. This is probably because the community is less disrupted by individual members who are psychotic or otherwise disturbed. Observing the retroflexive effect that such members had upon family and community, we drew attention in chapter 10 to the spiral of disintegration: social disintegration begets gross behavior disorder which begets more social disintegration. The deceleration of this sequence in the Kaiadilt could in part be attributed to extraneous factors, such as the death of one psychotic man who had formerly caused inconvenience (see the case of Q., chapter 10). In his last years the intensity of Q.'s disturbance had been relieved by tranquillizing medication and better social support. Some of the improvement may be attributed to psychiatric intervention, during and consequent upon our visit.

In order to examine the outcome of the transcultural psychiatric intervention inaugurated by the field team and then supervised by the settlement nurse, a case presented in chapter 5 (Depressive Pattern 4, M.Q., Kaiadilt) may be cited. In this brief account his totemic name, Casuarina (tree), is used. It will be recalled that he is a tall, distinguished-looking Kaiadilt who had been a leading man before the exodus from Bentinck Island. In his life on Mornington he had remained either morosely withdrawn, or agitated and fearful. On our visit we prescribed Amitriptyline (anti-depressant) medication, and we discussed the management of his condition in several mental health consultations with staff and elders.

After our departure Casuarina visited Miss Margot Holmes, nurse in charge of the clinic, every day with his wife and his children. He seemed perturbed about the health or safety of his family. In vernacular interspersed with fragments of English, a level of understanding was reached between them. Miss Holmes attended the wife and children before giving Casuarina his tablets. It had been suggested that the daily amount of the anti-depressant be given in one dose rather than in the divided doses usual in European clinics. (Most psychotropic drugs can be given in this way in non-literate communities where reliability is a problem; we have not found side effects more troublesome.) In the clinic he was courteous and dignified, described by the nurse as an "upright gentleman."

Shortly afterwards, Casuarina was admitted to the hospital for investigation of a pyrexia of unknown origin, which subsided, but Miss Holmes kept him loosely attached to the hospital. She felt it gave everybody more security at a time when the village people were asking whether he was safe to be at large, informing her that he had killed men on Bentinck Island and had tried to cut off his own nose on Mornington. He would go home to the village for a night's leave, but always returned promptly next morning. After waiting quietly until Miss Holmes had no more patients, he would then talk for as long as she had time to listen. He used mostly Kaiadilt and gestures, but had learned a few English words, such as "Sister," "tease me," "children." He appeared to be complaining about the children and especially about the young adults.

Miss Holmes had him helping with odd jobs around the hospital, such as making tea, and found him on the whole talkative and amiable. But when the young mothers came for treatment with their children, he would become agitated and begin gesticulating at the women. Then he would stride into her office, look her straight in the eye, and complain that he was being teased. The women invariably assured her that they were just talking and giggling amongst themselves.

One morning in the village Miss Holmes heard a commotion and found Casuarina surrounded by a ring of villagers standing at safe distance. He was yelling wildly, waving his arms in a temper. While the villagers screamed at her to keep away, Miss Holmes walked up behind him and tapped his shoulder. He swung around and shouted, "Go away, Sister. Me cranky." But he went to the clinic with her, talking loudly, while the people dispersed.

162

On Denham Island three nights later Casuarina lit a bush fire, and it was reported that he tried to kill his own son. The mission decided that it could not manage the situation and sent him to the nearest psychiatric hospital, Mosman Hall, at Charters Towers, about seven hundred miles away by air. He came home from the hospital on leave several times. Sometimes he acted strangely, keeping the villagers awake at night, accusing them of teasing him. He came several times to the hospital asking to be sent back to Charters Towers. Mostly, however, he seemed less agitated.

When the team member met with Casuarina in December 1970, he had been calm in mood and appropriate in behavior for several months. Dr. Huffer had already established some contact with him. Both Dr. Huffer and the team member were interested to find that they shared a similar protective feeling toward him, and tried to analyze its nature. They found they had an impression of his special dignity as a man— and maybe of his special value for science! Casuarina said that he had been sick because his second wife had left him, and he blamed his countrymen from Bentinck Island, who might be burning his "lavatory," or giving him *puripuri* (poison). He did not think leaving his homeland had made him ill; he was happy to come to Mornington and was never homesick. He said a few of the older Kaiadilt had been homesick—mostly women like Roonga and Maudie.

Casuarina considered Charters Towers hospital a splendid place— good food and good medicine. He had washed windows, and watered trees. Nobody had growled at him. He ate well there—better than the damper and tea on Mornington. He rarely eats meat or fish here. He complained he cannot hunt because of his eyesight, but could fish if he had a line and hooks, for which he asked. Nobody here lends him a fishing dinghy. He does not ask, because there is only one dinghy in the Kaiadilt community, and that is controlled by his countryman Wiley, not from his own group. We found that because of his poor vision he cannot identify children until they come fairly close. But only his children from his first wife come to him; the children of his dead brother's wives (who became his wives when his brother was killed on Bentinck Island) never come to him, except for one nephew, Roger.

Casuarina now spends some of his time visiting the house of Cora and Gully, his Lardil patrons. If Gully is working, Casuarina will help. Although Gully and Cora were his first contacts with the world outside Bentinck Island, and can interpret Kaiadilt, they do not know a great deal about Casuarina's former history, having mainly a nonverbal relationship with him. Casuarina likes to go more often now to Denham Island, which is a new island for him and gives him more enthusiasm for fishing and for cutting trees, the things he likes to do.

A letter was sent to the regional flying doctor based at Mt. Isa concerning several patients examined on this visit. The part about Casuarina read: "This psychosis is much improved, owing to regular medication and to some restoration of his former status through Sister's patronage, trips to Charters Towers hospital, and protection from the 'crazy' role in the village with the teasing that goes with it. You would hardly credit the good effect his improvement has wrought in the Kaiadilt community. I hope you will be able to put him on your visiting list and stimulate his rehabilitation, which has scarcely begun. You may be able to encourage his fishing and wood chopping, in which he has shown some interest. . . ."

THE CHARACTER OF (KAIADILT) DANGER

What factors led to the high level of social stresses among the Kaiadilt, contributing to the high levels of symptoms that we measured in our survey? The preconditions of mental ill-health in a primitive, basic society are of fundamental importance to psychiatry. Two hypotheses are favored on Mornington Island and have been outlined in chapter 10; during this follow-on visit these were explored further with Casuarina, with Gully and Cora, and with other local informants. The ecological hypothesis, associated with the work of Norman B. Tindale, first anthropologist to study the situation, relates the high level of stress to food and water shortages after a prolonged drought (Tindale, 1962b). The domestic hypothesis, preferred by the missionary, the Reverend Douglas Belcher, and by the Aboriginal men interrogated, relates the high stress level to persistent fighting over women, and its complications; this hypothesis disputes that hunger was important by comparison. It was questioned whether this was in fact a "non-argument." Certainly the distinction between the two hypotheses fades somewhat if women are regarded from an economic point of view, as a source of food and services. However, when this was pointed out to the male informants on the island, they emphasized that by "fighting over women" they meant the satisfaction of sexual desire, rather than the acquisition of economic security or social status. Since sexual desire and fighting over women are features of all societies, the problem concerns why "fighting over women" became especially intense among the Kaiadilt, at least in the recent years of which we have any knowledge.

This led to the consideration of some historical events, the significance of which may have escaped us on our first visit. In particular, the effect on Kaiadilt marital equilibrium of the interference from outside was explored, notably that of the white man McKenzie and his mainland Aboriginal helpers, who established a camp on adjacent Sweers Island around 1917. It will be recalled that McKenzie, with

Aboriginal helpers from the nearest mainland settlements, in 1916 to 1917 made a kiln on Sweers Island to produce lime for the refining of gold from the Croydon mines, at the base of Cape York Peninsula. Because he ran a launch, built a house, introduced horses and goats to Sweers Island, he might have made a substantial impact on Bentinck society. It seemed that if McKenzie's group had abducted enough Kaiadilt women, or by their killing had created enough Kaiadilt widows, this would change the existing Kaiadilt marital situation. Kaiadilt men might then have been obliged to secure replacement of missing wives, or to compete for the unassigned widows resulting from the massacres. Doing this by violent means would trigger the characteristic sequence that became disastrous for the Kaiadilt during the 1930s and 1940s. Thus we have to consider three hypotheses of Kaiadilt social disintegration at the time: ecological factors associated with drought; fighting for possession of women in a polygynous society; and intrusion of European influence upsetting the existing distribution of wives. It was hoped that further interviewing might reveal which hypothesis should be favored.

The chief Kaiadilt informant, Casuarina, was not born until 1922, five years after the McKenzie settlement. He was one of the first to make friends with Gully Peters in the early days of Gully's *bêche de mer* fishing around Bentinck Island. Later, Gully used to camp overnight on Bentinck Island on his boat trips to Normanton. Upon repeated visits, Gully recalls that Casuarina was usually the first to wade out to meet him. Cora and Gully recall that on one of the trips in the 1930s they were accompanied by Mr. Blakely,[1] a government man, who took gifts of tomahawks, cloth, fishing line and hooks, potatoes, and tomatoes. Cora relates that the Kaiadilt would not eat the tomatoes, threw away the hooks, and wound the cord around their waists. They were naked except for waist bands, and wore no pubic cover. They had mainly shells for tools, because the Bentinck Island stones were not hard enough. At that time, in 1932, Cora says she noticed the children showed evidence of malnutrition, with large bellies and thin legs.

On her early visits Cora feared Kaiadilt attacks, but Gully seemed confident that they would not attack him. On one occasion Cora and Gully proved it by coming up behind a group of Kaiadilt who were on the beach looking at their boat at anchor. Gully suddenly announced: "I'm here." The Kaiadilt threw their arms around them and "danced and danced," and then came to Gully's camp and ate all the food. Casuarina says he was about seven when he last ran away from

1. Undoubtedly J. W. Bleakley, who became chief protector of Aborigines for the Queensland government in 1913 and remained in charge of the department until 1940.

Gully's boat—about 1929. Gully says that even at that time there appeared to be incessant feuding between the two groups of Kaiadilt, the easterners or *Lealumben* (to whom Casuarina belonged) and the westerners or *Balumben*. Gully recalls that in the early 1930s an elderly Kaiadilt man, Wili, father of Darwin, had urged him to remove several young girls to the mission, saying that there had been a bad fight the previous night, and that he feared more killing. Gully declined the request on the grounds that Bentinck Island was the girls' country and that they should stay; privately he suspected that he would be accused of abducting the girls if he complied.

Gully and Cora say that during the 1930s and 1940s Casuarina was a "lively, happy man," though much involved in fighting. Kaiadilt raids took place at night, the man being taken by surprise. During one raid, Casuarina's brother was killed and his small sister abducted. Casuarina was speared in the left leg in this clash—he bears the scar today—but he was able to save his brother's four wives. In addition to his own wife, he now possessed his brother's four, making five women in his camp. There was one windbreak for all; he says they never fought among themselves. When his wound healed, he carried out his payback raid on a *Balumben* man. Casuarina says that on Bentinck Island, if a man wanted to marry a woman from the other group, he was liable to be killed by her parents—unless he killed the parents first. His account of Bentinck society at that time makes it seem that in order to marry, a man had to kill.

The possibility that this state of affairs might not have been perpetual, but was triggered by McKenzie's interference was explored. The Kaiadilt used to steal McKenzie's goats during his absences in Normanton. McKenzie's group abducted Kaiadilt women for their own camp. Casuarina knows of five women who had lived there for periods of time, including his own mother, Dougal's mother, Roonga, and Martha who now live on Mornington. They told him that McKenzie's men came over from Sweers Island with guns looking for women, shooting the Kaiadilt. On one occasion Gully saw four dead Kaiadilt men with their mandibles and kidney fat cut out. The mandibles would be traded higher up Cape York Peninsula for arm bands, and kidney fat was valuable for *puripuri*. Another group had been shot while in the water on the reef. It is not known whether men or women were the main targets of these massacres. Gully thinks that both sexes were equally involved, and that for a time McKenzie's object may have been to wipe out the Kaiadilt population. Only about twelve were killed in this way, and neither Gully nor Casuarina are inclined to attach much weight to the idea that these massacres and abductions sparked off the Kaiadilt warfare. It was "fighting over women" by men with strong sex motives.

The small Kaiadilt population of 120, approximately, was divided into eight classes or *dolnoro,* in theory owning separate sections of the island and its reef. In practice, the fighting was between the *Lealumben* (east) and *Balumben* (west) divisions. It is Cora's belief that the men fought over food supplies as well. Food resources such as *panja* (an onion tuber) were described by Cora as like private gardens, women being the collectors of the food. Collecting areas were usually acknowledged, but to emphasize ownership, Cora says the Kaiadilt women tied leaves around the plants in that vicinity as a sign to others. She said that stealing this food would lead to fighting. She thought it likely that in times of drought and poor harvest there would be more stealing and fighting because of this. The male informants, on the other hand, maintained that the fighting was because men wanted sex, and that women as a source of sex was the motive for killing, rather than women as a source of food or of children. Here were male and female perspectives of the same subject: the women seeing life as the search for security, and the men seeing it as the search for sex. If such a generalization were even partly valid, it would imply a deep ambivalence in the Kaiadilt men toward women. They craved them intensely as the source of sex and, presumably, solace for anxiety; but they feared them as the cause of fighting and death among themselves. Did the women's view have a different quality?

The sequence of killing and payback might have been interrupted if the mission had established an outstation on Bentinck Island in the 1930s. This outstation may have been contemplated, but the period was one of economic hardship for the Mornington mission when financial resources were particularly low during and after the depression. It was followed by World War II. It was not until after the war that a group of Kaiadilt was taken by Gully to Mornington Island as "tourists," to reassure them about the security to be found at *Gunana,* the Mornington village. The Kaiadilt elected to come to Mornington. The stresses of emigration were now added to what had gone before. Apprehensive and fearful, in poor general health and nutrition, the Kaiadilt established a camp on the south side of the Mornington village near the channel, looking over the water in the direction of Bentinck Island. At first they constructed horseshoe-shaped windbreaks made of branches and grass. To these materials they soon added, as we have seen, scraps of corrugated iron, canvas, and bark. The children defecated where they slept. It was the first experience of a fixed camp for the Kaiadilt, and they were not adapted to it. Their former animosity and suspicion persisted. Discrimination against them by the Lardil was widespread. The "Bentinck dogs" or "wild Bentincks" were not entirely welcome, though Christian motives decreed the charitable official attitude.

It is like a parable of man's brinkmanship to witness this tenacious branch of humanity, individually and collectively, attempting to resurrect itself from the edge of annihilation. In this process modern technology, including transcultural psychiatry, plays a crucial part.

John E. Cawte is an associate professor in the school of psychiatry of the University of New South Wales. Dr. Cawte received his medical degree at the University of Adelaide. He has been a fellow of the Commonwealth Fund of New York (Harkness Fellowships) to study social psychiatry at Johns Hopkins and Harvard universities. He is director of the New Britain Psychiatry Research Programme, and of the rural psychiatric epidemiology research program in the far west of New South Wales under the title "The Human Ecology of the Arid Zone." He has carried out transcultural psychiatric fieldwork in several regions of Australia and has published the material in such journals as *Oceania, The British Journal of Psychiatry, Psychiatry, British Journal of Medical Psychology, Social Science and Medicine, The Medical Journal of Australia,* and *The Australian and New Zealand Journal of Psychiatry.* He is coauthor, with anthropologist Robert Pulsford, of *Health in a Developing Country: Principles of Medical Anthropology in Melanesia* (Brisbane: Jacaranda Press, 1972).

Barry Nurcombe is senior lecturer in child psychiatry at the University of New South Wales, formerly medical director in the division of welfare and guidance, Queensland. He graduated in medicine from the University of Queensland. He received postgraduate training in psychiatry at the University of Melbourne and studied child psychiatry at the Judge Baker Guidance Center and Harvard Medical School under the auspices of the Commonwealth Fund of New York. Apart from his interest in transcultural psychiatry he is involved in research into schizoid sociopathy during adolescence. He has contributed articles to the *American Journal of Orthopsychiatry, Journal of the American Academy of Child Psychiatry,* and *Medical Journal of Australia.*

Geoffrey N. Bianchi is a research fellow of the New South Wales Institute of Psychiatry, formerly senior tutor in the school of psychiatry of the University of New South Wales. He graduated from the University of Queensland and subsequently obtained the diploma of psychological medicine. He received his medical degree from the University of New South Wales. Dr. Bianchi has published work in the fields of infectious diseases, mental subnormality and psychopharmacology. His present research is on psychogenic pain and hypochondriacal syndromes, and on depressive illness. He is presently a research fellow at the Institute of Psychiatry, University of London.

169

Douglas L. Belcher developed an interest in the emergence of native communities during his military service in New Guinea in World War II. He began work with the Mornington Island community in 1946 and was ordained in the Presbyterian ministry in 1952 in Sydney. He is now senior missionary in the Queensland zone of the Australian Presbyterian Board of Missions, having been intimately associated most of the time with the people of Mornington Island.

Michael I. Friedman came to the school of psychiatry, University of New South Wales, as an elective during his medical course at Stanford University. He participated in the school's field research programs on Mornington Island and in New Britain, and spent further time at the University of New South Wales transcribing his observations for this book. His observations on suicide in New Britain have appeared in the journal *Psychiatry*. In his premedical degree at Swarthmore he majored in philosophy and psychology, and he had some prior field experience in Ghana.

Leslie G. Kiloh is professor of psychiatry at the University of New South Wales and head of the departments of psychiatry at Prince Henry and Prince of Wales hospitals, Sydney. He graduated in medicine at the University of London. Although his main interests are the study of depressive illness and the quantification of psychiatric variables in relation to diagnosis, he has participated in the transcultural research program of the school of psychiatry. He has contributed sections to several books, and articles to numerous journals such as *The British Journal of Psychiatry, The British Medical Journal, Lancet, Brain, The Journal of Neuropsychiatry, The Medical Journal of Australia*, and *Social Science and Medicine*.

Donald W. McElwain is professor of psychology in the University of Queensland, having graduated from Wellington University, New Zealand, and from University College, London. He has held teaching positions in psychology in the University of Western Australia and Melbourne. His interest in transcultural psychology has led him to undertake fieldwork in New Guinea and in Australia. He was a collaborator in the "Report to the Commonwealth of Australia on the Mental Health of New Guinea Indigenes" (Sinclair, 1959). In recent years he has been active in developing tests of intelligence for use in communication-reduced situations, particularly the transcultural one; the test has been published in *The Queensland Test* by the Australian Council of Educational Research, Melbourne (McElwain et al., 1970).

Sardool Singh received his bachelor of science degree from the Punjab University and the master of science degree at the University of Sydney. He was a research student within the department of obstetrics of that university (cancer research and human chromosome studies). Since 1963 he has worked in the department of human genetics, the University of New South Wales, where his special interest has been dermatoglyphics.

Douglass Baglin, geographer-cameraman, did not accompany this expedition but visited Mornington Island a few months previous to it. He provided the photographs for this book to help convey the people, the level of material culture, and the ecological setting. Mr. Baglin's unique photography has illustrated a number of books about Australia.

Abbie, A. A.
   1969. *The Original Australians.* Wellington, New Zealand: Reed.
Adams, R. N.
   1959. *A Community in the Andes.* Seattle: University of Washington Press.
Australian Presbyterian Board of Missions.
   1949. *Friends from the Walkabout: Brief Studies of the Australian Aborig-*
          ines and of the Work of Presbyterian Missions in their Midst. Sydney:
          Assembly Hall.
Bateson, G.
   1936. *Naven.* Stanford: Stanford University Press.
Berry, J. W.
   1970. Marginality, Stress and Ethnic Identification in an Acculturated
          Aboriginal Community. *J. Cross-Cultural Psychol.* 1:3, 239–252.
Bianchi, G. N.; McElwain, D. W.; and Cawte, J. E.
   1970. The Dispensary Syndrome in Australian Aborigines. *Brit. J. Med.*
          Psychol. 43:375–382.
Blacket, J.
   1911. *History of South Australia: A Romantic and Successful Experiment*
          in Colonization. 3rd ed. Adelaide: Hussey and Gillingham.
Bowlby, J.
   1952. *Maternal Case and Mental Health.* World Health Organization Mono-
          graph. Geneva.
Brisbane Daily Mail.
   1917. Newspaper reports concerning Rev. Hall's death and Peter's trial.
          Nov. 5, 6, 7, 29; Dec. 7.
Brodman, K.; Erdmann, A. J.; Lorge, I.; and Wolff, H. G.
   1949. The Cornell Medical Index; Adjunct to Medical Interview. *J. Amer.*
          Med. Assoc. 140:530–534.
Brody, E. B.
   1966. Cultural Exclusion, Character and Illness. *Amer. J. Psychiat.* 122:852.
Carstens, Jan.
   1623. Quoted in English translation by Lt. Matthew Flinders, in *A Voyage*
          to Terra Australis (1814).
Cawte, J. E.
          Medicine is the Law. The University Press of Hawaii, forthcoming.
Cawte, J. E., and Kidson, M. A.
   1965. Australian Ethnopsychiatry. The Walbiri Doctor. *Med. J. Austral.*
          2:977.

Chance, N. A.
    1960. Cultural Change and Integration, an Eskimo Example. *Amer. Anthropologist* 62:1028.
    1962. Conceptual and Methodological Problems in Cross-Cultural Health Research. *Amer. J. Public Health* 3:410.
    1965. Acculturation, Self-identification and Personality Adjustment. *Amer. Anthropologist* 67:372.

Chance, N. A., and Foster, D. A.
    1962. Symptom Formation and Patterns of Psychopathology in a Rapidly Changing Alaskan Eskimo Society. *Anthrop. Papers University of Alaska* 11:32.

Collomb, H.
    1965. Bouffées délirantes en Psychiatrie Africaine. Mimeograph in French. Abstracted in *Transcultural Psychiatric Research,* April 1966, iii:29.

Conant, J. B.
    1964. *Slums and Suburbs.* New York: New American Library.

Cummins, H., and Setzler, F. M.
    1960. Dermatoglyphics of Australian Aborigines. In *Anthropology and Nutrition. Records of the American-Australian Expedition to Arnhem Land* 2:203. Melbourne: Melbourne University Press.

De Hoyos, A., and De Hoyos, G.
    1965. Symptomatology Differentials between Negro and White Schizophrenics. *Int. J. Soc. Psychiat.* 11:245.

Dubos, R.; Savage, D.; and Schaedler, R.
    1966. Biological Freudianism. Lasting Effects of Early Environmental Influences. *Pediatrics* 38:789–800.

Dunstan, D. A.
    1966. Aboriginal Land Title and Employment in South Australia. In *Aborigines in the Economy,* ed. I. G. Sharp and C. M. Tatz. Brisbane: Jacaranda Press.

Edwards, A.
    1957. *Techniques of Attitude Scale Construction.* Century Psychology Series. New York: Appleton.

Eitinger, L.
    1964. *Concentration Camp Survivors in Norway and Israel.* London: Allen and Unwin.

Elkin, A. P.
    1951. Reaction and Interaction: a Food Gathering People and European Settlement in Australia. *Amer. Anthropologist* 53:164–186.

Flinders, M.
    1814. *A Voyage to Terra Australis, undertaken for the purpose of completing the discovery of that Vast Country.* London: W. Bulmer. Our copy in Australiana Facsimile Editions No. 37 by the Libraries Board of South Australia, 1966. Original: London, G. and W. Nicol, Pall-Mall.

Freud, S.
    1912. *Totem and Taboo: Resemblances Between the Psychic Lives of Savages and Neurotics.* Trans. A. A. Brill. London: Routledge.

Gloe, C., and Weller, N. H. E.
    1949. *Water Resources of Mornington Island.* Report to the Queensland Irrigation and Water Supply Commission.

Group for the Advancement of Psychiatry (G.A.P.)
    1966. *Psychopathological Disorders in Childhood: Theoretical Considera-*

172

tions and a Proposed Classification. Report No. 62. New York: G.A.P.
Publications.

Gullahorn, J. E., and Gullahorn, J. T.
1968. The Utility of Applying both Guttman and Factor Analysis to Survey
Data. *Sociometry* 31:213–218.

Guttman, L.
1950. The Basis for Scalogram Analysis. In S. A. Stouffer et al., *Measurement and Prediction.* Princeton: Princeton University Press.

Hale, K.
1964. Australian Languages and Transformational Grammars. Paper read
at 63rd Annual Meeting of American Anthropological Association,
Detroit.
1965. Personal Correspondence on the Damin Secret Language to Rev.
D. L. Belcher, Mornington Island mission.

Hedley, C.
1903. A New Native Tribe Discovered. *Science of Man* 6:89.

Hollingshead, A. B., and Redlich, F. C.
1958. *Social Class and Mental Illness.* New York: John Wiley & Sons.

Holmes, M.
1964. *Australia's Open North.* Sydney: Angus and Robertson.

Honigmann, J. J.
1954. *Culture and Personality.* New York: Harper.

Hoskin, J. O.; Friedman, M. I.; and Cawte, J. E.
1969. A High Incidence of Suicide in a Preliterate-primitive Society. *Psychiatry, J. for Study of Interpersonal Processes* 32:2, 200–210.

Illustrated London News
1852. "A Black Camp" in New South Wales, after the Annual Gift of
Blankets from the Governor. April 24, p. 314.

Jose, A.
1928. *Builders and Pioneers of Australia.* London and Toronto: J. M. Dent
and Sons.

Kaelbling, R.
1961. Comparative Psychopathology and Psychotherapy. *Acta Psychother.*
9:10.

Keesing, R. M.
1953. *Culture Change: An Analysis and Bibliography of Anthropological
Sources to 1952.* Stanford: Stanford University Press.

Kerckhoff, A. G., and McCormick, T. C.
1955. Marginal Status and Marginal Personality. *Social Forces* 34:48–55.

Lambo, T. A.
1964. Patterns of Psychiatric Care in Developing African Countries. In
Magic Faith and Healing, ed. A. Kiev. New York: Free Press of
Glencoe.
1965. Psychiatry in the Tropics. *Lancet* 2:119.

Lebon, J. H. G.
1966. *An Introduction to Human Geography.* New York: Capricorn Books.

Leighton, A. H.
1959a. Mental Illness and Acculturation. In *Medicine and Anthropology,*
ed. I. Goldston. New York: International Universities Press.
1959b. *My Name is Legion: Foundation for a Theory of Man in Relation
to Culture.* Stirling County Study of Psychiatric Disorder and Sociocultural Environment, vol. 1. New York: Basic Books.
1965. Cultural Change and Psychiatric Disorder. In *Transcultural Psy-*

chiatry, ed. A. V. S. DeReuck and R. Porter. Ciba Foundation Symposium. London: Churchill.

Leighton, A. H.; Lambo, T. A.; Hughes, C. C.; Leighton, D. C.; Murphy, J. M.; and Macklin, D. B.
  1963. *Psychiatric Disorder Among the Yoruba: a Report from the Cornell-Aro Mental Health Research Project in the Western Region of Nigeria.* New York: Cornell University Press.

Leighton, A. H., and Murphy, J. M.
  1965. Cross-cultural Psychiatry. In *Approaches to Cross-Cultural Psychiatry,* ed. J. M. Murphy and A. H. Leighton. New York: Cornell University Press.

Leighton, D. C.; Harding, J. S.; Macklin, D. B.; Macmillan, A. M.; and Leighton, A. H.
  1963. *The Character of Danger: Psychiatric Symptoms in Selected Communities.* New York: Basic Books.

Leighton, D. C., and Leighton, A. H.
  1967. Mental Health and Social Factors. In *Comprehensive Textbook of Psychiatry,* ed. A. M. Freedman and H. I. Kaplan. Baltimore: Williams and Wilkins.

Lewis, O.
  1959. Five Families. *Mexican Case Studies in the Culture of Poverty.* New York: Basic Books.

Long, J. P. M.
  1970. *Aboriginal Settlements: A Survey of Institutional Communities in Eastern Australia.* Aborigines in Australian Society, no. 3. The Social Science Research Council of Australia. Canberra: Australian National University Press.

McElwain, D. W.; Kearney, G. E.; and Ord, I. G.
  1970. *The Queensland Test.* Melbourne: Australian Council for Educational Research.

MacIntosh, N. W. G.
  1952. Fingerprints of Australian Aborigines of West Arnhem Land and Western Australia. *Oceania* 22:299.

Mader, M. K.; Parsons, P. A.; Conner, M. A.; and Hatt, D.
  1965. Differences between Four Australian Aborigine Tribes as Revealed by Fingerprints. *Acta Genetica* 15:45.

Malinowski, B.
  1913. *The Family Among the Australian Aborigines.* London: University of London Press.

Mann, J. W.
  1958. Group Relations and the Marginal Personality. *Human Relations* 11:77–91.

Margetts, E. L.
  1959. The Future of Psychiatry in East Africa. *East Africa Med. J.* 37:443.
  1965. Transcultural Psychiatry. Editorial in *Canadian Psychiatric Assoc. J.* 10:2, 79.

Mead, Margaret.
  1956. *New Lives for Old.* New York: William Morrow & Co.

Meggitt, M. J.
  1962. *Desert People.* Sydney: Angus and Robertson.

Montagu, M. F. A.
  1937. The Origin of Subincision in Australia. *Oceania* 7:2, 193.

174

Munoz, L.; Marconi, J.; Horwitz, J.; and Naveillan, P.
    1966. Crosscultural Definitions Applied to the Study of Functional Psychoses in Chilean Mapuches. *Brit. J. Psychiat.* 112:1205.
Murphy, H. B. M.
    1961. Social Change and Mental Illness. *The Millbank Memorial Fund Quarterly* 39:385.
Oberg, Kalerbo.
    1960. Cultural Shock: Adjustment to New Cultural Environments. *Practical Anthropology* 4:177–182.
Oppenheim, A. N.
    1966. *Questionnaire Design and Attitude Measurement.* London: Heinemann.
Park, R. E.
    1928. Human Migration and the Marginal Man. *Amer. J. Sociology* 33:881–893.
Piaget, J.
    1957. *Logic and Psychology.* New York: Basic Books.
Pulsford, R.; and Cawte, J. E.
    1971. *Health in Papua New Guinea.* Brisbane: Jacaranda Press.
Queensland Aboriginals, Chief Protector.
    1908. Report in Queensland Parliamentary Papers of Eighteenth Parliament. First Session, vol. 2, 1909: 965–1027. Thereafter, annual reports from 1913 to 1964 in Queensland Parliamentary Papers.
Raman, A. C.
    1960. The Effect of Rapid Cultural Change on Mental Health. *World Mental Health* 12:1–11.
Rao, P. D.
    1964a. The Main-line Index and Transversality in the Palms of Australian Aborigines. *Oceania* 34:211.
    1964b. Fingerprints of Aborigines at Kalumburu Mission in Western Australia. *Oceania* 34:225.
    1965. Finger and Palm Prints of the Aborigine Children of Yuendumu Settlement in Central Australia. *Oceania* 35:305.
Redfield, R.
    1950. *A Village That Chose Progress.* Chicago: University of Chicago Press.
Robson, M. K., and Parsons, P. A.
    1967. Fingerprint Studies on Full Central Australian Aborigine Tribes. *Archaeol. Phys. Anthrop. in Oceania* 2:69–78.
Rodger, R. S.
    1967. The Generalized Median Test. *Aust. Psychol* 2:(abstract).
Roheim, G.
    1945. *The Eternal Ones of the Dream.* New York: International Universities Press.
Roth, W. E.
    1908. Australian Canoes and Rafts. *Man,* 8:161, plates.
Rowley, C. D.
    1962. Aborigines and Other Australians. *Oceania* 34:247–266.
    1966. Some Questions of Causation in Relation to Aboriginal Affairs. In *Aborigines in the Economy,* ed. I. G. Sharp and C. M. Tatz. Brisbane: Jacaranda Press.
    1970. *The Destruction of Aboriginal Society, Aboriginal Policy and Practice.* Aborigines in Australian Society, no. 4. The Social Science Re-

search Council of Australia. Canberra: Australian National University Press.

Schapper, H. P.
1968. Administration and Welfare as Threats to Aboriginal Assimilation. *Austral. J. Social Issues* 3:4, 3–8.

Sherwin, A. C., and Schoelly, M. L.
1965. Criteria of Psychiatric Disorder in Children. In *Approaches to Cross-Cultural Psychiatry,* ed. J. M. Murphy and A. H. Leighton. New York: Cornell University Press.

Simmons, R. T.; Graydon, J. J.; and Tindale, N. B.
1964. Further Blood Group Genetical Studies on Australian Aborigines of Bentinck, Mornington and Forsyth Islands and the Mainland, Gulf of Carpentaria. *Oceania* 35:1, 66.

Simmons, R. T.; Tindale, N. B.; and Birdsell, J. B.
1962. A Blood Group Genetical Survey in Australian Aborigines of Bentinck, Mornington and Forsyth Islands, Gulf of Carpentaria. *Amer. J. Phys. Anthrop.* 20:3, 303–320.

Sinclair, A. With the assistance of McElwain, D. W., and Campbell, E. D.
1957. Field and Clinical Survey Report of the Mental Health of the Indigenes of the Territory of Papua and New Guinea. Port Moresby: W. S. Nicholas, Government Printer.

Singh, S.
1968. Dermatoglyphics of Australian Aborigines, Mornington Island, Australia. *Archaeol. Phys. Anthrop. in Oceania* 3:41–48.

Smee, R. A.
1966. Special Survey of Persons of Aboriginal Descent Registered for Employment in New South Wales. In *Aborigines in the Economy,* ed. I. G. Sharp and C. M. Tatz. Brisbane: Jacaranda Press.

Spencer, B.
1914. *Native Tribes of the Northern Territory of Australia.* London: Macmillan and Co.

Stevens, F. S.
1966. The Role of Coloured Labour in North Australia. In *Aborigines in the Economy,* ed. I. G. Sharp and C. M. Tatz. Brisbane: Jacaranda Press.

Stonequist, E. V.
1937. *The Marginal Man.* New York: Charles Scribner's Sons.

Surya, N. C.; Datta, S. P.; Krishna, R. G.; Sundaram, D.; and Kutty, J.
1964. Mental Morbidity in Pondicherry, 1962–63. *Transactions of All-India Institute of Mental Health.* July, 50–61.

Tatz, C. M.
1966. The Relationship between Aboriginal Health and Employment, Wages and Training. In *Aborigines in the Economy,* ed. I. G. Sharp and C. M. Tatz. Brisbane: Jacaranda Press.

Territories, Department of.
1967. *The Australian Aborigines.* Issued under the authority of the Minister for Territories, the Hon. C. E. Barner, M.P., with the cooperation of the ministers responsible for Aboriginal welfare in the Australian states. Commonwealth of Australia. Sydney-Halstead Press.

Tindale, N. B.
1962a. Geographical Knowledge of the Kaiadilt People of Bentinck Island, Queensland. *Rec. South Austral. Museum* 14:259.

176

1962*b*. Some Population Changes Among the Kaiadilt People of Bentinck Island, Queensland. *Rec. South Austral. Museum* 14:297.

Warner, W. L.
1937. *A Black Civilization: A Social Study of an Australian Tribe.* New York: Harper and Bros.

Wilmer, H. A.; Marks, I.; and Pogue, E.
1966. Group Treatment of Prisoners and their Families. *Mental Hygiene* 50:380.

Winterbotham, L. P.
1959. Ceremonial Circumcision. *Med. J. Austral.* 1:412.

Wittkower, E. O., and Rin, H.
1965. Transcultural Psychiatry. *Arch. Gen. Psychiat.* 13:367.

World Health Organization.
1959. *Report of Proceedings of the African Seminar on Mental Health at Brazzaville.* Brazzaville: World Health Organization Regional Office for Africa.

Yates, F.
1934. Contingency Tables Involving Small Numbers and the Chi-Squared Test. *Supp. J. R. Statist. Soc.* 1:217–235.

Conant, J. B., 157
Cornell Medical Index (C.M.I.): limitations in scope, 80; modified for Aboriginal study, 71–73; modified for Eskimo study, 70; original health questionnaire, 70; presented as a graph, 73, 75, 76, 77; in principal components analysis, 95
Courtship, 109–110
Crime, incidence of, in community survey, 58
Cultural change: effect upon mental health of Aborigines, 136–137; significance for transcultural psychiatry, 84
Cultural contact, 144. *See also* Acculturation
Cultural exclusion: concept, 1, 60; as a factor in C.M.I. responses, 76; in personality disorders, 61
Cultural identity: cultural identity scales, 91; symptom levels and, 94. *See also* Acculturation, acquisition of Western culture
Cultural relativism, 112, 145
Culture shock: in Aborigines who emigrate, 50; in Europeans working with Aborigines, 27

De Hoyos, A. and G., 69
Delinquency: arising from stress between parents, 105; in tension-discharge syndrome, 120–122
Delusional states. *See* Transitory delusional states
Dependency, 61–62; of parents upon children, 161; of young men, 33. *See also* Inadequacy, 79
Depression: association with irritability, 80; C.M.I. questions, 72; C.M.I. responses, 79; key questions, 81
Depressive states: human ecology in psychogenesis, 67–68; occurrence in Kaiadilt, 67; patterns, 64–68, 79
Domestic conflicts: balance of domestic power, 49; killing as a preliminary to Kaiadilt marriage, 166; miscegenation, 48; monogamy enforced by mission, 47; psychiatric complications arising from, 48
Dormitory system of child-rearing: as a cause of parental deficiencies, 45; description, 103; as a factor in acculturation, 15
Dubos, R., 74
Dunstan, D. A., 158

Ecology: Mornington Island features, 12–14; natural hazards to life, 19–21
Ecology, human: determinant of mental disorders, 140–141; as a euphemism in psychiatry, 147; effect of fluctuating abundance upon, 140; succession, 140; zonation, 140
Economy: cattle, 17; craft, 18; pensions, 18; trepang, 17, 164. *See also* Poverty
Economic change, as factor in transcultural psychiatry, 142–143
Education: contribution of psychiatrist, 151; preschool training, 151; school system, 105–106, 109–110; of transcultural workers by universities, 152–153
Educational retardation: cases examined by the Queensland Test, 125; high incidence, 125
Eitinger, L., 141
Elkin, A. P., 56, 84
Emigration: economic necessity, 50; psychiatric disturbance, 50, 62; success and failure, 50–54
Emulation of Western culture, 87
Epidemiology, psychiatric: cultural level and, 84; pitfalls of statistics, 85; statistics available in settled society, 137; summary of basic findings, 129–130
Ethnic group, as a variable in symptom patterns, 76
"Evasion of confrontation": as an Aboriginal ethos, 44; as a character handicap, 46–47; as reluctance to dominate, 45. *See also* Character
Exploration in Gulf of Carpentaria: Carstens, 9; Flinders, 9, 11; Tasman, 9

Factor analysis, 95–97
Fatigue. *See* Lassitude
Fear: in childhood, 107; of supernatural, 59
Feuding, 163–166
Flinders, M., 9, 13, 17, 130–132
Freud, S., 2
Friedman, M. I., xv, 170

Genetics: blood groups, 22; fingerprints, 23–25; possible significance for emotional instability, 135; summary of distinctive gene frequencies, 133
Gross stress: in concentration camps, 141; in Kaiadilt, 80, 140
Gullahorn, J. E. and J. T., 97
Guttman analysis: design of scales for cultural identity, 86–90; with factor analysis, 97
Guttman, L., 89, 97

Hale, K., 12, 32
Hasluck, Hon. Paul, 155
Holmes, M., 17
Holmes, Nurse Margot, 162

Psychophysiologic disorder: childhood cases, 124–125; definition, 112
Psychotropic drugs: effectiveness as two-edged sword, 147; use in transcultural settings, 162
Puripuri: definition, 89; opportunity for mental health consultation, 148. *See also* Sorcery

Queensland Test, 125
Questionnaire methods: acquisition of Western culture scale, 85–86; Cornell Medical Index, 70–80; emulation of Western culture scale, 87–88; limitations of questionnaires in preliterate people, 85; retention of traditional beliefs scale, 89; retention of Western activities scale, 88

Racial discrimination: between Aboriginal groups, 29, 147–148, 167; complexity of, 153–155; persistence of, 153; in social disintegration, 137
Raman, A. C., 84
Rapport: assisted by offer of medical treatment, 58; between transcultural researchers and subjects, 145–147; sanctioned access to the sick by physicians, 5
Redfield, R., 84
Respiratory disorders: detection by C.M.I., 71, 77; high frequency in children, 118
Riots in the village: periodicity, 44; social pathology, 44; triggered by children's quarrels, 44–45; triggered by racism, 29, 149
Roheim, G., 2
Roth, W. E., 12
Roughsey, Dick, 33, 36, 38, 40–41, 145–146
Roughsey, Lindsay, 39, 41–42, 146
Rowley, C. D., 136, 150, 157

Schapper, H. P., 150
Schizophrenia: case of, presented as sorcery, 139; incidence, 60; mental health consultation, 149; transitory delusional states, 62
Sex: as source of feuding, 166; as variable in symptom patterns, 74, 80
Sex problems: recognition of, 58–59; sex education, 107–108
Sexual promiscuity: case of, 61; incidence, 58
Sherwin, A. C., 111
Simmons, R. T., 21, 22
Singh, S., xv, 21, 170
Smee, R. A., 145
Social credit network, collapse in Kaiadilt, 138

Social disintegration: comparison of communities, 56, 137; definitions (following A. Leighton), 55, 137; as a determinant of Kaiadilt mental symptoms, 137–138; mental disorders and, 55–56; rapid cultural change and, 84; Stirling County study, 55
Sorcery: complaints in mental illness, 138, 163; European misconceptions, 148; *malgri,* 89; as a measure of social disintegration, 137; not directed against children, 101; *puripuri,* 89, 163; retention of traditional beliefs, 89
Spencer, B., 145
"Spiral of disintegration," 139
Stevens, F., 157
Stonequist, E. V., 61, 85
Stress: high levels of, in the Kaiadilt, 164, 167; human ecology, 140; reactive disorders in childhood, 118–119. *See also* Gross stress
Subsection system: as cause of marriage problems, 47; contemporary difficulties, 104; structure of the family, 98
Suicide: active, 64; attempted, 64; "partial" type, 64–65; "voodoo" type, 64
Surya, N. C., 68
Symptoms: evaluation in transcultural setting, 69, 70; key questions to elicit, 81

Tasman, Abel, 9
Tatz, C. M., 74
Teasing, 105, 161
Technological change, personality difficulties and, 84–85
Tension-discharge syndrome: case histories, 120–122; definition, 113; high prevalence, 120, 128
Tensions: detection of, by C.M.I., 71, 79; in the village, 27
Territoriality: crowding and tensions, 29; in traditional life, 15; residential clusters in village, 27–29. *See also Malgri*
Tindale, N. B., 12, 13, 16, 20, 164
Traditional culture: conflict between traditional and modern, 39–41; retention by Aborigines of activities, 88; retention by Aborigines of beliefs, 89, 93–94
Transcultural psychiatry: anthropology and, 2, 6; definition, 1; epidemiology and, 3, 6; human ecology and, 3
Transitory delusional states: case histories, 63–64; in culture contact, 62; in emigrants, 50. *See also Bouffée délirante;* Schizophrenia
"Twenty Questions": to detect adult behavior disorders, 57; to detect childhood behavior disorders, 116; to detect personal discomfort, 81, 82